The Trickster
in Ginsberg

The Trickster in Ginsberg
A Critical Reading

KATHERINE CAMPBELL MEAD-BREWER

McFarland & Company, Inc., Publishers
Jefferson, North Carolina, and London

Excerpts from "Howl" and "Footnote to Howl" from *Collected Poems: 1947–1980* by Allen Ginsberg. Copyright © 1955 by Allen Ginsberg. Reprinted by permission of HarperCollins Publishers.

Excerpts from "Howl" and "Footnote to Howl" from *Collected Poems: 1947–1997* by Allen Ginsberg. Copyright © 1956, 2006 by Allen Ginsberg, LLC, reprinted throughout the UK and British Commonwealth by permission of the Wylie Agency LLC.

LIBRARY OF CONGRESS CATALOGUING-IN-PUBLICATION DATA

Mead-Brewer, Katherine Campbell.
    The trickster in Ginsberg : a critical reading / Katherine Campbell Mead-Brewer.
       p.   cm.
    Includes bibliographical references and index.

    ISBN 978-0-7864-6469-2
    softcover : acid free paper ∞

    1. Ginsberg, Allen, 1926–1997—Criticism and interpretation.
2. Ginsberg, Allen, 1926–1997. Howl.   3. Beat generation.
I. Title.
PS3513.I74Z736 2013
811'.54—dc23   2013013937

BRITISH LIBRARY CATALOGUING DATA ARE AVAILABLE

© 2013 Katherine Campbell Mead-Brewer. All rights reserved

No part of this book may be reproduced or transmitted in any form or by any means, electronic or mechanical, including photocopying or recording, or by any information storage and retrieval system, without permission in writing from the publisher.

On the cover: Danny O'Connor, *Allen Ginsberg*, acrylic, 30" × 40", 2008

Manufactured in the United States of America

McFarland & Company, Inc., Publishers
  Box 611, Jefferson, North Carolina 28640
  www.mcfarlandpub.com

For my family and all of its new members

Acknowledgments

I would like to thank the wonderful professors who made up my thesis committee, who guided me along the way, who provided me with new texts and avenues, and who lovingly put up with my weekend and summertime barrage of worries, ideas, and questions. Thank you, Professor Bednar, for your good humor and unfailing support. Thank you, Professor Gaines, for your crazy-wisdom and goodwill. Thank you, Professor Tahmahkera, for your gentle advice and constant flow of ideas. And thank you, Professor Mello, for your patience and your honesty. You have all shown me truly great faces of academia, civic action, and the importance of reaching out to others and encouraging them in those pursuits that give them personal joy, growth, and meaning.

Thank you also to Gary Mitchem whose prompt and cheerful e-mails kept me optimistic in times of doubt. I also want to extend special thanks and gratitude to my parents and fiancé whom I often subjected to both my laughter and tears over this research and struggle. You are truly the finest collection of individuals I have ever known, and I could not be more grateful to have you in my life as my support system. Extra appreciation is also in order for Professor Traci Giuliano, without whom I probably would not have made it out alive — thank you for your constant care and attention to all of my needs and concerns along the way.

Thank you also to Alexandra Levenberg at the Wylie Agency and Peter London at HarperCollins; you have both demonstrated a profound generosity and patience with me as I stumbled through my first steps and experiences in the wild world of academic publishing and permissions. A special thank you also to the lovely Haylie Swenson, Devin Proctor, and Craig Mariconti — you are all wonderful teachers full of invaluable insight.

Quite sincerely, I could not have done this without you. Thank you all.

Table of Contents

Acknowledgments	vi
Preface	1
Introduction	9

PART I : ALLEN GINSBERG AND THE TRICKSTER

1. I Am Large. I Contain Multitudes.	29
2. Considering Coyote	57

PART II : COYOTE-ING "HOWL"

3. Space, Place, and Traversing Boundaries	99
4. "Howl's" Appetite	125
5. A Trick and a Trap	138
6. Smearing Borderlines	147
7. Transformation: Madman Bum and Angel	163

Epilogue	172
Notes	177
Bibliography	195
Index	203

"Kali, Durga, Ram, Hari, Krishna, Brahma, Buddha, Allah, Jaweh, Christ, Mazsda, Coyote, hear my plea!"
— Allen Ginsberg

Preface

In Tom Spanbauer's *The Man Who Fell in Love with the Moon*, the protagonist, a young half–Native American, bisexual boy named Shed, begins the tale by relating his understanding of the differences between Native and non–Native (specifically *white* non–Native) stories. According to Shed, white stories are about "how [white people are] going to be," and he laments that it is "as if they weren't even living yet ... [and are] 'afraid of being who they are right now.'"[1] Native stories, on the other hand, are "about how the world is."[2] And while I largely agree with Shed's assessment, I firmly believe that Allen Ginsberg is an exception to this rule. Ginsberg was a white, Jewish, homosexual, activist, Buddhist, poet-man, who wrote about how the world for himself and his people, his Beat people, and the other worlds surrounding them *were* as well as what he hoped they might be and what he hoped they might rise up in protest for. Ginsberg celebrated a certain state of being that was already in motion as well as spoke out against a certain state of being that was actively working to stifle that motion. In other words, he spoke in a way truly redolent of the Native American trickster Coyote, as Coyote especially celebrates and argues for the thrill of impermanence, celebrates and argues "for things as they *are*."[3]

I hope that through this work you will come to see this extraordinary part of Ginsberg's writing style that, I believe, connects his "Howl" in unique ways, however tenuously at times, to the Native American trickster. "Howl" entered the world's stage on October 7, 1955, when Ginsberg stepped forward with Part I in hand to perform for some of those "best minds" of his generation at the Six Gallery poetry reading in San Francisco. But even Ginsberg (who well acknowledged and appreciated his own genius) could not have anticipated that these "best minds" would come to encompass such a wide circle of individuals, rippling into a sphere of influence that stretched overseas and through governments to France, Romania, Japan, China, and so on until it eventually came to be published and translated into 23 different languages.

During the process of writing "Howl," Ginsberg also traveled extensively, connecting himself with authors, poets, and tricksters of all shapes and sizes, and it is this spirit of travel, adventure, and tricky playfulness that Ginsberg poured into his poetry in *Howl and Other Poems*. These myriad influences have not, however, been extensively explored in relation to the poetry of "Howl" specifically so much as in relation to the life and biography of Ginsberg. Beyond this surprising gap, there exists little to no current scholarship or consideration concerning Ginsberg's interests and connections to Native American cultures despite the variety of fascinating interrelations Ginsberg shared with Native American trickster narratives. Therefore, this study seeks to begin addressing this missing piece within the existing Beat conversations. As Ellen Rosenberg states in "Native American Coyote Trickster Tales and Cycles," "all things in the universe are ... interrelated," and it is with this concept in mind that I approached this work in examining the possible relations between Ginsberg's "Howl" and the Native American Coyote.[4]

And, considering Coyote, it is important to note that while I do lack the depth of cultural knowledge and understanding of a Native studies expert as well as the more intimate understanding or grounding of a Native American tribal citizen, I want to stress that, though this study does incorporate a significant amount of Native studies discussion, it remains a study of Ginsberg's "Howl" and how his interpretations and exposures to Coyote may have impacted that poem. It is through this focus on "Howl" and Ginsberg's own interpretations, letters, histories, and experiences that I hope to offer a new, broader view of "Howl" and widen the scope of cultures considered in its poetic makeup.

When I was an undergraduate junior, I took a course with Professor Kenneth Mello entitled *Topics in Religion: Native American Religions in Unexpected Places*. During that semester I also participated in a class with Professor David Gaines concerning the study and analysis of 20th century American writers. Through my experiences with these professors in these classes and times, I came to recognize an important new piece of myself, one that was enamored with Allen Ginsberg and fascinated by Native American religions. Every once in a rare while, I have found myself gifted with a professor or mentor who cares so deeply about their work that I find that care somehow transferred or suddenly inspired within myself. This phenomenon occurred between Ginsberg's poetry and myself during that semester with a newfound appreciation for his life, his writing, and his humor. Growing up, most of the literature that surrounded me, that I understood as "Literature," consisted of primarily British and early American histories, novels, and legends, whereas the more Beat and Bob Dylan style tended to be affectionately deemed as "the destruction of literature" and so remained largely unread.

When I gave my first hard, considered look at Ginsberg's *Howl and Other Poems*, what most struck me was simply the loveliness of the actual page with his frequent pauses and sweeping cadences. As Ann Charters phrases it in *The Portable Beat Reader*— Ginsberg acts something like "a jazz musician" in how he utilizes "triadic verse ... extending the line out to the length of his own long breath, thinking of himself."[5] And showing it physically upon the page, composing jazz of carefully timed stanzas and wild chants seemed to make "Howl" into a fluid motion and sound, something akin to a train whistle bowling down a city street. The loveliness amid the humor, blood, and grinding teeth was immediate simply because I knew I was looking at a new type of music-language filled with odd symbols, lines, jerks, pauses, and beginnings— what Ginsberg called "eye-page artistic balance" and "breath stop and speech-mind hesitancy."[6] And as I began to read and reread and reread his poetry, the beauty transformed for me, bloomed, into something I would not call lovely at all, but simply *changing*, something that changed in and of itself with each reading, growing in size, scope, and perspective with each new look. This was the first voice I had encountered in my young life that struck me as something truly different from what I had been reading and truly necessary; I knew immediately that Ginsberg was a man who had something to say that I would not hear anywhere else and that he was saying it in a language I did not recognize at first yet fell into with stunning pleasure.

However, even with this newly kindled interest in Ginsberg, Jack Kerouac, Gary Snyder, and the whole wild Beat crew, it took a research assignment from Mello—*discuss an aspect of religion you find in an unexpected place*—to prompt me to consider connecting these newfound interests in Beat literature and Native American cultures. The paper started out as a meager 11-page piece of personal curiosity but quickly ballooned into a 131-page honor thesis, enabling me to depart from undergraduate school with a book contract under my belt and an unnerving feeling that I was forgetting something gigantic, that I was misjudging just how much I still knew I did not know.

This work involved not simply the physical labor of researching and writing, but also the mental labor and deliberation as to whether or not I, as a non–Native, non–doctoral student, non–Beat, a non-really anything had the right to continue with this project. I struggled for months to determine whether or not I had the ability, background, and vocabulary to pursue such an intercultural work. To help me answer this ethical dilemma, I sought out the guidance of everyone from my undergraduate professors (Native and non–Native alike) as well as other experts in a variety of fields including Professor Gary Snyder, Professor Gerald Vizenor, and James Luna.

The question of whether or not I could approach these other, intensely diverse, non–WASP (sub)cultures and literatures without acting unintentionally as a force of colonial intrusion or appropriation, or simply of basic misinterpretation, went essentially unanswered despite these efforts to appease my own conscience. However, as I spoke more with Luna (who is a Luiseño performance and installation artist), he shared a piece of his own experience with me that has remained in the forefront of my mind throughout the ensuing research for this study:

> I'm using Allen Ginsberg; I'm using Jack Kerouac; ... I'm stealing and I'm proud of it. No one's going to tell me I can't use it because it's part of my culture.... But you understand the resentment and the anger [among some Native Americans], that's fair because of the injustice that's been done.... So, I think it's all in how it's approached. I don't have a problem with it. I think I did and then I realized what I was doing.[7]

I remain mindful of the fact that Native American cultures and traditions are not my own and that my language still hurts for words and phrases, that my understandings and interpretations still want for different perspectives and comprehensions. I understand that my usage of Native American narratives here are inauthentic and that many of them, given my focus upon Ginsberg's interpretations and encounters with them, are decontextualized from their true Native origins and are thereby sadly stripped of certain meanings and traditions. However, hearing Luna discuss his change of mind in regard to non–Natives approaching issues and ideas of Native Studies has given me great comfort and encouragement. This is beside the fact that he also acknowledges a certain level of appropriation or "stealing" of another culture within his own art and works (such as in his short film, *Indian Having a Coffee with Jack Kerouac, Allen Ginsberg and Ernest Hemingway*). And, in fact, he is not the only one to discuss these ideas. Consider Simon J. Ortiz's "Towards a National Indian Literature: Cultural Authenticity in Nationalism," wherein he explains that many Christian rituals brought to the pre–American Southwest in the 16th century,

> are no longer in Spanish. They are now Indian because of the creative development that the native people applied to them. Present-day Native American or Indian literature is evidence of this in the very same way. [Thus,] ... it can be observed that this was the primary element of a nationalistic impulse to make use of foreign ritual, ideas, and material in their own — Indian — terms. Today's writing by Indian authors is a continuation of that elemental impulse.[8]

Relatedly, in an interview with Joy Harjo, she critiques those who assume the identity of "'The White Shaman'"—"an Anglo poet who writes versions of American Indians poems"—and says,

> It's a matter of respect to say, "I'm borrowing this from this place," or "I'm stealing this from here," or "I'm making my own poem out of this," but the white shamans don't do that. They take something and say it's theirs....[9]

Perhaps the most famous critic of the "White Shaman," however, is Geary Hobson, explaining in his article, "The Rise of the White Shaman: Twenty-Five Years Later," that he and his colleague, Leslie Marmon Silko,[10] sought to

> address the proliferation of White poets who were suddenly calling themselves shamans, and by and large embarrassing/amusing/angering Indian people by their pretensions to Indian sacred knowledge and ceremonialism as they paraded such hucksterism in their various publications and public performances.[11]

Part of what was "stolen" from Native cultures (to use Luna's terminology), has also been incorporated or appropriated into modern, mainstream American culture — parts like Coyote, who may now be seen everywhere from popular children's cartoons to college mascots. This does, certainly, change Coyote and shift his significance for some, insofar as how non–Natives may proceed to (mis)understand him. Moreover, I hope to not "steal" parts of Coyote here but to examine the parts of Coyote that Ginsberg may have stolen in order to address Coyote's connections to Ginsberg's "Howl" rather than to Native cultures.

The new forms of research I encountered through this project, approaching the interdisciplinary, often posed more puzzles and problems than helping hands. For example, examining texts such as Henry Nash Smith's *Virgin Land* in hopes of discerning some greater foundation in the early myth and symbol school as well as some grounding concerning any sort of "traditional" methodology in the American studies discipline yielded little more than further frustration. Beyond this, finding and determining credible resources to contextualize my analysis in history and fact became increasingly more difficult to extricate as I hit wall after wall no matter where I turned. Take, for instance, the peculiar case of Edmund White. In his introduction to *Allen Ginsberg: Spontaneous Mind*, White writes of a sexual relationship he once had with "a handsome Native American from Colorado" who was also a wrestler, a writer, a deeply paranoid individual, and one who was always given "a place to crash" by Allen Ginsberg.[12] In consideration of pursuing this possible lead for another, more direct and physical connection between Ginsberg and Native American cultures, I knew that further details regarding any relationship between this mysterious "handsome Native American" and Ginsberg were necessary.

After all, to say that a relationship with one anonymous Native American man suggests a rich intercultural experience is to suggest that any relationship with anyone amounts to such an experience. Thus, I searched throughout White's many works before finally finding some potential answers in his *The Farewell Symphony*. Though he makes no mention of ever "crashing" with Ginsberg in this work, White does mention Tad, the "sleepy-eyed Native American" with whom he enjoyed a sexual relationship and who was also "completely crazy," entertaining "a paranoid fantasy about a cult of Hollywood actors who wanted to sacrifice him to the devil."[13] Regardless of this discovery, however, the details of this relationship stretch no further, nor does White pursue any greater discussion of the mysterious Tad in regard to Ginsberg. In this way, White allowed the trail of Tad and his possible relationship with Ginsberg to fall cold. Without any further knowledge of Tad's relationships or his Native heritage, opinions, background, or even last name, the clue becomes more of a contextual question mark than a thread of illumination. Tad became, for this study, a gray spot in the periphery, a cautionary tale and admonition against false leads and hopes of the like which I, as a young and primarily literary scholar, had never before encountered. Still, learning to weave around these labyrinthine relationships, search out clues, and rearrange old pieces of various different puzzles together fascinates me and has since drawn me more intensely into this new type of interdisciplinary scholarship, despite however constantly it may have stopped me in my tracks and forced me to retrace them.

However, the words and writings of many major Native American scholars (such as Craig Womack, Robert Allen Warrior, and Tol Foster) continue to sit on my shoulders, continuously helping me realize and reconsider the extent of my own prevailing misconceptions of Native Studies and literatures. As Fran Lebowitz explains in *Public Speaking*, "If you're young, everything's new to you, so you don't know that it isn't new."[14] These authors have helped me recognize my own assumptions about what was new, about what had been ignored, and about what others already did and did not know, and were and were not talking about. In Womack's *Art as Performance, Story as Criticism: Reflections on Native Literary Aesthetics*, his frustration with the constant focus and fascination, cultural fixation on tricksters is made abundantly clear in passages such as the following aside: "The trickster (I tried to make it through the book without saying that word) in...."[15]

Of course, when considering my point and purpose for writing this book, I find it was not to reveal or suggest any new expertise to the world. I am only 23, after all, and the world remains new to me and, I imagine, the world remains rather dubious and entertained by my contributions thus far. The point of writing this book was simply to examine the intersections between two distinct topics in a uniquely American Studies way. I hope to illuminate an interconnection between the Native trickster Coyote and Ginsberg's "Howl," revealing that perhaps we are not so different, that we all steal, learn, and hope for many of the same things and outcomes. The primary goal and purpose of this work is to reimagine the cultural giant of Allen Ginsberg's "Howl" through the lens of the Native American trickster, Coyote.

Introduction

On October 7, 1955, at the Six Gallery in San Francisco, a young Allen Ginsberg helped open new avenues and possibilities for the North American literary canon with the first public reading of his soon-to-be-infamous "Howl." Before an audience of other young artists including Gary Snyder and Jack Kerouac, with jugs of red wine passed around and around, Ginsberg performed his new (yet still incomplete) protean poem. Ginsberg was a poet and activist best known and studied for his connections with the Beat, gay, Buddhist, and Jewish (sub)cultures. However, while his poetic works are thickly bricked by these interests and personal experiences, I contend that Ginsberg's mortar of humor and wisdom, tricks and traps, liminality and transformation, may also be considered through the equally broad and influential lens of the trickster, and, more specifically, that of the Native American Coyote. Ginsberg was surrounded by Native American cultures in manifold ways throughout his life, from witnessing Pueblo initiation dances to the fainter background cracklings of the work of friends like Gary Snyder. Due to this atmosphere and these experiences, one may rightly expect to see these cultures influence his writing in much the same way, if not as obviously or intentionally, as did his Jewish heritage or his Zen Buddhism.

This work examines Ginsberg's "Howl" through the lens of the Native American trickster Coyote by identifying and tracing the four core trickster traits inherent in the trickster archetype throughout "Howl's" three parts. *Endless appetite* is a core trait of the trickster and is exhibited again and again within Coyote narratives as he recklessly and endlessly pursues another meal or another sexual encounter. Possessing a *proclivity for creating and falling into tricks and traps* is another of the four primary, inherent trickster traits, pointing to Coyote's talent for innovation and invention and simultaneous tendency to become a victim of his own ambitions found therein. The trait of *boundlessness* highlights Coyote's liminal nature and ability to traverse virtually all boundaries whether they be geographic, cultural, supernatural, spatial, identity related, or otherwise. The fourth and final trait is that of *transformative power*; this characteristic stems from Coyote's ability to change the shape, identity, culture, and/or role of himself and others.

These four traits (identified by David Leeming and Jake Page in *The Mythology of Native North America*[1]) are central to the identity of the trickster and, as such, will make up the framework upon which I construct my analysis of "Howl." I elected to focus predominantly on the trickster dynamic within "Howl" instead of upon Ginsberg himself because of the historic tendency of the literature of the Beats—and especially of Ginsberg—to be often overshadowed by its authors and surrounding (sub)cultures. Nonetheless, the overlap between author and authored is often nigh indistinguishable, especially so in the case of Ginsberg, given his desire to depict the world precisely as he saw and experienced it. Due to this, a certain amount of biography is still incorporated within this study but only for the purposes of laying an analytic foundation, contextualizing a poetic phrase or for establishing a greater link between Ginsberg and Coyote. However, to begin to introduce a topic so seemingly simple and yet so widespread across a variety of dimensions will require a bit of jumping and skipping around at first—stick with me though; this is about to get a little funky, but it will (hopefully) get easier as we go.

In *Knave, Fool, and Genius: The Confidence Man as He Appears in Nineteenth-Century American Fiction*, Susan Kuhlmann follows the archetype of the Confidence Man throughout various works of American literature. She follows the figure as a dynamic American cultural force working through these literatures as well as a character continuously popping up, some grand literary inside joke for the sake of social criticism. She considers various aspects of the role, elements of the identity, and patterns of the behavior of the confidence man in order to trace his movements and influences, not chronologically, but regionally in order to better understand American literary classics. However, where Gary Engle and other critics may view this decision as a weakness, I see this as a fascinating choice to remain uniquely planted in the American sense of a constant New Frontier, of a pastless body of immigrants seeking land, opportunity, and the ability to live by their own realities—not heritage.

Introduction

By this method, Kuhlmann is able to discuss not only a variety of texts from a new perspective but also to effectively examine a much subtler connection between the symbol and the authors themselves who utilized these symbols within their texts. She is able, in other words, to manage the complexity of her argument by focusing on a single common dimension across a variety of categories or, in this case, authors and texts. In this same fashion, I examine elements of the role, identity, and behaviors of the trickster (utilizing the Native American Coyote as an anchor and focus) throughout "Howl" rather than actually seeking out a glimpse of the specific character Coyote within the poetry. I also similarly engage with a uniquely spatial argument, examining "Howl" as a spatial construct inhabited as well as created by Ginsberg, Coyote, and other readers.

There are three major stages within "Howl": Part I, which focuses upon the best minds of Ginsberg's generation, utilizing the "who" phrase as an anchor to allow for repeated flying off into other realms and histories; Part II, which focuses on the monster of Moloch and its many forms and invasions; and Part III, which focuses on Ginsberg's relationship with Carl Solomon (a man Ginsberg befriended while institutionalized and to whom "Howl" is dedicated). The trickster characteristics most prevalent within each stage of "Howl" shift dramatically as "Howl's" tricks and traps also vary in style and purpose from part to part, ultimately transforming "Howl" as a whole into a liminal space dotted with a variety of exuberant, humorous, ironic, and terrifying places.

Terrie Waddell also, perhaps more forthrightly than Kuhlmann, approaches this spatial element of arts and stories by focusing upon the spatiality of the trickster within her *Wild/Lives: Trickster, Place, and Liminality on Screen*. In *Wild/Lives*, Waddell traces the element of the trickster throughout a variety of modern television programs and films including *Lost* and *Grizzly Man*. She argues that the trickster emerges within these visual texts "as an energy permeating every facet" therein, extending "from music, set design, dialogue, casting and editing to the intricate relationship of viewer and viewed," of reader and read—"it's trickster who cements the bond between a film," or text, "and its audience" for Waddell.[2] In other words, the trickster is not only a liminal entity existing simultaneously within the text and its various components, the author and its audiences, but is also not necessarily a character in and of itself. Similarly, though I focus on the trickster within "Howl," neither the trickster nor Coyote appear within "Howl" as a named or solid character. However, there are

Introduction

other solid trickster characters present in the poem (such as Neal Cassady, one of the other "best minds of [Ginsberg's] generation," and even the reviled Moloch). These entities and pervasive energies, when considered together, culminate into a new trickster force, into the force that is "Howl." In other words, this trickster Coyote, Ginsberg's Coyote, is one existing in contact and conversation with Kali, Brahma, Christ, Jaweh, Snyder, Kerouac, and the rest of those figures presented in my epigraph. As I am attempting to promote the consideration of such a symbol as Coyote within Ginsberg's "Howl," these relations and interpretive twists must be kept in mind. This is my own interpretation of Ginsberg's interpretation (however conscious or subconscious). And I carry this thought process and methodology (similar to Waddell's) into this work, examining the elements of trickster throughout both the construction and execution of "Howl" in order to expand traditional methods of reading and understanding this timeless text.

However, I seek to manage my complexity by focusing more precisely upon the multiple dimensions of the trickster symbol across the single category of "Howl" and through the single personification of Coyote. This narrowing of both poetic and archetypal scope enables me to focus not only more keenly upon the unique element of America and regionalism within "Howl" but also enables a more intricate examination of Ginsberg's heretofore unexplored relationship with Coyote specifically. Exploring this relationship is of particular interest here given that most texts concerned with the trickster as an archetype utilize an almost "universal trickster" approach rather than focusing upon a single, unique entity. The universal approach's cogency is founded within the truth of the archetype's globalism, as most cultures possess their own version and personification of the trickster. In fact, different scholars "including Laura Makarius, have suggested that one could use such shared characteristics"—those outlined by William J. Hynes or by Leeming and Page—"as a matrix by which to survey all known examples of tricksters"; however, as Hynes explains, "one should be cautious about the imposition of communality from without."[3] Besides this caution, focusing upon Coyote to examine the trickster elements within Ginsberg's "Howl" is further supported by Ginsberg's own letters, journals, and interviews wherein he reflects upon the trickster broadly but will also, on occasion, call this entity out by one of its various names (including, specifically, Coyote). This reveals both Ginsberg's own unique interpretations of these trickster characters as well as his detection of the

Introduction

clear distinctions between them despite any archetypal similarities. Therefore, this work utilizes Coyote for three primary reasons: its regional connections to the American Southwest, Ginsberg's invocations of Coyote on several occasions in letters and journals, and the fact that Ginsberg's connections to Native American concepts and figures have yet to be examined as possible influences upon his writing. Recognizing my own shortcomings in this area, I hope to here set the groundwork for other scholars with greater understandings and resources regarding Native Studies and cultures to further explore how these topics relate to others of Ginsberg's works, the works of other Beats, and how these may have also influenced Native authors of the 1950s and today.

As Ginsberg himself once ranted, "[I am] not saying that either Olson or Howl are Lorca or Pound — I'm saying there's a recognizable continuity of method," and this is the thrust of my feeling and pursuit in this ensuing study.[4] I do not mean to suggest that Ginsberg or I are Native Studies Scholars or Native at all or even that either of us possess greater understandings of ourselves compared to others who also continue to benefit from histories of colonization and genocide. I am simply saying that there is a recognizable continuity of method existing between some elements of the Native American trickster, Coyote, and the images, evocations, stories, and phrasings of "Howl" and that by Ginsberg's own recognition of Coyote, the connection — as a means of further exploring "Howl" — ought to be examined. Thus, as Daniel Morley Johnson wrote in "(Re)Nationalizing Naanabozho," "I position myself as peripheral to the conversation, not as an expert, but as an obviated visitor,"[5] one who is simply attempting to apply the core concepts or components of a Coyote both Native and non–Native to the bones and makeup of "Howl."

As Steve Heine expounds within his book, *Bargainin' for Salvation: Bob Dylan, a Zen Master?*, "a characteristically ironic saying in the Zen tradition celebrates the need to see reality from every possible perspective while in the end remaining unbound by any particular viewpoint."[6] "Howl" is a poetic work that, if truly as influenced by Buddhism as it is understood to be, not only deserves but requires and even celebrates being viewed from new perspectives, such as that of the trickster. The methodology of this project flows similarly to Heine's in his study of Dylan, as he deftly reins in a work of great intersectionality. He divides the argument into two primary segments: "Dylan & Zen," which provides background on both subjects or categories, followed by "The Zen of Dylan" where Heine recombines the component parts and analyzes them as a complex whole, analyzes the multiple dimensions shared across these categories. This work is divided similarly between the primary spheres of "Ginsberg and the Trickster" and of "Coyote-ing 'Howl.'"[7]

Heine, however, also raises (as many authors and critics have) the question of Zen's influence upon Dylan and Beats such as Allen Ginsberg. For example, while constant motion and traveling is a key aspect of Coyote's trickster nature, the art of journeying is also a deeply engrained characteristic of Zen Buddhism. Heine explains that a "Zen-like outlook" encouraged within Dylan "the quest to find a haven of solitude and detachment in a world where the boundary between reality and illusion is continually breaking down with each act of social or personal injustice, hypocrisy, and inauthenticity."[8] He also includes the talent and "attitude of 'seeing things as they really are,'" as Buddhist in nature and reflective of Dylan's Beat influence, whereas I have already argued that the work to see and understand the world as it is today is also quite peculiar to much of Native American literature and poetry.[9] However, there are key differences here between our interpretations of journeying, understanding the world as it is, and participating or not participating in the breaking down of boundaries. Where Heine seems to paint these boundary crossings and deteriorations as results of violence and injustice, I contend that the disruption of boundaries can often be done in service of society, in the attempt to release society from its own "incomprehensible prisons," as Coyote so often demonstrates within his own adventures and as Ginsberg illustrates within "Howl":

> Moloch the incomprehensible prison! Moloch the crossbone soulless jailhouse and Congress of sorrows! Moloch whose buildings are judgment! Moloch the vast stone of war! Moloch the stunned governments![10]

Of course, these types of understandings and connections are not the only ones shared or similar between Zen and Coyote, and, in fact, some have already suggested that perhaps Coyote was also a bit of a Buddhist himself, or, perhaps, that there is a bit of Coyote in Zen.[11] However, these similarities do not in turn negate the presence of Coyote or Native American cultures within Ginsberg's life or poetry. Instead, these ideas, figures, narratives, connections, and concepts may have been complemented and supportive of Ginsberg's exploration and inclusion of Coyote.

Introduction

As the dust and smoke of this interdisciplinary undertaking dissipate, it becomes clear that this study is not situated solely in the realm of the literary but also in cultural history. As Richard Slotkin defines it in *Gunfighter Nation*, cultural history focuses upon "giving a historical account of the activities and processes through which human societies produce the systems of value and meaning by which they explain and interpret the world and themselves."[12] However, this work remains located predominantly in that of the literary, combining this method with a more traditional literary analysis. I seek to contextualize and understand "Howl" through its location in Ginsberg and history (as well as Coyote through his location and transformations within Ginsberg's work) while also attempting to interpret the poem as a new entity through a commixed utilization of reader-response theory, cultural studies, and certain methodological elements of queer theory. Due to this literary focus and objective, I find no squeamishness or uncertainty with utilizing the work of Leeming and Page to create the backbone and framework of this study. While I do agree with Gregory E. Smoak's critique in that Leeming and Page problematically sacrifice Native cultural contextualization of both narratives and traditional figures, even Smoak concedes that "from a literary perspective [their] divisions might make sense," although their categories (presumably referring to their decision to divide *The Mythology of Native North America* into three parts: "Heroes and Heroines," "Cosmos," and "Pantheons") hold, at best, questionable "salience among historic or modern Indian peoples."[13] However, in this study, though I do aim to take a more explicitly literary approach (and certainly one from a Euro-American perspective given the focus upon Ginsberg's poetry), I only utilize the categories they map insofar as the trickster is concerned (appetite, boundlessness, transformative power, and tricks and traps).

Given my significant focus upon how this text, this "Howl," has interacted with its author as well as other authors and readers (including myself) to recreate itself over the years, refresh itself with new meaning in each ensuing reading, the utilization of reader-response theory proves almost intrinsic. This approach presumes the dominance of readers (including Ginsberg himself) and their decoding of "Howl" over authorial intent. I contend that, given Ginsberg's many varied interpretations of his own work over the years, the moment he ceased writing "Howl" he ceased being simply its author and was transformed into another of its readers, working to find his way back into the poem by constantly decoding and re-decoding it. The incorporation of cultural studies works to illuminate the transformation of symbols over time (namely, Coyote) and how "Howl" promoted such transformations through its origination on the margins of society. Queer theory, on the other hand, came to bear significantly on the formation of this study, as I am primarily concerned with reinterpreting "Howl," not through a gender studies lens but through a trickster lens. I will examine how "Howl" may have been subconsciously coded by Ginsberg (who is an American neo-trickster himself) and thus implement the method of "queering" or, in this case, Coyote-ing.

Jonathan Goldberg and Madhavi Menon eloquently detail this method of "queering" texts and histories in their article "Queering History." They explain that to queer something such as history is to attempt to change the ways people traditionally view that history (or text); it is to suspend the idea that the history is either strictly in the past as "wholly other" or as something that can be "assimilate[d] ... to a present assumed identical to itself."[14] They proffer a new option outside of the traditional, comfortable binary: a vast "reconsideration of relations between past and present that would trace differential boundaries instead of being bound by and to any one age," or, for the purposes of this study, by any one idea, time, or interpretation.[15] Thus, by utilizing both queering and reader-response theory (though this may seem counterintuitive in some aspects), we are able to examine "Howl" both within the 1950s and as a part of the present, something constantly shifting and moving through time. Through these theories, we are able to step outside of the Euro-American, linear time construct and apply ideas and influences from other time periods to "Howl."

In conducting this interdisciplinary analysis, Leslie McCall's *The Complexity of Intersectionality* has also proven highly influential as a means of acquiring both a firm foundation and vocabulary. She laments the frustrations of working as an interdisciplinary researcher, of feeling the pull to either provide expertise in all areas and methods of an interdisciplinary project or to keep from using them at all. In an effort to outline a variety of means of approaching this issue, she defines the concepts of *intersectionality* ("the relationships among multiple dimensions and modalities of social relations and subject formations") and *intracategorical complexity* (which "interrogates the boundary-making and boundary-defining process itself ... [though] it acknowledges the stable ... relationships that social categories represent at any given point in time").[16] In other words, inter-

Introduction

sectionality is the overlap of different sectors of individual and societal identities and/or formations, and intracategorical complexity is both a means of approaching academia as well as a trickster project—troubling the categories of our paradigms and ways of thinking while still embodying and existing within several of these categories (and thereby defying them all over again). For the purposes of this study, intersectionality pertains to the cloverleaf of Ginsberg's "Howl" and the trickster archetype. Intracategorical complexity, on the other hand, is a means of approaching and managing the complexity of such intersectionality by questioning the boundaries of these two subjects—the poem and the symbol/archetype—while still utilizing them as separate categories in order to understand how they overlap and intersect. This work depends upon the intracategorical approach as a foundation for examining two inherently complex and independent entities "'whose identit[ies cross] the boundaries of traditionally constructed groups.'"[17]

The poetry analysis of this project is conducted by means of dismantling "Howl" into its component parts and examining their similarities in method, moral, and content with those of Coyote, whose unique characteristics I establish through a similar examination of various Native and non–Native trickster narratives. Due to this chosen course, a variety of other topics must also precede this analysis in order to explicate and subtilize the details of why Native American interpretations of the trickster archetype were selected over other cultural portraits as well as to provide a finer understanding of the historical and cultural contexts of Ginsberg's poetry. "Howl" is thus assayed step by step in order to examine wording, historical and biographical context, symbolism and meaning, to demonstrate connections between the poetry and the trickster archetype. Through these procedures, in conjunction with other cultural, literary, and even mystical theories (such as the notion of *cosmic consciousness* presented by Richard Bucke), a greater interdisciplinary understanding of how and why "Howl" may possess elements of the trickster archetype may be achieved.

"Howl" is a revolutionary work written to communicate a radicalism of the self, an idea rooted deeply in a thoroughly "American tradition." This "American tradition" is, ironically, one of revolution and change stimulated by cries for greater intellectual and spiritual sovereignty and for expanded individual liberties. Through meticulous examination of

"Howl," Coyote, and Ginsberg's various connections with Native American cultures, I posit that the trickster archetype acts in Ginsberg's poetic work as a sort of shadow-benefactor of his humor and "holy fool" trickster-wisdom.[18] By "shadow-benefactor," I mean that it is due to the nature of the trickster dynamic that Ginsberg is able to so eloquently utilize the types of humor and ironic wisdom within "Howl," often in the space of a single phrase, without his purposefully working to incorporate the trickster into the poetry.

Granted, this argument becomes tricky (no pun intended) given the decision to focus on "Howl," one of Ginsberg's earlier works. He composed "Howl" during a time when even Gary Snyder recalls that Ginsberg probably did not yet "have much sense of the 'Old Doctor Coyote' or 'Coyote Old Man' motif and stories."[19] This chronological vagueness concerning Ginsberg's recognition of Coyote does not erase the stunning similarities running through this trickster and poet. Instead, this vagueness means that this work is not about arguing Ginsberg's intentional employment of Native tricksters, but about looking at "Howl" through the context of new cultural influences and theories, and through Ginsberg's own obvious intent to promote conversation and connection between many different peoples and cultures. Establishing this keynote distinction liberates many new possibilities for analysis, enabling this study to not only expand upon a revolutionary poem but to also consider it through the lenses of other cultures and ideas the author may not have originally intended.

Anne Waldman essentially affirms this assessment in "Premises of Consciousness," explaining that "Howl" is not a poem bound by any particular era, translation, culture, or understanding. "Howl" is, in a sense, meant to speak to and charge up a multitude of cultures and experiences through its ability to permeate the consciousnesses of numerous individuals and populations. "Howl," she asserts, "moves beyond literal historical time."[20] "And what makes the poem seem more and more, over time, like a sacred text, a sutra, a ritual"—and a part of an oral tradition, such as that which has kept Coyote continuously transforming and traveling through time—"is that as it is read silently or aloud, 'Howl' is reactivated."[21] In other words, readers are able to return to "Howl" again and again and come away with new realizations, interpretations, and revelations each time through its capacity, like Coyote's, to seep into a culture's consciousness and change it, influence it, and encourage the exploration of new perspectives.

Introduction

However, this ability to permeate cultural consciousnesses extends beyond simply Coyote as many aspects of various Native American cultures have come to impact and influence other modern American cultures, whether by the effects of assimilation, appropriation, familial integration, or otherwise. Examples of this may include the resurgence of "aboriginal philosophies of respect for ... the earth" in the late 20th century as a part of the early stages of national "environmental awareness"; recharged mainstream interest in Native narratives generally, however often problematically due to rampant oversimplification and presumptiveness; the proliferation of stereotypes such as the "Noble Savage"; and the general misinterpretation and White-washing of narratives and histories.[22] These are, of course, dangers that arise whenever an outsider approaches such insider texts and topics, although these dangers should not undermine the weight of these insider influences. Many native narratives, including those tied up in Coyote, attempt to express "the realities of the present for the sake of the future" rather than romanticize nostalgic, idyllic pasts or fantastical, utopian futures.[23]

These elements of influence may be keenly observed within the archetype of the trickster, and, by extension, Coyote specifically. He continuously acts as the catalyst of progress and invention while simultaneously symbolizing the past. However, despite his wisdom, Coyote also remains trapped by his own preoccupation with instant gratification and the rewards of the present. This pattern of focus on the present as a means of affecting change in the future, of entrapment in the paradox of being both an elder filled with wisdom and a youth full of creativity and desire for self-gratification, is also clearly reflected in Ginsberg and his poetry. After all, Ginsberg is widely considered — despite Kerouac's being the first to coin the term *Beats* — the father of the Beat generation, one of the first and founding Beats who proved himself to be a surprisingly effective catalyst for change and action in more than simply poetry but in grassroots activism for multiple causes such as censorship issues.

These early elements of Coyote and Ginsberg's poetic talents expressed in "Howl" also allow for a better understanding of the poet's role as activist. As Adrienne Rich explains in her article "The Hermit's Scream," poets are uniquely qualified for activism due to the supposition that "poetry, in its own way, is a carrier of the sparks ... seeking connection with unseen others," perhaps even seeking connection with a starry dynamo in the machinery of night.[24] And Ginsberg's unique qualifications for activism (as both a poet and an "actual" activist) are evidenced by the many people who found themselves rallied and inspired to action via powerful rhetoric and, specifically, "Howl." Andrei Codrescu reminisces how "Howl" influenced him and his friends in 1960s Communist Romania: "Clearly, we could no longer simply ... hope that the masses would be illuminated by sudden understanding of our metaphors. We had to act as well as write."[25] Of course, Mark Doty clarifies that poetry is actually more "a form that tends to be a far advance scout of culture rather than an actual agent of change."[26] Poetry incites others to action; "Howl," a clarion yawp for change, both enacted its tricksterhood as well as revealed to others the ability and necessity of doing so.

I intend to apply this amalgam of factors in a series of close readings and analytic study of "Howl" and highlight components of Coyote and the trickster hitherto largely unconsidered. This creates a steep and challenging slope to navigate, especially considering Ginsberg's sometimes almost cruel pleasure in having his poetry misinterpreted by fellow academics.[27] The primary frustration he and other Beats faced in this regard was similar to that censoring sin committed against many Native narratives and poems—that their works were angry first and foremost, obsessed with death and depression rather than with hope and humor, that their work was "a *revolt against* rather than a *protest for* something."[28]

However, as Ginsberg concedes, there is a certain amount of unavoidable secrecy to art and literature due to the natures of symbolism, voice, and influence. Ginsberg himself once admitted that his poems resulted from his "own reflections of [his] own state and the state of the cosmos, and are written in a secret language," but this awareness seemed to grow slowly more and more uncomfortable for him as he approached the construction of "Howl."[29] While he viewed the journeys and works of a poet as a means of gaining personal vision or epiphany, he eventually realized that if he allowed his symbols and language to so obfuscate his meanings and messages, then there could be no expectation or enjoyment of wider audiences for his future career.[30] This reveals another clear trickster grin within Ginsberg's poetry. Just as Coyote is wise, he is also constantly foiled by his own exploits and actions. Likewise, Ginsberg occasionally set traps for his readers in the form of complex metaphors or obscure references only to fall occasionally victim to them himself by sacrificing reader respect and numbers as well as by constantly changing his own public interpretations regarding "Howl." In this way, Ginsberg often found himself caught between his own unique style, slang, and message and the audiences he, like most authors, so desired.

However, of the many studies of Ginsberg and his wily ways, most scholars are more concerned with the historical changes and events occurring around and because of him rather than with his many literary and poetic contributions specifically. As Nancy Grace recognizes in "Seeking the Spirit of Beat: The Call for Interdisciplinary Scholarship," "even when a concerted effort is made to illuminate the literature, doing so is difficult: the romance of the Beat life threatens to subsume the project."[31] This dearth of "concerted efforts" is a partial cause for this research, bearing in mind the unusual nature of this project even among the few texts that do reinterpret Ginsberg's poetry. These texts primarily do so by examining Ginsberg in relation to or conjunction with the works of other Beats and artists (such as Jack Kerouac or William Burroughs), creating a pastiche of Beat works, purposes, and influences. However, simply because they worked so closely and intimately with one another in the construction and promotion of their works does not mean that the Beats all thought as one or wrote to accomplish the same goals or by the light of the same influences. And these types of works appeared in droves all throughout the 1980s and 1990s as biographers, publishers, and critics "lined up to interpret" and judge the lives of the Beats rather than focus upon or attend to the many contributions of their writings.[32]

Though I do employ a wide breadth of elements within this study, I have reined myself into the narrower focus of "Howl" and Coyote specifically to avoid this type of interdisciplinary trap. Instead, I attempt to produce what Grace identifies as "scholarship that combines both the perspectives and methods of two or more disciplines to ... answer questions that are beyond the scope of a single discipline."[33] Therefore, smaller discussions of Ginsberg's biography, the Beat movement, censorship issues, Native American literatures and religions, and recent interview material of Ginsberg's are all included, lending multiple perspectives for the construction of a more complete cultural context for the study of "Howl." In other words, I utilize the history and biography as tools to probe the poetry rather than as subjects of analysis. This poetry analysis is thus grounded and validated by the incorporation of literary, anthropological, historical, and political perspectives to present the fullest possible view of "Howl" through the proposed new lens of the trickster.

The book is broken into two primary parts: "Allen Ginsberg and the

Trickster" and "Coyote-ing 'Howl.'" The first part examines Ginsberg and his connections to Native America before, during, and after the writing of "Howl," setting the stage for the larger poetry annotation and analysis. This part then transitions into a larger conversation of Coyote, thereby establishing the necessary explanations and examinations of the core trickster traits through which "Howl" is analyzed. As the book moves into its second part, however, the full bulk of the poetry analysis begins. In the first chapter, "I Am Large. I Contain Multitudes," I principally examine Ginsberg and his work in creating "Howl" by exploring his personal history, his history with censorship, and his collaborative process with other Beats such as Kerouac. I utilize a variety of other authors and interviewers, such as Tom Robbins and John Lofton, in order to explicate Ginsberg's possible understandings and definitions of the Coyote trickster as well as his growing and shifting interpretations of "Howl." Discussing these possible understandings of Coyote and "Howl" at various points throughout Ginsberg's life provides us with a clearer framework for exploring the influences of the trickster throughout his poetry.

Upon establishing a working understanding of Ginsberg's concept of Coyote and "Howl," I move into an examination of a variety of Native American and non–Native American Coyote narratives stemming from the late 19th century (which are often translations or reinterpretations by anthropologists) to the modern day (which are often modern narratives or poems by Native and non–Native scholars) in Chapter 2, "Considering Coyote." Through a series of close readings, I work to provide a balanced understanding of the Coyote trickster (as it is understood by a variety of Native communities as well as by non–Native communities, as a both sacred and profane archetype capable of both blessings and curses, of wisdom and foolery). However, this section focuses primarily upon understanding Coyote through its four core traits as posited by David Leeming and Jake Page's *The Mythology of Native North America*: appetite, boundlessness, a proclivity for setting and falling victim to tricks and traps, and transformative power. It is important to bear in mind for this section that I only include these narratives and close readings for the purposes of highlighting certain aspects of Coyote's character; how he may be differently interpreted from group to group (and therefore should not be understood as solely a simple fool, charming buffoon, gluttonous villain, or any other such oversimplification); and how these relate to the trickster archetype in "Howl."

Introduction

In the third chapter, "Space, Place, and Traversing Boundaries," I work to transition this discussion from existing with each foot in a different realm to instead existing fully within a liminal zone. Through an examination of both "Howl" and the trickster's shared liminal natures, I begin to discuss the poetry in terms of Coyote, utilizing both literary and space/place theories alike to foreground this icebreaker. From this examination of their shared liminalities, the work shifts into a series of close-readings of "Howl" structured upon the four core trickster characteristics beginning with appetite and so works its way through each major component, tricks and traps, smearing borderlines, and, finally, transformative power.

These connections between the trickster and the works of Ginsberg ultimately lie in their liminal natures as practitioners of humor, their embrace of bodies, their embrace of the unknown, innate curiosity, joys, radicalism, and taboos to encourage the rest of us to begin living by our wits and reconsider old assumptions and practices.[34] If we continue to drown out these voices and trickster influences both within our literatures and our lives, to drown out our own hungers and drives, then how will we ever move forward? Ginsberg recognized a necessity for a new impetus in American culture; he recognized a suppressed albeit deep hunger for the extension of freedom to all human beings, for the freedom to live by new rules and perspectives. He managed to put a voice to this great need by defying many social and cultural boundaries, setting tough-loving traps for his opposition, employing humor both medicinally and ferociously, and by transforming "Howl" from a diary entry into an epic liberty bell.

Due to these striking qualities, it seemed only appropriate that "Howl" should be my poetic focal point for this analysis, however chronologically odd it may seem. I opted for "Howl" over many of Ginsberg's later works (where the Native American influences may be more clearly and definitively seen) for many of the same reasons I chose Coyote out of all other tricksters of the world. "Howl" is probably the most popular, or at least the most recognizable, of Ginsberg's works. It also made the largest cultural stir, prompting a new wave of insightful and exuberant critiques, reflections, and scholarly essays throughout the literary world. The prominence and pervasiveness of "Howl" are instrumental to my analysis of the poem. The same follows in Coyote and how he sneakily pervades much of American culture through his general popularity and false simplicity. I also selected "Howl" knowing it was probably less directly affected by a concrete knowledge of Native American mythologies. This is a suggestion for a simple reconsideration of the cultural giant that is "Howl."

Thus, it should be kept in mind that Ginsberg's direct knowledge and application of Coyote is not what I am attempting to prove. I only propose that this poem was intended to reach, speak for, speak to, and rally up an American audience of various cultures. Considering other poems Ginsberg included within the full *Howl and Other Poems*, such as the blunt "America" (which contains multiple references to Native Americans through both the simple calling out of "Indians" as well as the brief, satirical utilization of what is commonly referred to as "Hollywood Injun English"[35]), highlights his intention to address the entire nation in his poems, not simply his niche of friends or the New York poet-rebel community. By doing so, he created a revolutionary, protean voice and poetry in "Howl."

This work requires consideration from more than simply a handful of disciplinary and historical perspectives in order to avoid becoming limited by those perspectives, a cage of set voices and influences by which we limit the possibilities of "Howl." This is a poem both intended for and deserving of scrutiny through a multitude of cultural lenses and symbols. To this end, the symbol of the Native American trickster lends itself as an ideal new lens given its multitude of not-so-surprising commonalities with "Howl." And so, throughout the course of this work, much as my predecessors and contemporaries have been queering literatures for a new perspective, I will be Coyote-ing "Howl" in hopes of better understanding "Howl," along with its multitudes, and thus, hopefully, expanding our understanding of its possible cultural impacts and influences.

"Howl" is a poem composed of a wild cultural and spiritual blend and patchwork, experimenting with and deeply questioning Western, non–Native perceptions of time, civilization, progress, and social acceptability. In this poem Allen Ginsberg poured his most secret feelings, fears, loves, and shames, and when he first paused from pounding the keys— though he may not have realized the full implications then and though there were to be years of editing to come — he had produced something simultaneously protesting, romantic, hyperbolic, and significantly, frighteningly true.

> who dreamt and made incarnate gaps in Time & Space through images juxtaposed, and trapped the archangel of the soul between 2 visual images and joined the elemental verbs and set the noun and dash of consciousness together jumping with sensation of Pater Omnipotens Aeterna Deus[36]

to recreate the syntax and measure of poor human prose and stand before you speechless and intelligent and shaking with shame, rejected yet confessing out the soul to conform to the rhythm of thought in his naked and endless head,
the madman bum and angel beat in Time, unknown, yet putting down here what might be left to say in time come after death[37]

Part I

Allen Ginsberg and the Trickster

Chapter 1

I Am Large.
I Contain Multitudes.

> *These novels will give way, by and by, to diaries or autobiographies — captivating books, if only a man knew how to choose among what he calls his experiences, that which is really his experience, and how to record truth truly.* — Ralph Waldo Emerson

In February of 1952, Kerouac sat in San Francisco, a full continent away from Ginsberg holed up in drunken Paterson, New Jersey, and wrote to him of their separate works, encouraging Ginsberg and seeking encouragement for his own self as he compared Neal Cassady to a grinning coyote madman in *On the Road*. Through their letters, these young men forged their own transcontinental railroad, flying critiques, suggestions, and gasps of love steaming across America's broad chest. Ginsberg's March response highlighted his appreciation for Kerouac's blooming style and made special mention that the inclusions of "coyote with dog grin" and "Coyote" had caught his eye.[1] And it is only cogent that it would attract his attentions as he was already in the process of learning to poetically grin himself, sending pieces of "Howl" to Kerouac as he wrote them.

Ginsberg began to recognize early on the power of frankness as an art and lifestyle. He used the varying inertias, energies, and works of those powerhouses about him in order to explore this method further within his own writing. His father (Louis), William Burroughs, Kerouac, Lucien Carr, Neal Cassady — they were all so many minds either possessed by madness, grasping wildly at the status quo, working toward a new language, moving into violence, or moving into silence. And Ginsberg saw it as his task to address and depict them all, to realize a new and entirely true form of self-expression, multitudinous and flexible, which might enable him to encompass his people, his politics, his hopes, and his secrets. Due to this, "the publication of *Howl* in 1956 is often used to signify the arrival of the Beat Generation," these "best minds" "of alienated young people who expressed contempt for sterile mainstream society and bourgeois values."[2]

Ginsberg credits his friendships with Kerouac and William Burroughs as the forces that kept him from "developing into a Columbia College prick" and who, instead, made him feel "honored" and turned on by his own "personal eccentricities."[3] This trio made up the foundation of what would grow into the Beat Generation. Ginsberg discusses all the variations on this label in his foreword to Anne Waldman's *The Beat Book: Writing from the Beat Generation*. "Beat generation" as a label, he explains, originated from a conversation, from one "between Jack Kerouac and John Clellon Holmes in 1948" while "discussing the nature of generations."[4] It is this nature of creation through conversation, this dependency upon frankness, openness, and the influence of the group that I explore in this chapter.

The Beat poets and writers depended greatly upon the inspiration and motivation derived from intelligent conversation and collaboration, from their own peculiar versions of salon, and thus, ultimately, from each other. Kerouac, especially, worked with Ginsberg on this front. Kerouac began experimenting with new forms of poetic style and voice in his writing before Ginsberg, developing and playing with possibilities such as his "spontaneous 'bop prosody'" that helped inspire Ginsberg's own desire to utilize a franker, more musical vernacular in his poetry.[5] Kerouac himself was oddly interested in certain myths and mainstream versions of Native America, obsessing for a short period over his own putative Native ancestry, and bringing to the Beat movement a call for "respect for land and indigenous peoples and creatures," making "The Earth Is an Indian Thing" the slogan for *On the Road*, one also repeated in his *Lonesome Traveler*.[6]

Kerouac is responsible for a great deal of the editing that went into Ginsberg's "Howl." Kerouac and Ginsberg also, in a way, co-authored certain poems. A clear example of this phenomenon lies in poems such as "FIE MY FUM" and "Pull My Daisy." "FIE MY FUM" is a short poem written via collaboration between Kerouac and Ginsberg with a few different versions floating about in different anthologies. "Pull My Daisy" is a collaborative poem made by Kerouac, Ginsberg, and Cassady all together and, in fact, reads like a variation in and of itself of "FIE MY FUM." In these attempts and collaborations appears Coyote, appears the trickster. Coyote depends upon his connections with others as he desires to impress them, help them, best them, take from them, and play with them; all contribute to his creativity, inventiveness, and constant humming action. Despite his often asocial and selfish behavior, Coyote relies upon others to feed and, perhaps more importantly, to feel his impetus. Of course, it is in some ways a much simpler task to connect the dots between Coyote's actions and those who help to inspire his actions than it is to illustrate his impact upon others such as Ginsberg.

After all, the trickster, the wisdoms and histories of the Beat subculture, and the vast Native American cultures do, as Walt Whitman first said, contain multitudes. They acknowledge and embrace the humorous, interpersonal, and complex in order to keep from becoming "tied down by any one set way of doing things."[7] Ginsberg manages this both in his humorous, revolutionary writing style as well as within his own lifestyle choices from his travels about the world to his persistent adoption of new identities to his social activism. Many Native American cultures exemplify this not only in their own community differences but also in their continuous application of humor within sacred stories and their inclusion of "complex conceptual schemes, equality, and forgiveness" within this "comic vision" as both a worldview and a literature.[8] Thus Ginsberg starts off already sharing with Native American cultures a certain unique perspective on the usefulness of accepting the complex, the humorous, and the mythic as vital tools for survival and, for Ginsberg, the poetic.

And the connection between the trickster and the poetic works of Ginsberg lies also in the "enigmatic invitation" they both extend through their use of humor, embrace of bodies, and liminality "to rethink the meaning of existence."[9] Author Tom Robbins defines this characteristic in his article "In Defiance of Gravity." He describes it as a "*divine* playfulness intended to ... [encourage] 'the rapture of being alive,'" citing Zen and Taoist teachings.[10] He unfortunately neglects to mention any Native American cultures specifically but nonetheless explains that it is the humor and the trickster who take the darknesses and harsher physicalities of life and create something new, create "what the Tibetans call 'crazy wisdom' ... the holy fool"—the Trickster.[11]

Ginsberg offered his own definition of trickster humor to John Lofton, both a self-proclaimed Puritan and ex-columnist of the *Washington*

Times in a 1989 interview.[12] The interview begins with Lofton misquoting the first line of Ginsberg's "Howl," which Ginsberg coolly corrects. And from the misquoting of this line — substituting, "I saw the best minds of my generation destroyed by madness," for "the best *young* minds" — Ginsberg creates a gateway to expound the complexities of tricksterhood and paradox within himself and within his poetry as well (emphasis added). He begins by explaining that his opening line in "Howl" is not exclusive in who it refers to but "could apply to ... anybody," including himself.[13] However, he clarifies, or rather stipulates, that it is a reference primarily for those "who survived" and thrived "in a basically aggressive, warlike society."[14] Ginsberg also extends the opening line to people "who freaked out" or who "were traumatized," but what is particularly interesting about this clarification is what comes next: according to Ginsberg, "There's an element of humor there."[15]

From the very start of this interview, Ginsberg extends the voice and meaning of his poem to many various peoples. Many Native Americans have certainly been traumatized by a "basically aggressive, warlike society," which systematically stripped their cultures down through attempted genocide, censorship, the institution of poverty, and governmental neglect. What is more, as we know through Ginsberg's many letters and testimony, by 1989 Ginsberg would have been keenly aware of these facts in regard to Native American cultures. His important nod to humor must not be overlooked, as he consistently utilizes it as a means of communicating to and for the "traumatized" and "freaked out," for the survivors of cultural trauma.

Lofton, however, hooks into Ginsberg's inclusion of himself as a possible best mind destroyed by madness and asks him if this inclusion means that he is confused over whether or not he is mad. Ginsberg's answer to this question — "I mean everybody is a little mad" — reveals a bit of the creativity and wisdom that also belongs to the cultural hero Coyote, asking, *Who knows if they're mad or simply beyond another's borders of sanity?*[16] And, at Lofton's behest, Ginsberg expounded further that madness is not a simple, stagnant, uniform entity, that there is also "divine madness" along with many others; "reality has many aspects."[17]

Here Ginsberg seems prescient of Robbins' observation regarding "divine playfulness," playing with Lofton's own words to create a poetic trap. This is a clever incorporation and recognition of the chaos that exists within the trickster archetype: the creature of madness, humor, and play.

By this interview, Ginsberg also possessed knowledge of Native American tricksters and of Coyote specifically. But even with this under our belts, the fact that Ginsberg would be willing to look back on past works like "Howl" and apply trickster characteristics to them reveals his own tendency to view literature and history as fluid, with the present and future influencing the past just as definitely as the past influences the future. It reveals Ginsberg as the reader reflecting upon the work of Ginsberg the author.

This is made evident also by Jonah Raskin's *American Scream: Allen Ginsberg's* Howl *and the Making of the Beat Generation*. He illustrates how, over the years, Ginsberg continuously added new facets, perspectives, and interpretations to his "Howl," transforming himself into a reader, unveiling the traveling truth of authorial identity. In 1956, Ginsberg told Richard Eberhart he wrote "Howl" in an attempt to "persuade [his readers] that they were 'angels,'" but a decade later he described "Howl" as "an homage to art."[18] In 1974, by Ginsberg's own words, "Howl" was a literal "coming out of the closet" and became an "acknowledgement of the basic reality of homosexual joy."[19] In 1975, it became "about [his] mother" before he called it, in 1986, an "emotional time bomb that would continue exploding ... [the] military-industrial-nationalistic complex."[20] As Ginsberg grew to better know his own multitudes, so "Howl" grew right along with him.

"Howl" may thus be realized as a shape-shifter, a transformer, amorphous and multitudinous. Raskin said it best with his observation that "whenever [Ginsberg] peered into [*Howl*] he saw another side, another aspect. Readers around the world, too, brought their own cultures and histories to *Howl*, reading it in the context of their own lives"—just as Ginsberg hoped they would, creating for it "the legacy of its legendary status from Prague to Peking, Barcelona to Budapest."[21] In essence, "Howl" functions both for its author and for its readers as a continually evolving text, simultaneously dismantling and disrupting more comfortable social norms and complacencies in favor of instituting grittier creative progress. Due to this state of almost constant transformation, examining Ginsberg's reflections under the purview of a reader-response theoretical framework combined with cultural studies (so that we may better know the reader in question) becomes especially valuable in order to imagine "Howl" as a trickster in and of itself.

As their interview progressed, Ginsberg instructed Lofton to "dig this"—*this* being a quote of Whitman's in which he declares—"'I contradict myself. I am large. I contain multitudes.'"[22] Lofton, apparently uncertain of the validity of even Whitman's writing, responds rather sassily, doubting that even Whitman put meaning in his words. This denial of message, this unwillingness to deem even Whitman as worthy of decoding suggests a quick obstinacy to all things touched or appreciated by Ginsberg. Lofton then hotly demanded of Ginsberg how he could possibly know what Whitman meant, and Ginsberg, laughing, simply replied, "Because I am large. I contain multitudes."[23]

It is not surprising that Ginsberg would so focus upon Whitman as a kindred spirit given how deeply influenced he was by this American Renaissance poet. However, this concept of "multitudes" touches on a subject peculiarly trickster in nature. It is a notion approached in Richard Bucke's philosophy of *cosmic consciousness*. Bucke was a contemporary and friend of Whitman's and one particularly impressed by him and his poetry.[24] Cosmic consciousness, he explains, clearly applies to Whitman and William Blake, two inspirations for Ginsberg. Due to this, it is quite possible Ginsberg was also aware of this term and concept, which may aid in explaining his prescient enjoyment and employment of trickster elements as well as his many personal transformations and certainty of his own genius.

Cosmic consciousness, briefly defined, "is a higher form of consciousness than that possessed by the ordinary man," that is beyond simple self-consciousness.[25] It is a "consciousness of the cosmos" stemming from an "intellectual enlightenment or illumination [placing] the individual on a new plane of existence."[26] This is an apt descriptor of tricksters that are not only immortal but are also able to move between times and spaces others cannot, undaunted by borders of the "normal" or "noncosmic" consciousness and reality. Thus, it may also be a sort of "Coyote consciousness," something cosmic and possibly dangerous. By applying this type of consciousness to human beings (as Bucke does with several people including Whitman, William Blake, Mohammed, Ralph Waldo Emerson, and Moses), it creates within them the same mythical and transformative mindset as exampled by tricksters like Coyote. Granted, this type of consciousness may be more easily and credibly translated as simply "genius." However, by any term, it explains Ginsberg's ability to describe, demonstrate, and write with Coyote trickster traits before actually meeting the Old Man. This is not to imply that Ginsberg knew *Coyote* before knowing *of* Coyote but simply that Ginsberg began recognizing and embracing the dynamic of the *trickster* before officially "knowing" Coyote.

And when Ginsberg told Lofton that, *of course* he will contradict himself, just as Whitman had conceded before him, Lofton accuses Ginsberg (and Whitman by extension) of offering only "gibberish."[27] To this, Ginsberg references John Keats' concept of "negative capability," explaining that "the quality of a very great poet like Shakespeare was his ability to contain opposite ideas in the mind without an irritable reaching out after fact and reason."[28] He expounds that this "reaching out" for reason is a part of the smaller mind, the narrower, more judgmental part and that it is the "larger mind" that "notices that it contradicts itself."[29]

The attention Ginsberg pays here to the element of the contradictory, of negative capability, is a deeply important theme within both his poetry and the trickster. *Negative Capability* was Keats' neologism for the ability of some to accept life and the world as entities of inherent contradiction and paradox. Keats may have named the concept, but it belonged to the tricksters long before his time. Coyote exists as a contradiction, one who is hero and anti-hero, fool and medicine man, revered and derided. This is an element of humanity Ginsberg fought to come to terms with as he bushwhacked through oddball identities and relationships with friends that would oppose war, the bomb, or the working stiff but murder their own wives or stab a gay admirer and throw his body into the murk of the Hudson River. All of this strife and Greyhound bus baggage comes to task in the revealing and inherently paradoxical nature of his poetry. As Raskin observed, "*Howl* is a work of synthesis," a pastiche of different elements, experiences, identities, and friends of Ginsberg's life including "the sacred and the profane, the prophetic and the self-promoting."[30]

The employment of these other wordsmiths (Whitman, Shakespeare, Keats, and Blake) does not exclude the trickster from the conversation; it simply indicates that the trickster may be hidden within some part of their works as well. Consider, for example, the fact that Whitman and Native American cultures are hardly unconnected. Whitman's life was, after all, "framed by two of the defining events in nineteenth-century Native American history," the Trail of Tears (1838) and the Wounded Knee Massacre (1890).[31] Beyond this, Whitman had personal experiences with Native Americans both "as a boy on Long Island and as a young editor in New Orleans," as well as when he acted as "the only major American poet to work in the Indian Bureau of the Department of the Interior (1865)."[32]

These connections between Native American cultures and Whitman are clear, concrete, and probably did not go unnoticed by one of Whitman's largest, most multitudinous fans, Ginsberg.

Ginsberg constantly drew multicultural connections both in his journals and his poetry. On March 25, 1962, Ginsberg added a new entry to his *Indian Journals* in which he called out to Coyote specifically alongside a number of other deities.

> Kali, Durga, Ram, Hari, Krishna, Brahma, Buddha, Allah, Jaweh, Christ, Mazda, Coyote, hear my plea![33]

Ginsberg calls out across a craze of cultural boundaries and dimensions to enter a plea for help as he finds himself suddenly awake in Jaipur, Rajasthan, India, and tackling the questions of who and why he is the person he is, and what he should do with his life now at 37, "half over" yet "half begun"; moreover, he finds himself calling out to, of all people, Coyote the Trickster for answers. This illustrates an attempt by Ginsberg to call to Coyote for a greater understanding of the self— of *his* self— across all boundaries (cultural, geographical, spiritual, societal, and individual). This attempt also displays the many transformations of the self, of Ginsberg, even as it hungers to so collect itself into some cohesive instrument capable of beneficially impacting society, of impacting its Beat fellows. Nevertheless, this hunger is stifled and prolonged by the recognition of the traps self-set and self-sprung over the years, as Ginsberg seems to recognize here as he questions his own paths, decisions, choices, and actions while feeling his "fleeting life surveying its twinkling away."[34] This complex combination of transformation, journeying, boundlessness, traps, and appetite is a rough example of Coyote in action within Ginsberg even as Ginsberg calls upon him. And though, of course, 1962 is a few years past the publication of "Howl," it demonstrates a growing personal knowledge and application of Coyote as well as traces of Coyote tricksterness already engrained within Ginsberg and his ways of thinking. However, to more clearly see Coyote's influence we must begin to turn away from Ginsberg himself and examine the poetry he produced using these influences.

All throughout "Howl," Ginsberg utilizes the crossing of borders and the proliferation of travels as a means of revealing the inherent interconnectedness of disciplines of thought, peoples' lives, national ideals, and our own vices and virtues coexisting within a body of identities. Ellen Rosenberg speaks to this in her article, "Native American Coyote Trickster

Tales and Cycles," when she states that "all knowledge is integrated" and that "all things in the universe are ... interrelated."[35] This is an inescapable philosophy once realized, and one, it seems, that Ginsberg most certainly ascribed to in approaching his writing (one which is, undoubtedly, also shared and further strengthened by Zen Buddhism). Of course, as may also be witnessed within Ginsberg's outcry to Coyote, this is a concept deeply interwoven with Buddhist ideology as well. Yet, as the concept itself suggests, such a similarity does not equal the prominence of one over the other in Ginsberg's mind but rather the inherent interconnectedness of the two.

In October of 1955, Ginsberg was 29 years old and had only performed his poetry in public once before — this was to be "Howl's" debut (however incomplete it remained at that time, as it still missed Part II, Part III, and its Footnote). Looking younger than his age and skinny in his coat and tie, large, dark square frames turning his face into a cubist dream, and already buzzing from the generous flow of Kerouac's sauce, Ginsberg stepped up to perform his soon to be infamous "Howl"— one of laughter, one of pain, and one of desperation. The Six Gallery gathering was not a nostalgic salon thrown by classically romantic poets celebrating other classically romantic poets with bouquets of basil. It was something much more akin to a boozy five-part play with wide dips and shifts in style from Michael McClure's sobering reading of "The Death of a 100 Whales" to Ginsberg's more exuberant performance of "Howl" fed by Kerouac's "shouts and whoops in the manner of a raucous bebop jazz performance."[36] In Bill Morgan's words, Ginsberg kept nothing "hidden behind a veil of poetic rhetoric" but kept his feelings, opinions, and impressions of the world, of how things immediately were, "laid bare, undiluted and direct, exposing society's raw nerve" to his Six Gallery audience.[37]

And it all almost didn't happen. In a letter to friend John Allen Ryan (September 9, 1955) regarding the planning processes of this event, Ginsberg confided that Wally Hendrick[38] had asked him (possibly much earlier than September) if Ginsberg would be interested in helping him to "organize a poetry reading at the Six."[39] To this, Ginsberg originally responded in the negative, explaining that he was not aware at the time of "any poetry around worth hearing."[40] However, fortunately, Ginsberg did end up changing his "fucking mind" and assured Ryan that "the tradition [would continue] with a Gala" in the near future.[41]

These sentiments are significant for a number of reasons: not only do they reveal some of Ginsberg's own prejudices regarding the quality of poetry at the time but also that the act of Beats performing their poetry for each other was already a well-established "tradition" between them. It was not until Ginsberg had Kenneth Rexroth, McClure (no matter how "tightassed" Ginsberg thought his poetry was—"that's maybe the way god built him"), "Howl," Philip Lamantia, and Snyder lined up that he felt comfortable enough with the "worth" of the poetry to warrant a full-fledged performance.[42]

This style of storytelling—poetic, performative, honest, direct, and consumed with how the world, how he and his Beat fellows, came to be the way they were—revealed a sharing of "innermost thoughts in a way that had never been done before" yet which is, in some ways, quite akin to the style of many traditional and modern Native narratives.[43] A poignant example of this similarity may be seen in the work of James Luna. According to Luna, it was while brainstorming about the nature of speech and natural, intimate communication with others, specifically with other men, that he began to think more about Allen Ginsberg and Jack Kerouac, the "heavyweights"—a brainstorm perhaps in part responsible for his film, *Indian Having a Coffee with Jack Kerouac, Allen Ginsberg and Ernest Hemingway*.[44]

Ginsberg explained in one interview with author Nancy Bunge (1981) that those who think it improper or unnecessary to perform poetry or read it aloud "are also the ones who have a limited idea of what's classic and what's traditional."[45] This statement came only minutes after a wider discussion of Coyote and his relation to the "academic scene," which ought to lead one to consider if Ginsberg may have been quietly nodding to certain Native American oral traditions in this reflection.[46] Snyder, most certainly, had also already made Ginsberg aware of such traditions many years before. Of course, one need not be a professional performance artist (like Luna) or a renowned poet (like Ginsberg) to participate in this performative, oral tradition. In her short story "Claire," Coeur d'Alene author Janet Campbell Hale depicts her young character sitting up during the summer evenings (although, she concedes, usually storytelling is done during the wintertime) with her grandmother and beseeching her to tell her stories

> "about the frog girl who didn't want to marry Coyote. Tell me about the time Coyote pretended he was dying and wanted to apologize to the rabbits for always chasing and killing them. And the time he traded places with the sun

and ended up telling everyone's embarrassing secrets, including his own. And the time he decided to get rid of Bear once and for all."
And she would.[47]

From revered community elders to revered familial elders to bebop poets to Buddhists to Native Americans to performance artists, this tradition of oral storytelling is one that follows Coyote. It is the one that gives Coyote life and the ability to keep turning up alive again and again, no matter how many times he winds up dead, misinterpreted, or appropriated.

"Howl" is obviously influenced by a multitude of other writers and cultures from Whitman to William Carlos Williams to Hart Crane. However, as I have already postulated, Ginsberg calls on many elements and ideas in this poem that were presented by some Native American trickster narratives long before his conception of "Howl." All of this began what was to become a pattern of cultural "smorgasbording" (to borrow a term from Ari Goldman's concept of "Smorgasbord Jews") all throughout Ginsberg's poetic career.[48] "Smorgasbording," in regard to Native American tricksters, is not synonymous with appropriation or its contingent dangers, as Ginsberg never directly references Coyote or the trickster within his poem. As Goldman explains it, "smorgasbording" is a method by which many modern American Jews, rather than completely following every Jewish religious tradition or practice, "take the items [or traditions] that are most meaningful to [them], and that will," they believe, "make [them] better Jews."[49] In a similar fashion, Ginsberg reflected upon and sifted through the sum of his life experiences and cultural and literary interests constantly and continuously. And he chose, from among those "items" that held the most meaning for him to give meaning to his poetry, and to also, he seemed to believe, make himself a better poet, make "Howl" a better poem, and make America a better America. These "items" consist of many different materials and moments, from letters to Gary Snyder to journaled moments regarding events such as his mother's lobotomy. Much as Luna suggests for the "items" taken into his work, "I'm using Allen Ginsberg; I'm using Jack Kerouac; ... ; I'm stealing and I'm proud of it."[50] From these "items" of memory, culture, and meaning came a dependence upon collaboration and poetic performance.

Salon-like conversation and connectivity are major building blocks of Beat literature. The famous first public reading of "Howl" was in its own way a part of a major conversation stretching out, Coyote-like, between different generations, disciplines, and mediums. This reading was at once an act of poetry, of performance, and part of an ancient oral tradition — a similar tradition by which stories of Coyote were spread and adapted between many Native American communities. And this connection between Ginsberg's chosen method of howling and a prominent method of Native American storytelling is not one to be ignored. After all, to return to Whitman, a figure with an even more concrete connection with Native American cultures and lives (and who more obviously influenced Ginsberg's poetry) and famous for the "oracularity" of his poetry:

> [Whitman's] desire to reach people directly, led him so far as to assert the importance of understanding his poetry as essentially not "literary." ... Abraham Lincoln is reported to have read aloud from the book [*Leaves*] — an "unusual" occurrence ... [with *Leaves* though] he "read with sympathetic emphasis verse after verse." ... Henry James ... [at least] according Edith Wharton, was cured of his stammer when reciting Whitman, whose lines poured fluidly.[51]

This oral method of performance, of sharing by word of mouth rather than by bookstore or television, is an inherent connection between Coyote and "Howl" responsible for much of their growth, adaptation, and power.

But there is more to this part of Coyote's relationship with "Howl" (and with Ginsberg generally) than a method of communication; there is also the method of creation. The Beats, and especially Ginsberg and Kerouac, depended upon conversation and an environment of intellectual generosity in order to create new poems. In other words, they relied heavily upon the interests, knowledge, and ideas of each other in order to build and polish their own projects. Kerouac is responsible for much of the editing that went into many of Ginsberg's poems and especially for many of the stylistic shifts Ginsberg underwent as a young writer. Ginsberg, likewise, is responsible for a significant amount of early *On the Road* brainstorming. Kerouac and Ginsberg also, perhaps more deliberately, co-authored several other shorter poems such as "Pull My Daisy." In this same fashion, many Native American myths (from all over the country) often end up being nearly identical in plot and moral, at times only differing in details such as which trickster did the tricking or trapping.

Oral traditions are particularly adept at enabling stories to change, grow, and spread, creating mythologies about the stories and poems themselves, such as has happened with both Coyote and "Howl." In this way, the creation and proliferation of the larger cultural identities of both "Howl" and Coyote and the performative nature of their proliferation inherently connect them. It is also worthy of note how both of these tricksters have also managed to utilize these same methods and ideas in order to quietly (and in some cases, such as the obscenity trial, not so quietly) reshape aspects of American culture. As Robert Bednar explains, a major component of "culture is the production"—and, I would add, the proliferation and adaptation—"of stories," whether it be "Howl," Coyote narratives, or even biblical parables or the first Thanksgiving.[52]

Ginsberg wrote voraciously throughout his life but not simply poetry—he was also an avid letter and journal writer. And it is due to these habits that many of his more concrete connections with Native American cultures, and Coyote specifically, survive. These letters help illuminate some of the extent of Ginsberg's knowledge or at least his familiarity with Coyote. Ginsberg's friends and Beat colleagues were not much for keeping works and ideas to themselves. They wrote to each other constantly and were not at all squeamish about working with each other on their artistic pursuits, crafting poems and prose, bolstering careers, and sharing in experimentation. Knowing this propensity for collaboration, the fact that two of Ginsberg's close friends, Kerouac and Snyder, possessed knowledge of Native American mythologies pre–"Howl" presents a clue to Ginsberg's Coyote prescience. Kerouac "had studied Native American mythologies as early as 1947."[53] And Snyder had, long before "Howl," already studied and written works which "blend[ed] Native American imagery"[54] with other cultures and politics.[55] It is also likely that Ginsberg and Snyder conversed about, at least, Snyder's interests in Native American Studies while "Howl" was still in progress, and even before its debut at the Six Gallery performance. In a letter to friend John Allen Ryan, Ginsberg, during a discussion of his work helping to stage and coordinate the Six Gallery gathering, mentioned

> a bearded interesting Berkeley cat name of Snyder, I met him yesterday [September 8th, 1955].... [He is] hungup on Indians (ex anthropology student from some Indian hometown) and writes well.[56]

In a later letter from Snyder in early January of 1957, it is revealed that Ginsberg has apparently been in possession of a copy of his manuscript, *Myths & Texts* (the corresponding letter from Ginsberg is missing from the record, but it would appear from Snyder's following letter that Ginsberg provided some "assurance that the manuscript [was] safe" or, as Snyder put it, "still with this world").[57] This book (which Snyder worked on during 1952 and all the way into 1956) was eventually published, and, while pieces of it certainly drew upon Snyder's Zen fascinations, Snyder explains that it is partially based upon "the songs and dances of Great Basin Indian tribes [he] used to hang around."[58]

These links and letters evidence the Beats' predilection for open discussion of ideas as well as their culturally omnivorous ethos. Given these documents and trails, it seems likely that Ginsberg and Snyder may well have discussed shared interests in aspects of Native cultures and narratives in the earlier years of "Howl's" conception and delivery (although the extent and depth of these conversations is lost to the hollows of history).

On May 8 of 1967, in a letter to Snyder, Ginsberg wrote that he had met with Larry Littlebird (Santo Domingo/Laguna Pueblo) for ten days. Littlebird showed Ginsberg around, demonstrated how to properly shoot arrows, and even took Ginsberg to witness a Pueblo girls' "initiation dance" which Ginsberg describes as "tremendous—falsetto clowns instructing [the] girls" to begin exploring their newfound sexuality with them.[59] Littlebird, "a screenwriter and a painter, a storyteller and a hunter," as well as a friend of Ginsberg's, often presented his work publicly to "the people of Taos Pueblo," including work such as "his traditional 'coyote stories' and tales [which] are those told to him by his own and other tribal elders."[60] Littlebird's brother and poet, Harold Littlebird, also recalls meeting and becoming influenced by Ginsberg and Michael McClure—"who came to New Mexico 'seeking nirvana without any strings'"—while living with (Larry) Littlebird in El Rito, New Mexico (he had moved in with Larry during 1963 but does not mention when specifically he became acquainted with Ginsberg).[61]

Throughout Snyder and Ginsberg's letters, trails of conversations about Coyote may be found. For example, on July 20, 1968, Snyder wrote to Ginsberg, updating him on the events and transformations of fatherhood, and mentions a trip to Japan during which he participated in a special "fire ceremony" conducted by "the Master of Ritual, a tiny old coyote-man."[62] In this instance we may see Snyder combining (and thereby comparing, connecting the dots between) some of his and Ginsberg's Japanese influences and beliefs with their knowledge of certain Native American narratives and figures, such as Coyote. Moreover, what may be most interesting about this reference is that through this Coyote name-drop, Snyder points to the expectation that Ginsberg would have well understood his reference to the southwestern trickster.

On September 17, 1971, Snyder wrote again to Ginsberg, this time

1. I Am Large. I Contain Multitudes.

concerning a forest fire he had helped put out that was "nearby after [Ginsberg] left" on "our neighbors', the We'pa's, land."[63] This reference to the We'pa is a Nisenan or Southern Maidu term meaning "coyote."[64] This suggests that not only would Ginsberg have understood what *We'pa* refers to but that he may also have spent some time on Southern Maidu land (presumably with Snyder and Southern Maidu). In another letter (June 28, 1971), Ginsberg compliments Snyder on his continuous progress and improvement upon his "Coyote/Ananda" poem (likely referring to Snyder's "The Forest Fire at Ananda").[65] In response to this letter, Snyder informs Ginsberg that he is hoping to spend some time tripping up to Higher Sierra (a site of Maidu communities that stretches from the "crest of the High Sierra, west to the Sacramento River, and south to the Consumnes River").[66]

Six years later on November 11, Ginsberg wrote to Snyder again, this time in response to Snyder's general catching up and discussion of his own work "on the prose book about Asia" (a book that was never completed).[67] In his letter, Ginsberg speaks to the character of Gregory Corso, explaining that there was certainly "enough element of Coyote in his social person that makes him valuable local genius as well as sonofabitch," and, as if recalling more and more of Coyote as he went on, Ginsberg refers also to Coyote's "irreducible orneriness," "human stupidity," and "spirit of genius," before asking, "Didn't Bear or others get so mad at Coyote they wanted to kill him?"[68]

These passages are significant because they, along with many other of Ginsberg and Snyder's letters, clearly display not only a certain understanding of the trickster dynamic, in this case specifically that of a distinctly Native American trickster, but also an everyday implementation of that knowledge. Snyder also made certain to connect Ginsberg with others involved with Native American cultures, including Franco Beltrametti (a professor at Polytechnic College, San Luis Obispo) and the mysterious Jaime de Angulo (who was "an author and expert in anthropology and Native American culture").[69]

In effect, much of Ginsberg's early poetry may possess Native American influences via secondhand stories and ideas. In "Consumption, Addiction, Vision, Energy: Political Economies and Utopian Visions in the Writings of the Beat Generation," Allan Johnston explains that "any reader ... knows the role that continuous, intense conversation played in Beat culture ... even if some Beats only knew of each other through friends."[70] This web of conversation and knowledge "very possibly encouraged the development of a common pool of ideas," which they very possibly poked their toes and dipped their hands into subconsciously.[71] After all, the invisible hands of friends, community, culture, economy, religion, and like forces affect people daily and usually without their full realization of these invisible forces.

Ginsberg also journaled vigorously for many years. He recorded endless helpful clues and insights to the colorful and complex intricacies of his mosaic life. In entries such as that of March 12, 1952, he reflects on an evening spent with William Carlos Williams, his longtime mentor and friend. They met in March of 1950 after Ginsberg heard him speak at the Guggenheim Museum and later introduced himself to the renowned American poet via a letter. Williams went on later to pen the introduction to Ginsberg's *Howl and Other Poems*. According to Ginsberg's journal, during their evening together in March, Williams spoke with Ginsberg about everything from why they write to Ginsberg's personal "interest in Southwest Indians."[72]

His next entry does not come until just over a full month later, where he describes his first experiences with peyote.[73] Peyote is a drug of particular interest due to its inherent connection with certain religious practices of some Native American communities as well as with part of Ginsberg's creative process in constructing "Howl." This drug serves as another bond, however tenuous, between them. Ginsberg acquires the peyote from an old harpsichord-building friend, Bill Keck, who describes peyote as God, though Ginsberg later disputes the statement. However, though Keck did not speak of peyote in the same religious sense as some Native Americans do, the way he did speak of it — as a door to a new understanding of the universe, a new reality or way of being — is inherently spiritual and related to the religious belief of visions. This, in its own way, connects Ginsberg that much more to Native American cultures and religions he would continue to learn progressively more and more about throughout his lifetime.

In "Howl," a poem of both private-diary desperation and endlessly hopeful jubilation, Ginsberg takes the serious, the sexual, and the painful and turns them on their ears, using humor to spread hope and point out the light at the end of our haphazardly gouged American tunnel. In the 1994 BBC Jeremy Isaacs interview, *Face to Face with Allen Ginsberg*, Ginsberg explains how "Howl" went from a not-to-be-published diary poem to a rooftop yawp, how he stumbled upon his own transformation into a trickster.

> I figured ... "Well, then I'll just write writing for myself." ... So I started writing ... ["Howl"] and I went on to catalogue a series of almost grotesque, ironic, mocking, serious, sincere, ... psychologically or mythological gossip that I heard of and when it got to my own "got fucked in the ass by handsome sailors and screamed with *joy*" rather than screamed with pain or agony, I realized how funny it was.[74]

The humor exists in moments like "who let themselves be fucked in the ass by handsome sailors, and screamed with joy," where something so out of the blue and graphic may be declared joyful rather than painful or taboo; these are the same moments in which Coyote and the trickster force become most apparent. This particular line from "Howl" later changed to "fucked in the ass by saintly motorcyclists, and screamed with joy"; this switch, however, does not change the sex and humor combination, though it does change the method of transportation to something peculiarly rebel-American in flavor, capitalizing on the cultural valence existing between "sailor" and "motorcyclist."[75] Ginsberg's acknowledgement of the "mythological gossip," vague and yet useful, further strengthens the argument that in every moment of sexual, violent, political, moral, poetic humor, we may also see the words shape about the trickster's smoky grin.[76]

In this same interview, Ginsberg also briefly addresses Bob Dylan's comparison of him and "the trickster hero,"[77] where "the question of tricksterness and joke" becomes a connection between the trickster and Ginsberg himself as well as with his poetry.[78] This bond is also recognized by Lewis Hyde in his *Trickster Makes This World*, where he claims that "Ginsberg is prophetic the way that Coyote is, getting out of his cage by calling down the chaotic Everything."[79] However, this argument leans less on prophecy and more on the humor mentioned by Dylan.[80]

"Howl" is unique in its ability to act both as a lament as well as a humorous poetic rant. In many ways, "Howl" is a deeply depressed and embittered poem. Consider these illustrative stanzas:

> who cut their wrists three times successively unsuccessfully, gave up and were forced to open antique stores where they thought they were growing old and cried,
> who were burned alive in their innocent flannel suits on Madison Avenue amid blasts of leaden verse & the tanked-up clatter of the iron regiments of fashion & the nitroglycerine shrieks of the fairies of advertising & the mustard gas of sinister intelligent editors, or were run down by the drunken taxicabs of Absolute Reality[81]

These stanzas demonstrate negative capability in just how deftly they exemplify both desperation/tragedy and ironic, trickster humor. The gruesome humor exists in watching those who had wished to die but were "forced" to grow old in someone else's American Dream, all amid the militant language (indicative of the military industrial complex) of "iron regiments," "nitroglycerine shrieks," and "mustard gas."[82] Although, as Ginsberg explains in his 1975 addendum to his earlier letter to Eberhart, "the drunken taxicabs of Absolute Reality" was also a *prophetic* line, foretelling the fate of those "historians apologizing for Indochinese & Middle East Hot Wars, scientists inventing Napalm and Plutonium..., CIA sponsored editors ... all these madmen" to be run down by the "post–Watergate" taxicabs.[83]

These darknesses within "Howl," however, are tempered by a continuous stream of humor and satire: the bleak hyperbole of these young Beats comparing grievances against "fashion" norms regarding poetry and lifestyle ("iron regiments of fashion") to the wars abroad; the black humor of being bogged, blinded, and censored by those with other ideas regarding writing, poetry, and the world via mustard gas rather than through a pen, opinion, or contract ("the mustard gas of sinister intelligent editors"); and the absurdity of being "forced to open antique stores" after the attempt to kill oneself to escape just such a fate. In these stanzas, Ginsberg effectively displays both the grim and the funny that may result from clashing cultural beliefs, norms, and mores and the fight therein for assimilation rather than coexistence. Thus, Ginsberg embodies the Coyote trickster through "Howl," using it to escape from his cage by poetically dismantling and critiquing the world responsible for constructing it.

In this way, "Howl" utilizes its wealth of sex, humor, and religion/spirituality in ways similar to those utilized by the trickster—for playing tricks, gaining empowerment, helping others, and providing enlightenment. Through these ingredients, "Howl" becomes an amalgam of not only humor and severity but of all four of the trickster requirements: appetite, tricks/traps, boundlessness, and transformative power. James Breslin comments on this type of unique combination in his article, "Allen Ginsberg: The Origin of 'Howl' and 'Kaddish.'" He suggests that "Howl," like "Kaddish," represents "a key place in the evolution of [Ginsberg's] personality, developing out of a time in his life when his creative impulses came into something like a balance with his propensities for self-destruction."[84] In other words, he seems to suggest that "Howl" emerged from a

1. I Am Large. I Contain Multitudes.

careful and growing creativity (manifesting both humorously and spiritually in the poem and in Ginsberg), which was keenly tempered with both accidental and purposeful tendencies toward self-destruction. This combination is particularly similar to the totality of Coyote as he represents the constant commix of wisdom, creation, and destruction.

Furthering this similarity is Coyote's proclivity for beginning his stories by wandering, traveling, moving, and that "Howl" was born of and during one of Ginsberg's most influential journeys, that of his move from New York to San Francisco, taking place in 1953, smack in the middle of "Howl's" composition. And this tendency toward beginning already in motion, beginning with a wanderer's eye, follows throughout "Howl," with those "best minds" so constantly journeying, seemingly without possibility or consideration of rest. In this similarity, I posit, exists a unique trickster relationship between nomadism and creative destruction.

These diverse elements appear in unique form throughout "Howl." Consider, for example, these stanzas from Part I:

> who howled on their knees in the subway and were
>   dragged off the roof waving genitals and manu
>   scripts.
> ...
> who blew and were blown by those human seraphim,
>   the sailors, caresses of Atlantic and Caribbean
>   love,
> who balled in the morning in the evenings in rose-
>   gardens and the grass of public parks and
>   cemeteries scattering their semen freely to
>   whomever come who may,
> ...
> with the absolute heart of the poem of life butchered
>   out of their own bodies good to eat a thousand
>   years.[85]

Ginsberg begins with the best minds howling — perhaps in laughter, perhaps in pain, perhaps both — as they appear in two places, in two positions and actions at once: on their knees in a subway while waving about on a roof. Not only are they depicted as a part of an underground movement but also as a part of protests on the higher ground. They are pleading and desperate as well as combative and ardently bellicose, waving procreative organs as well as creations. This begins to illustrate the feelings and instances of creative destruction combined with the need for movement, for journeying forward.

Ginsberg progresses onward with his pun of sexual and artistic creation with "blew and were blown," combining the possibilities of sexual acts with the winds used by a sailing ship, caressing a wide ocean, a lover, or a work of art. Within this complex comparison, Ginsberg also utilizes the paradox of "human seraphim." He artfully poses the issue of humanity versus heavenliness or the angelic, highlighting the inherent differences between the two, while also suggesting that his best minds possess both the enlightenment of the seraph and the needs and desires of the human. This is precisely the combination Coyote celebrates as he constantly strives to fulfill his desires while the world benefits through his pursuit of these wants (as his narratives provide new wisdoms and insights into how the world came to be the way it is today).

The sexual references continue with "balled," "rose," "scattering their semen," and "come." This stanza makes living of the dead by pouring fresh, warm creative juices upon the cold and forgone, suggesting a form of rejuvenation and timelessness; Coyote experiences this phenomenon throughout a number of his adventures as he returns from the dead and brings both death and new ways of life to others. In this section, Ginsberg also experiments further with journeying and the reach of boundaries as he moves seamlessly both through time, "in the morning in the evenings," as well as through space, "in rose-gardens," "public parks," and "cemeteries," with a call for all others who are able to come to join him in these travels. The line, "whomever come who may," is of particular interest as it demonstrates Ginsberg's recognition that not all may move through the boundaries separating these different spaces of exploration and enlightenment. Not all have or recognize the power in the trickster characteristic of boundlessness, as preconceived boundaries may lend reality structure and dimension, even if those structures demonize certain hungers, desires, philosophies, or lifestyles.

And it is the feeling of this demonization that Ginsberg explores in the final of these stanzas, "with the absolute heart of the poem of life butchered." Ginsberg unveils here the need to rip "the poem of life" from one's own body, to be willing to endanger and move into new, frightening, painful worlds before having something meaningful and powerful enough to sustain oneself through the restructuring, through the liminality, and through the violence of being "dragged off" by the forces of the establishment, of those who may not come.

These stanzas are all moments of intended humor, hyperbole, and

1. I Am Large. I Contain Multitudes.

satire, similar to what happens in many Coyote narratives. But these are moments used to address important and persistent social problems, such as the persecution of others with "unpopular" ideas and/or lifestyles (i.e., homosexuals, Jews, communists, and so on). This persecution may be seen in how they were "*dragged* off the rooftops" and suffered the "poem of life" to be "butchered" out of them (emphasis added). Ginsberg chose to laugh at their persecutors and stick out a penis rather than a tongue, to show that sex in itself is not evil, that humor in itself is not evil, that difference in itself is not evil. It is how these things are advertised, twisted, used, and misunderstood that is the danger, that provides the potential for evil. This example is well found in Native American tricksters, characters of unceasing craze and creation — "scattering [his] semen freely to whomever come who may" — as well as of potential danger and deceit. This twist of humor, severity, and satire in the same fashion as the trickster flows all throughout "Howl" and into its postlude, "Footnote."

"O victory forget your underwear we're free!" is one of Ginsberg's ending lines transitioning him from "Howl" to the holy-orgasmic "Footnote" where the faux stream of consciousness lets loose a chant of 111 *Holy!*'s, declaring with humor, triumph, and Coyote-confidence,

> the tongue and cock and
> hand and asshole holy!
> Everything is holy! everybody's holy! everywhere
> Is holy! everyman is here! everyday's eternity!
> everyone's an angel! ...
> Holy the sea holy the desert holy the railroad holy
> the locomotive holy the visions holy the omens
> holy the hallucinations holy the miracles holy
> the eyeball holy the abyss!
> Holy forgiveness! mercy! charity! faith! Holy! Ours!
> bodies! suffering! magnanimity! Holy the
> supernatural extra brilliant intelligent kindness
> of the soul![86]

"Everything is holy! everybody's holy! everywhere is holy!" — here in the "Footnote," Ginsberg promulgates the pantheistic truth of our sacred places, environments, and ecosystems, which is certainly conceptualized within many Native American cultures considering the predominance of regional religions. Being friends with Gary Snyder, Ginsberg was most likely also acquainted with this concept. Snyder's knowledge of Native American mythologies and the cultural importance of their relationship with ancestral or tribal lands[87] may have very well influenced Ginsberg's famous chant. And Ginsberg's inclusion of "everyday's eternity!" showcases yet another trickster notion. For a being that cannot die and yet dies constantly, every day becomes an eternity, an eternity of new possibilities, ideas, races, obstacles, and tricks. This fits very well with Coyote's unusual sense of time and boundless nature as it does not conform to the typical Euro-American linear sense of time (which is riddled with beginnings and endings).

Then here, "the tongue and cock and hand and asshole holy!" is a moment of great humor over an obvious trickster play: he gets you cracking up before you realize the actual practical joke you've been missing out on. Ginsberg takes advantage of our preconceived notions and tendencies to find humor in sexuality before revealing to us that these are our own cultural biases against our own bodies. Ginsberg has moved past the satire and sarcasm of "Howl" and here flatly proclaims that these are all natural pieces of our lives and bodies made evil only by our minds and media, our Moloch.[88] The idea and identity of Moloch becomes especially central in Part II of "Howl." Moloch, a pagan deity once worshipped by the Israelites and to whom they would sacrifice children (usually by burning), is mentioned over and over again like a protest chant in Part II of "Howl" in metaphorical, accusatory reference to the United States and all of its more tyrannous and hateful characteristics and arbitrary borderlines.

"Worlds Can Also Collapse"

Lawrence Gross explains that a "primary means by which humans construct worlds is with myths or sacred stories" and it is through the persistence and maintenance of such constructs that humans may survive the collapse of worlds.[89] However, the many forces of Ginsberg's Moloch, after years of trying to keep the trickster tales swept dry of all meat and humor and sex, of all real, gritty, and beautiful humanness, continue to go after our modern-day trickster storytellers. By banning poems and books, throwing up obscenity trials, and polarizing literatures as strange or sexualized, we are only, ultimately, fighting against ourselves. And these problems of censorship and media are ones endured by both Ginsberg's poetry and Native American narratives alike. Ginsberg's poetry as well as the literatures, causes, and cultures of Native Americans have faced

1. I Am Large. I Contain Multitudes.

the friction of censorship and media neglect over the years, particularly during the 1950s and 1960s. As observed in *The Rhetoric of Agitation and Control* by John Bowers and colleagues, the media teach us "'how to succeed, how to love, how to buy, how to conquer, how to forget the past and suppress the future. We are taught, more than anything else, how not to rebel.'"[90]

How media effectively dictate American "collective" thought and thus bog down modern protest within America is an issue deeply entrenched within many conversations regarding Ginsberg's poetry and Native American cultures. This common enemy serves as another important part of the shaded middle ground in the Venn diagram of Ginsberg's "Howl" and Native American trickster narratives. Thus, it is important to address this other major connection between them in order to fully understand the natures of "Howl's" and Coyote's tricksterhoods.

To understand the greater extent of the damage wrought by censorship and the selective elimination of humor, I must first stress just how vital humor is to both groups. Humor functions as our humanity's white blood cells, an inner warrior or medicine; it is one of the most important tools we utilize for our daily survival and progress. Humor, especially when considering its relationship to the trickster, "reflects the human mind's creative abilities and helps ease the burdens of human sociocultural existence."[91] This peculiar, playful part of life has been recognized by many cultures and writers as an important means of explaining, fighting against, and coping with the violence and evils of the world. Many Native American communities, with a variety of oftentimes regional religions,[92] utilize humor in their parabolic, sacred, and/or mythological narratives. As Lawrence Gross explains in his article "The Comic Vision of Anishinaabe Culture and Religion," humor is often employed to help communities overcome the social traumas of the past and present, to make sense of the hardships and confusions of an ever-changing landscape and social-scape, and to "explain how [they] are managing to survive."[93] He notes several key elements to this "comic vision," including great tolerances for disorder and ambiguity, "divergent thinking," "nonseriousness," a willingness to embrace anti-heroism, disavowal of rules in favor of "situation ethics," and the courage and willingness to question both "authority and tradition."[94] Many of these elements also appear in Beat actions, lifestyles, and writings, including "Howl," which may further highlight their own version and need to escape to somewhere between the mainstream apocalypse and its conformity. As evidenced by Ginsberg's many hails to sex, danger, and drugs coupled with his pervasive religious rhetoric and hopefulness in "Howl," we may see a streak of the anti-hero, situational ethics, a tolerance for and deep infatuation with disorder and ambiguity, divergent thinking on nearly all levels, and a severe yet good-humored severance with all manner of tradition and traditional authority.

Ginsberg discusses humor explicitly and often, lamenting in a later note that "the element of parody and humor in [*Howl*] ... has been missed, even by members of a later generation schooled in Acid madness ... and misinterpreted as 'anger.'"[95,96] Kerouac similarly lamented that "Beat" "stood not for 'beat down' but for 'beatific.' I want to speak *for* things.'"[97] This almost willful misinterpretation on the part of non–Beats reached its zenith in the late 1950s, just after the publication of "Howl," "in a 1958 *Partisan Review* review of *On the Road* by Norman Podhoretz" because, where "*Life* had compared the beats with communists and anarchists, Podhoretz grouped them with Nazis and Hell's Angels."[98]

However, it is of great importance that these cross-purposes— Ginsberg's utilization of humor to aid in the survival and overcoming of various social oppressions and Gross' explanation of humor utilized by the Anishinaabe — are not confused with any sort of equality or congruency of experiences, traumas, or cultural/political complexities. As Gross goes on to explain,

> The loss of land, resources, relatives, and heritage all contributed to a shattering of the Anishinaabe world. Though fragments remained that would aid in the later reconstruction of the culture, the totality added up to an apocalyptic experience from which the Anishinaabe are still recovering.[99]

Despite Ginsberg's Judaism[100] (and the obvious histories of genocide and Diaspora suffered by the Jewish people), I argue that the suffering and pains he describes in "Howl" remain in no way comparable to the sorts of injustices and brutalities Gross depicts here. Gross even goes so far as to term the phenomenon "post apocalypse stress syndrome" (PASS).[101] This syndrome reasserts humor as one of the most important medicines and cultural survival kits available to us all.

Coyote possesses a unique mastery of this survival-by-humor concept (whether he is aware of it or not). As Jeanne Reesman recognizes in the introduction of her *Trickster Lives: Culture and Myth in American Fiction*, the trickster is "the exponent of all possibilities"; he is a figure "simultaneously hilarious and repulsive."[102] The Coyote trickster exemplifies how wit and wisdom may be foiled by foolishness and fault, how wisdom may sometimes come from those we would sooner consider fools, and how humor may arise from both scenarios to simultaneously lighten and highlight their consequences. Tricksters thrive upon humor and the wisdom derived from it. Whether the humor is at their own expense or simply scatological, the trickster (and absolutely the specific trickster, Coyote) thrives upon the humorous paradox inherent in its identity as both the cultural hero and the social deviant. After all, humor is necessary not only to help us through the painful times but also as a means of rallying sensibility, rationality, and truer understandings of ourselves and of the world around us.

However, much of this humor within Native American mythologies and folklore now fights for its own survival. Many of the "scatological and sexual aspects" of these stories were censored out from the beginning by the non–Native and Native American ethnographers, missionaries, and academics reporting them.[103] But this censorship did not simply take the form of creative editing; it also materialized through the ethnocentric practice of trading out the metaphorical and comedic characteristics for purely literal translations and explanations. These attacks allow and encourage dangerous feelings of supremacy and paternalism among non–Native scholars newly introduced to the recorded and translated material.[104]

Of course, this type of censorship is not suffered by Native American cultures alone. Many other arts and peoples have suffered these injustices in recent history, from the obscenity trial endured by "Howl" to today's textbook and anthology editing atrocities. During the time of "Howl" and the Cold War, the U.S. government "regarded writers as dangerous."[105] Dylan Thomas, Arthur Miller, Dashiell Hammett, and W.H. Auden all endured governmental scrutiny or interference in some form whether by the denial of passports or FBI investigations; even "in academia and in the leading literary magazines of the day, teachers and critics warned against innovation and radicalism."[106]

In recent years, there has been much improvement in the Beats' literary reputations, many of their works being included in college-level courses and becoming the basis for other academic explorations. However, many traditional biases against their literary contributions persist. "Howl" is still often kept out of many high schools while others decry its validity as even a poem at all. Anne Waldman, co-founder (with Ginsberg) of the

Jack Kerouac School of Disembodied Poetics at Naropa University, explains that "Ginsberg fought his whole life for the right of free speech, for the unfettered articulated power of the imagination."[107] Even by the end of his life in 1997, "readings or recordings of 'Howl' could not — and still can't — be broadcast on daytime radio in the United States."[108]

In "Milestones of Literary Censorship," Nancy Peters explains that, during the early Cold War era, "no matter how beautifully written or ethical its viewpoint, if a work of literature employed frank sexual language or depicted sexual acts, it [would be] considered obscene and banned in the U.S.," a ban applicable to Native American and Beat literatures alike.[109] From the moment of "Howl's" publishing, it was labeled obscene, and its publisher, Lawrence Ferlinghetti, was promptly arrested. Ferlinghetti explained that "the 'Howl' that was heard around the world wasn't seized ... just because it was judged obscene by cops, but because it attacked the bare roots of our dominant culture, the very Moloch heart of our consumer society."[110] However, Ginsberg's case with *Howl and Other Poems* also became the first to employ "the Roth standard[111] ... [which] enabled the ACLU [American Civil Liberties Union] to argue that *Howl* as a whole had literary merit and did not appeal to prurient interest."[112] "Howl" became the first American poem to face the legal literary litmus test for threats of obscenity instead of being simply burned or banned outright. Fortunately, Judge Clayton W. Horn found that its literary merit outweighed its putative threats to American decency.

And, in fact, even the wording of Judge Horn's court decision seems redolent of Old Man Coyote:

> Even the word itself has a chameleon-like history through the past, and as Mr. Justice Cardozo said: "A word is not a crystal, transparent and unchanged. It is the skin of living thought and may vary greatly in color and content according to the circumstances and the time in which it is used."[113]

Coyote works in just this way, beclouded and metamorphosing as the shifting skin of living trickery, wisdom, and humor. However, in recent years, he has been stretched into what is now popularly perceived as the non–Native American (but "American") symbol of the inventive fool, reduced to a cartoon stumbling and laughing onward after a roadrunner. But when Coyote is examined and approached with the sincere knowledge that one does not understand him or his significance, he may begin to reveal his complexities bit by bit. Coyote is thus evocative of all the playful rage, protest, and optimism Ginsberg attempted to eschew in "Howl" though it was first received (and is often still received) with poor if any attempts to understand and accurately represent it. Of course, the fact that this court case even came to be reveals a peculiar cultural misunderstanding of "Howl"; it reveals a belief in members of the mainstream (both academic and layman) that "Howl" was somehow dangerous, something the American public needed protection from. This obscenity trial reveals a desire to harness the attitudes and ideas of the American public. In this way, this case also speaks to the many misunderstandings of minority ideas and beliefs (such as those faced by Native American tricksters) which keep them from becoming a part of our general cultural rhetoric and education. Ginsberg addresses these issues of cultural miscomprehension (or perhaps even *in*comprehension in some instances) and censoring of humor within his letter, "Reintroduction to Carl Solomon," written in February of 1986:

> May this writing sweep away Clouds of Ignorance
> From sentient beings too much in pain to see dream humor
> Metaphor & hyperbole as comedic personae of the Muse
> & for those ill-affected by "Howl's" text, redress the karmic balance.[114]

Ginsberg recognizes that it is often due to fear, prejudice, or being "too much in pain" that people may miss the "dream humor / Metaphor & hyperbole as comedic personae of the Muse."[115] He does not blame others for these pains and flaws but acknowledges them *as* flaws in an attempt to heal or correct them with his words and works—words and works that he defends as possessing a sense of humor requiring acknowledgement in order to be properly understood, appreciated, and edifying. What is particularly interesting about this piece, however, is his concern with righting the "karmic balance," recognizing "those ill-affected by 'Howl's' text as well as the possible karmic consequences he may thus face. However, despite this recognition, he still seems unwilling to accept blame or demonstrate remorse for upsetting this balance; this displays the trickster within Ginsberg himself as he begins to acknowledge that what he perceived as his great gift to the world may not have turned out quite as he had planned and, in fact, may have taken on a life of its own.

Of course, the rewrites of interpreters and translators and the attempted legal banning of certain forms of language are by no means the only forms of censorship. Early 20th century Native American author Christine Mourning Dove admitted she often edited out instances of sexuality and excretory events within her own folklore anthology, *Coyote Stories*. Dove explains that some stories were not recorded in their fullest traditional form because of threats that "the authorities would 'put her in jail.'"[116] There are also occasions where personal concern dictated the final production of these translations. These occasions make sense when we consider that much of Dove's audience consisted of, what she likely perceived to be, conservative and possibly ethnocentric white Americans. However, most scholars' critiques of Dove's *Coyote Stories* stem from her collaboration with L.V. McWhorter whose various "intrusions" stilt the stories and may have also led Dove to try too hard to "satisfy [both] white and tribal literary requirements."[117] Jay Miller points to many of the resulting "ethnographic inaccuracies and omissions in his introduction to the 1990 reprint" of Dove's works.[118]

This type of editing crops up in stories such as "Coyote and the Buffalo." In this story, Dove decided not to mention that while Coyote took revenge against Buffalo by kicking and spitting at his skull, he also urinated upon it.[119] And in her version of the story, "Coyote Meets Wind and Some Others," she opts not to explain that the fog Coyote creates, he creates via ejaculation.[120] These are unfortunate censorships not only for the story's sake, but also for the sake of the Native American cultures they originate from, as these omissions both change the nature of the stories and wrongly suggest that such details are embarrassing or somehow inappropriate. This latter issue of appropriateness is one of particular importance to Ginsberg. He purposefully included such language and content within his poetry in an effort to restore or create poetry that celebrates and depicts the true joyfulness and problems of the body and life at its most fundamental.

Fortunately, despite these hurdles, the ipseity of these cultures and their literatures persisted and persist today. Native American tricksters survived the Euro-American invaders with their castrating prejudices just as Ginsberg's work managed to stay afloat amid a sea of 1950s and Cold War intolerances and fears. These wisdoms and histories, translated into stories and poems commingled with humor and trickery, are meant to "encourage us to live by our wits."[121] They both acknowledge and embrace the complex in order to keep from becoming "tied down by any one set way of doing things."[122]

Chapter 2

Considering Coyote

The Chemehuevi tribe explain that Coyote "embodies all *the human traits: laziness and patient industry or frantic exertion; foolishness and skillful planning; selfishness and concern for others.... He is the incomplete and the imperfect.... Coyote has fun.... What he lacks in dignity he makes up in sheer exuberance."*—Jay Miller, Introduction to Mourning Dove's *Coyote Stories*

It is the tricksters who survive to build a new world on the ashes of the old.—Lawrence W. Gross

Barry Lopez offers a particularly interesting introduction to Coyote in his book *Giving Birth to Thunder, Sleeping with His Daughter: Coyote Builds North America.* He explains that Coyote came to be "at a time in the history of man when there was no rigid distinction between good and evil," and that, nowadays, there is no other figure "as old, as well known, or as widely distributed among the tribes as Coyote," lending him the peculiar power to exist without "strict physical dimensions."[1] This is also referenced by Gerald Vizenor and Franchot Ballinger who describe the trickster as being "like a subatomic particle" because "he defies final definition of time, place and character."[2] Thus, it is commonsensical that the Coyote is a trickster not limited to any particular tribe, as will be further illustrated by the various tribal narratives that are drawn upon in the course of this analysis. The trickster narratives examined in this chapter do not privilege any specific tribal interpretation over another nor does this study necessarily favor a Native American interpretation of Coyote over a non–Native interpretation (after all, this study is focused upon the interpretation or use of Coyote by a non–Native within a non–Native narrative).

This chapter works to explicate the four primary trickster characteristics (appetite, boundlessness, transformative power, and the proclivity within Coyote for setting up and falling into tricks and traps) through a variety of narratives. Some of those discussed are presented in their entirety and others are provided only in fragmentary form. This was a difficult methodological decision to make given the great importance of Coyote's origins to understanding Coyote. However, to effectively Coyote "Howl" and thereby understand some of the interpretative and intercultural shifts "Howl" underwent during its construction, it is necessary to acknowledge some of those shifts within Coyote (due to shifts in American popular and scholarly culture). As Snyder recognizes, "Of all the uses of native American lore in modern poetry ... the continuing presence of Coyote, is the most striking."[3] The popularity of Coyote specifically, in other words, is striking given the universal nature of the trickster archetype. He goes on to explain,

> in folklorist terms [Coyote is] a trickster, and the stories of the far west are the most trickster-like of all. He's always traveling, ... he's kind of bad, ... [but] he's done some good things too, [such as when] he ... taught people which were the edible plants.[4]

Notable here is that Coyote is specifically defined as *folkloric*. If we are to begin to understand what this can mean, however, we must first consider the nature of folklore itself. Folklore has been defined in myriad ways depending on who is providing the definition (whether they identify themselves as folklorists, linguists, anthropologists, or otherwise), with attempted definitions ranging from William Bascom's "myths, legends, folktales, proverbs, riddles, verse, and a variety of other forms of artistic expression whose medium is the spoken word" to Gertrude P. Kurath's a "science of traditional popular beliefs, tales, superstitions, rimes, all dealing preeminently with the supernatural" to Charles Francis Potter's succinct, "a lively fossil which refuses to die."[5] However, the primary obstacle or criticism facing most literary analyses of texts which may fall under the category of folklore is that "too many studies of folklore in literature consist of little more than reading novels for the motifs or the proverbs" while ultimately failing to "properly identify folkloristic materials before commenting upon their use."[6] In other words, while literary scholars have established a history of attempting to analyze or utilize various motifs, characteristics, and concepts of different groups' oral, mythological, legendary, folkloric, or sacred texts, they have rarely worked to also contextualize these concepts within the environments and purposes of their originating cultures. This is often the case with Coyote specifically (and is, in fact, largely the case in this work as well).

A rather famous folklore example of a similar scholarly dilemma played out in the works of Barre Toelken, a folklorist who became quite renowned for his study of Navajo culture(s). Toelken outlines the obstacles he faced in his pursuits in his article "The Yellowman Tapes, 1966–1997." This article succinctly captures the ethical dilemmas involved in the study of cultures one is not a part of, especially when such studies are combined with new technologies (such as audio recording equipment). Toelken well states that "folklorists"—and certainly all scholars—"stand to learn more and do better work when scholarly decisions are guided by the culture we study, even when taking this course causes disruption in our academic assumptions."[7] Sharon Sherman also bravely takes up this conversation in her "Who Owns Culture and Who Decides?" in which she briefly discusses Toelken's ethical quandary. After his interviewee, Hugh Yellowman, passed away, Toelken grew uncertain of how to ethically handle the stories Yellowman had left behind, sacred stories that were now recorded for the world to hear regardless of tradition and context. Sherman asks, "Did [the tapes] really belong to [Toelken]? They captured someone else's voice, and the coyote tales were only to be played, or Coyote even mentioned, in winter."[8] As such questions continued to plague Toelken, he eventually decided not to pursue a study of Navajo witchcraft[9] (to the significant upset of some of his colleagues), "believing it dangerous and not to be shared outside of Navajo culture" out of respect and deference for that culture.[10] Such questions and considerations have also posed obstacles to this work as well, as I am well aware that Coyote narratives are not meant to be shared at certain times of year. However, just as Luna has borrowed things and changed them in his own narratives, just as Ginsberg borrowed voraciously from cultures around the world, I have decided that, for the purposes of this inherently literary (and *not* folkloric) study, I will share and even reproduce here some Coyote narratives as they have been shared by others. I thus often utilize Coyote and elements of him as motif, take him out of context, and draw conclusions regarding him and his actions for the sole purpose of illustrating how Ginsberg did so within "Howl." In other words, I attempt here, not to validate the appropriation of Coyote by non–Native authors, but to explore how Ginsberg may have drawn on Coyote and employed elements of this trickster within "Howl." By exploring some of the shifts and transformations from narrative to narrative through stories of the Coyotes of various Native communities as well as of the Coyotes of non–Native communities, we are able to better contextualize the meaning of Coyote as a poetic tool for Ginsberg specifically.

Katrina Schimmoeller Peiffer uses a similar method within her work, *Coyote at Large: Humor in American Nature Writing*, wherein she simply states that she does not attempt to contextualize Coyote within any of the Native communities he hails from due to a simple lack of resources, citing the ultimate undoing of much of Toelken's work to discuss the Coyote figure in Navajo culture as justification for not including cultural or tribal contextualization. She explains that because Coyote is so deeply and intricately involved with the cultures that originated him, it is virtually impossible for a non–Native author (non–Native of those tribes and communities which have Coyote narratives at all) to not "inevitably trail behind" in research and understanding, remaining "forever shy of the full story."[11] I am inclined to agree with her sentiments and thus share this element of her methodology. Given this Peiffer method and related obstacles, this chapter will not attempt to frame the narratives discussed within their originating cultural contexts but will begin with a brief framing of Native American conditions and issues during the time of "Howl's" construction before moving into the analysis of specific narratives. However, I must also note that even as I utilize this method, the problems inherent within it are not lost on me. Native Studies scholars are, after all, not calling for isolationism or exclusivism, nor are they outrageous or unfair in their call for honest, intensive, and humble scholarly approaches and considerations. In fact, they are quite clear in their rightful demand for "a meaningful, informed engagement with Indigenous peoples and their texts."[12]

Of course, upon examining the other major element of Snyder's statement, we find the figure of Coyote being explicitly linked to the far west ("In folklorist terms [Coyote is] a trickster, and the stories of the far west are the most trickster-like of all"), not only in cultural origin but also in the popular mindset and modern American poet.[13] In fact, Snyder explains further that this mainstream (some might say *white*stream[14]) obsession with Coyote is also in large part due to the classic American obsession with the larger Myth of the (Western) Frontier. In other words, Coyote has transformed over time as he has come to traverse the boundaries of culture and tradition, existing now both on traditional, perhaps more strictly "Native terms" as well as on nontraditional, "non–Native whitestream terms."

Of course, this is not to say that the trickster or Coyote has somehow become or is becoming a non–Native figure — the Coyote and other Native tricksters are inextricably Native American. I proffer that, similarly to Judith Leggatt's readings of different Anishinaabe trickster narratives, though there does emerge "a cross-cultural trickster poetic," it does not result in a "hybrid culture."[15] Rather, it enables authors (in Leggatt's case, Native American authors) to "reimagine the meeting between worlds in a way that privileges the comic vision of Anishinaabe" and other Native tribes' "trickster discourse[s] over the tragic vision applied to the meeting [of narrative or discourse interpretation] by most social science and other academic approaches."[16] In other words, the trickster enables Native authors to play with "signs of continued cultural existence" as well as "ways of negotiating cross-cultural communication."[17]

Terminology is of the utmost significance in these conversations given the intensive intermixture of languages, translations, reiterations, reinterpretations, and censorings. To be a non–Native, white American writing about Native subjects, narratives, and topics is to be set within a constant struggle to overcome issues of colonizing language, presumption, and basic misunderstandings. As Vizenor suggested in an interview with A. Robert Lee (regarding Vizenor's views toward anthropology), we must

> consider the arrogance of a culture that believes in outside experts ... over natives, over the wit and wisdom of native stories, and the cultural predators who reduce the original, mythic, and ironic perceptions of natives to mere material evidence. Consider the cruelty of a culture that converts native reason and tricky stories into dumbwaiter theories and celebrates museum simulations over a native presence.[18]

Although I would contend that the idea of one, singular "culture" acting as a cruel and arrogant thief is problematic, the heart of his purpose here is more than valid — it is accurate. Considering, however, these cruel and arrogant cultural actions, it is necessary to bear in mind that while I am a non–Native scholar, I am not attempting to suggest or offer any expertise regarding Native Coyotes, but to trace how, perhaps through a variety of these "outside experts" and others, Coyote may have shifted in meaning along his way down the telephone line to Ginsberg's "Howl." Thus, in order to examine some of those "outside experts" who have shaped "outside" understandings of Coyote, I have incorporated a mixture of older, modern, Native, and non–Native Coyote narratives. However, Vizenor's statement also prompts the questions, who is an "outside expert," what are they experts of, what precisely are they outside of, and who gets to decide who is on the outside? While it is clear from the interview transcripts that he was responding to a question regarding anthropologists at the time, his word choice in "culture" may suggest either an anthropological studies culture or something larger; he prompts questions leading into the heart of many Native Studies discussions and controversies.

In an attempt to avoid making the problematic assumptions he outlines and engaging in the same practices as these "outsiders" (though, despite the vagueness of the term *outsiders*, I am certainly a part of the outside in this conversation), the stories and narratives discussed are presented as closely and honestly as possible to their original presentations by their various translators, writers, and transcribers. Whenever a quote is given in this chapter, it is to signify that it is directly as its author presented it down to spelling and capitalization. Whenever a story is paraphrased, I have worked to reproduce the meaning and content without embellishment or change of tone or meaning. However, this still means that one should approach these narratives and interpretations with the knowledge that they are constantly growing and shifting and have grown and shifted through these, my own retellings as well. Given these decisions, these stories come in a variety of narrative styles due to a variety of circumstances, authors, and choices. In order to attend to these differences, I have included stories from a diverse body of writers published all throughout and some prior to the 20th century. This is not to suggest, however, that issues of style are privileged or of equal significance to content here, as my argument remains primarily concerned with attempting to analyze and understand these narratives as they pertain to and are illustrative of the four core trickster traits in the decontextualized fashion that Ginsberg would have likely encountered and understood them. After all, it is the understanding or establishment of these traits that enables an effective comparison and examination of "Howl" under this same framework.

Marginalization and Termination

In 1946, the Truman Administration turned its attentions upon Native Americans with a call for the termination of all federal aid to reservations (a call first put forward by the Hoover Administration with the

Hoover Commission Report and a call that would continue into the Eisenhower Administration as well).[19] This decision could, as Peter La Farge[20] put it, create "a crisis more acute than any that has faced Indians in our time."[21] And during the 1950s and 1960s, Native American resistance to other U.S. policies "was galvanized by [this] common threat of termination of reservation and tribal status" which sought, rather than equality as the prevaricating rhetoric of the House Concurrent Resolution 108 seems to suggest, "to detribalize and liquidate Indian land, directly abrogating federal treaties and agreements."[22] While stripping many people of vital services and protection, it simultaneously encouraged new racist rumors about Native American laziness, "free lunches," and "handouts" as justifications for the detrimental action. Utah senator Arthur Watkins, one of the loudest voices against the Native Americans at the time, claimed, "Native tribes no longer needed federal protection and that joining the American mainstream could easily solve the problems rampant in reservation life."[23]

This marginalization and institutionalized oppression of Native Americans overlaps with a great deal of open and obscene anti-homosexual, anti–Communist, anti–Other campaigns unleashed during this period, as many similarly argued that if only nonheterosexuals could join "the American mainstream," they could "easily solve the problems rampant" in their lives. During this period (1940s), there simultaneously arose the "Lavender scare"[24] and mainstream prejudice against Communism, alongside powerful voices in favor of sexual liberation and tolerance, such as the Kinsey reports of the 1940s and 1950s and the Mattachine Society.[25] Politicians and media thus worked to slide prejudices against nonheterosexuals and nonwhites into the same arena as the perceived Communist threat in order to encourage the popular criminalization of nonheterosexuals and nonwhites, resulting in stories like the *New York Times*' "Perverts Called Government Peril" and eventually in public service announcements like the Sid Davis Productions' *Boys Beware* in 1961. This is not to mention the cultural consequences of the Cold War, leaving the entire country with plenty to fear as putative leaders such as Albert Canwell, a legislator from Spokane, Washington, and chair of "the Washington State Legislative Fact-Finding Committee on Un-American Activities," proclaimed that, "'If someone insists that there is discrimination against Negroes in this country, or that there is inequality of wealth, there is every reason to believe that person is a Communist.'"[26] Other powerful forces, like the FBI, were also quick during this time to not only equate Communism with all things "loathsome" but to also "connect a commitment to racial justice with political subversion."[27] All of this authoritative, Molochian mess ultimately amounted to riots, prolonged segregationist policies and other systematic racial and social discriminatory practices.

In other words, beginning in the 1920s and stretching all the way into the 1960s, the answer to the issues faced by many Native Americans, Beats, and many American citizens generally seemed clear: *assimilate or starve.* However, Native communities suffered uniquely during this time as their suitability for American citizenship as an identity remained in question, a question that began to serve as a justification for swift and ruthless government abandonment and neglect.[28] And on August 1, 1953, Congress passed the House Concurrent Resolution 108:

> to make the Indians within the territorial limits of the United States subject to the same laws and entitled to the same privileges and responsibilities as are applicable to other citizens of the United States, to end their status as wards to the United States, and to grant them all of the rights and prerogatives pertaining to American citizenship.[29]

This piece of legislation, though at face value it may seem like a grand display of national pride or generous bestowing of rights and citizenship, in actuality serves simply as an excuse for seizing Native American lands, denying tribal sovereignty, and stripping funds and special protections owed them due to years of attempted genocide, degradation, enslavement, and exile. This legislation devastated many Native communities; it hurt already subpar education and healthcare systems, and was successfully contested by only a few tribes, as only the "larger tribes were able to raise sufficient funds to lobby members of Congress to save their lands and government."[30] It took until 1975, after what has been deemed "the termination era (1953–1968)" and the enactment of policies like the Indian Self-Determination and Education Assistance Act, for the United States government to finally begin to recognize and aid some of the Native American nations it had for so long purposefully neglected (whether by forcing many onto reservations or by seeking to "eliminate [their] special limited-sovereign legal status").[31]

Into Coyote

Coyote, as characterized by Barry Lopez, is an entity that exists in the world without strict physical dimensions, boundaries, or rules—a figure that remains unbound by colonialist rule, exile, or imprisonment. A trickster like Coyote, Raven, or Iktome (all examples of Native American tricksters) is an entity whose exact identity varies from community to community. For example, for the Anishinaabe, whose "cultural life kept time with the changes of the seasons," "the cycle of the trickster myths and other powerful stories, known as the *aadizookaanag*, were to be told only when snow lay on the ground."[32] And in fact, "in most Native North American cultures, winter (not summer) is the storytelling season."[33] This reveals not only a fascinating aspect of the Anishinaabe's relationship to the trickster but also of their trickster's relationship to certain times and places within their lives. Of course, the identity of the trickster can also vary dramatically within tribes and communities as well.

The Hopi, for example, went through several distinct, historical shifts in the way they viewed Coyote. In some of their older narratives, it seems as though Coyote may have been regarded as "one more akin to a divine hero-god" only to grow more "secularized at a later time."[34] However, in some of the slightly younger narratives as well as through some interviews conducted by Ekkehart Malotki in the early 1980s, it would seem that, as the Hopi migrated further south, they began to regard Coyote more as a part of the "sinister and destructive side of Hopi life."[35] However, according to Malotki's study, the predominant Hopi opinion seems to be that Coyote is more of an entertainer than one to be revered as either a hero or a villainous "sorcerer."[36] In fact, Coyote is better linked today in much of Hopi culture with the traditional clown "whose sacred duty it is ... to hold up a mirror to the foibles ... of the Hopi audience."[37] Of course, as mentioned, even clans within a certain tribe may differ dramatically in their interpretation of Coyote. This may be seen in clans such as the Coyote clan who are "fellow tribesmen" to the other Hopi clans but who are more likely to regard Coyote as "a good hunter" or as one who "ponders every aspect" of any situation or circumstance he finds himself in (two traits that are the precise opposite of the views of some other Hopi tribesmen).[38]

However, even within these layered and seemingly opposing viewpoints of the trickster's identity within a single tribe, there still exists every element of the trickster's *archetypal* identity. This identity may be best summarized as an entity who exists simultaneously within the worlds of humans and the divine or, as the Navajo (the Diné) explain it, who exists at once with the Earth People and the Holy People, and who both creates and falls victim to tricks and traps.[39] Native tricksters often demonstrate how human wit and cleverness may be foiled by human foolishness and fault, how wisdom may sometimes arise from the mouths and doings of those we would sooner ridicule than honor or respect.

The trickster's is an identity not truly definable, though many have attempted to do so (as I have similarly attempted). In Jay Miller's introduction to Mourning Dove's *Coyote Stories*, he defines the Coyote trickster as

> a complex figure, often baffling to a white audience ... more anti-hero than hero.... He is Everyone, a native version of the medieval European Everyman, expanded beyond the human species to encompass all of sapient life.[40]

Dove elaborates that Coyote played the most vital role of all the "Animal People." Once he was charged with his identity and purposes, he became one of the primary actors involved with making the world into a livable place for the new humans. What's more, it was only when he did not busy himself by doing these good works that he "amused himself by getting into mischief and stirring up trouble."[41]

Anthropologist Paul Radin, responsible for one of the first comprehensive trickster studies with his *The Trickster: A Study in Native American Mythology* (1956), defines the trickster as

> at one time creator and destroyer, giver and negator, he who dupes others and who is always duped himself ... know[ing] neither good nor evil yet ... responsible for both ... possess[ing] no values, moral or social, is at the mercy of his passions and appetites, yet through his actions all values come into being.[42]

Lewis Hyde, author of *Trickster Makes This World: Mischief, Myth, and Art*, defines the trickster as "a boundary-crosser" who is simultaneously a "cultural hero and fool," the mythic figure who "threatens to take the myth apart," a definition that continues to develop and widen throughout his entire book.[43] However, Hyde agrees that the trickster's appearance in the modern world is ambiguous at best, either being everywhere or nowhere at all. This lends Coyote and other tricksters a peculiarly strong relationship with the notion of America as a whole. In his introduction, Hyde even goes so far as to say that if we think of America as a place of immigrants and "opportunists," then "'America' is his [Coyote's] apotheosis."[44] Thus, it makes sense that the nature of Coyote would influence and exist within the multicultural quilt of America, including Ginsberg's "Howl," which grew out of a confluence of his multicultural American experiences.

According to Leeming and Page, tricksters, despite their malleability or particular culture, nearly always possess the same quartet of core characteristics. As explained earlier, the four central traits may be best defined as: the "denial of boundaries" (such as the ability to move between the mortal or natural world and that of the supernatural, or between identities such as the wise/medicine man and the fool); "unbridled human desires" (which extends to all desires though lust and gluttony seem to be the two predominant extremes exemplified in the trickster Coyote); the "powers of transformation" (with the transformation from animal to "human" or that from fool to sage being the most prevalent examples); and, finally, the talent for creating and the tendency for falling victim to tricks and traps.[45]

These traits are the perfect recipe for wisdom via humor. Each attribute plays neatly into creating a character too flexible and paradoxical not to be hilarious as well as wise, possessing characteristics of genius in its ability to, as a whole, understand the world(s) from seemingly contrary perspectives, both the heroic as well as the reviled. According to Ellen Rosenberg, Native cultures often value and utilize humor as a means of communicating "behavior or attitudes dangerous to the well-being of the society."[46] Humor, she explains, in Native narratives often functions as a means of highlighting social aberrance as well as a means of dealing with and learning from any hardships that may arise due to miscreant or dangerous behavior. Thus a revival of traditional Native cultural practices and narratives may help reconnect younger generations of Native Americans with trickster narratives and this understanding of humor, of the trickster dynamic — an understanding and utilization very similar to that which Ginsberg employs within "Howl" for the benefit, harbinger, and encouragement of other young people.

However, these traits may also be illuminated or, at least, may be lent a bit more explanation by first considering what Vine Deloria Jr. calls part of "Native American Spirituality" in his *For This Land*. He explains that from an ethic of treating others with dignity stems "the American Indian understanding of human personality and the meaning of life."[47]

> Individuals strive as best they can to deserve the dignity which the community gives them and it is extremely embarrassing to be praised and honored by one's better while failing to perform according to expectations.... A person hailed as wise, strives to be wiser, a person acclaimed as brave, seeks to be braver.[48]

Given this engrained Native American communal value and ethic of bestowing dignity as both an honor as well as a means of encouraging others to strive to be worthy of said honor (defaulting to a respect of others rather than a disdain, contempt, or ridicule), Coyote's tendency to be honored and yet constantly, often *greedily*, seeking out greater and greater honor becomes even more complex and humorous, offering a parallel and satirical version of society in which basic cultural mores and beliefs are played with for a variety of purposes.

When all borders, whether roads or realities, are wiped away from an entity, its existence becomes defined by torrential desires and constantly shifting identities. Of course, this broad definition applies to certain mythological figures from almost every culture, not exclusively Native American. This point thus prompts the question, what differentiates Native American tricksters from those of other cultures to the extent that one might say, *that's a Native American trickster* as distinguished from *that's trickster mythology*?

The simple truth is that every trickster is nuanced differently; from the ever-popular Native American Coyote to France's Reynard the Fox to Irish leprechauns to China's Monkey, they all share some common traits. And yet all have definite important differences in their purposes and parables as they work within their specific cultures to explain certain specific aspects of life for the people within those cultures. The trickster, in this way, is simultaneously a very regional and very universal character. Think of each trickster as simply of a different culture, each working to explicate nuances of their culture's place and function within their environments and histories. However, Barry Lopez posits a slightly different type of trickster transformation in Giving Birth to Thunder. He suggests that, perhaps, given Coyote's nature as Imitator, Trickster, and Creator, he is also the main "figure of Paleolithic legend among primitive peoples the world over," surviving today in a variety of cultures from that of the Native Americans to even African folklore.[49] Of course, it is important to also note that Coyote is only one form, version, or manifestation of the universal archetype of the Trickster. However, for the sake of managing complexity, maintaining a focus upon the North American region, avoiding the issues inherent in presuming equation of cultural tricksters through their universal similarities, and honoring Ginsberg's many references to Coyote specifically, I have chosen to make Coyote and Coyote narratives the trickster focal point of this piece.

It would be almost impossible to go through each and every individual trickster and dissect their differences, drawing lines between their similarities and origins. A study that massive and specific would result in a

2. Considering Coyote

different book altogether. Instead, I opt to simply select a key Native American trickster (Coyote) and briefly explain what makes him unique among the masses and most significantly influential throughout Ginsberg's hefty body of works. In this way, I will not only utilize the broader characteristics of tricksters (appetite, tricks/traps, boundlessness, and transformation) to frame my discussion but also continuously refer back to specifically and exclusively Coyote stories in order to highlight this particular trickster's relationship to Ginsberg's poetry.

Tricksters are of great significance to many Native American cultures as both agents of chaos as well as "the creators of culture," who not only stole and distributed different goods and wisdoms from other worlds for the benefit of humankind, of the New People, but also as creators who worked to "shape this world so as to make it a hospitable place for human life ... in spite of all their disruptive behavior."[50] However, due to the great and wide variety of tribes, lifestyles, and environments throughout the North American continent, Coyote bends toward different ends of his spectrum for different tribes and nations. For primarily agricultural cultures, Coyote tends to be regarded as "a crude and dispensable pest," whereas hunters and gatherers typically regard him as "resourceful" and strong willed, who, "just like humans, ... is sometimes the victim of his own devious ways."[51] However, thanks to the trickster's aforementioned inclination toward chaos (and thus, in some cases, toward evil), his identity has also been known in some tribes to roll into whole other identities altogether. Native American clowns are a prime example. Tricksters and clowns are like cousins, like two whirlwind cousins who are perhaps more similar to each other than they are different.

Clowns vary widely from culture to culture and community to community, but may be roughly described as entities "who display the open sexuality and gluttony associated with tricksters, but are confined within ritual ceremonies and therefore rendered less dangerous."[52] Where the trickster's greatest importance to Native American cultures may lie in his ability "to mediate between the human world and the divine, to call attention to the element of disorder — even death — that makes the world real and alive," clowns can play a more educational role, and tend to be more bound and defined by ritual.[53]

But this, the importance of death as an enhancer of life, is another trickster trait Ginsberg was well aware of. When asked by fellow poet Kenneth Koch what was necessary to open oneself up enough to produce good poetry, Ginsberg responded, "A little glimpse of death. And the looseness and tolerance that [it] brings."[54]

Gary Snyder also acknowledges this aspect of Coyote and death in his *Back on the Fire*, explaining that "sometimes he [Coyote] is even the outright principle of evil, the devil."[55] However, Snyder also makes certain to clarify that death in itself is not an evil. He illustrates this through the relationship of Earthmaker and Coyote who, according to some interpretations of Maidu (northern California Sierra) narratives, created the world together and bickered constantly the whole way through. Earthmaker had proposed a world of immortals, a world without sex or pain or death in opposition to Coyote; Earthmaker was suggesting "an ideal," but Coyote created "the phenomenal"—the world which both provides the perfect environment for and, perhaps, the world which most needs vibrant poetry.[56] The world of the phenomenal, of Coyote's choosing, is one simultaneously "fluid, shape-shifting, role-playing, painful and dirty, but also cheerfully transcended."[57]

However, despite their differences, it becomes easier to see how some tricksters may have been rolled into clowns over the years. This establishes an important link between the humor and wisdoms of tricksters and the risks that can accompany said wisdom in the form of chaos, disorder, and social change; this marks the thin albeit vital line over which both Coyote and Ginsberg skate for our benefit, our enlightenment, and (hopefully) our escape from "the spiritual death of a mechanized world."[58]

However, these transformed tricksters have not attained the same widespread popularity as those who tend to remain essentially themselves despite the differences found from tribe to tribe and region to region — those such as Coyote. "No region in the world, with the possible exception of Africa, is so trickster-oriented as Native North America," where Coyote acts as one of the more predominant fulfillers of the archetype.[59] He is perhaps the most (in)famous of the tricksters who haunt (primarily) the far West, Southwest, and some areas of the Great Plains of North America. According to Richard Erdoes and Alfonso Ortiz in their comprehensive *American Indian Trickster Tales*, stories of Coyote "are told from the Arctic down to Mexico," and all across the continent; they even posit that there "are probably more tales about Coyote than there are about all the other Native American Tricksters put together."[60] Duane Niatum even goes so far as to suggest that "Coyote is rapidly becoming, in art and literature, a pan–Indian character."[61] It is important to note here that though the humor and sexual freedoms expressed by this entity will be focused on for the purposes of their relation to Ginsberg and his motives, Coyote is not purely a fool or scapegoat to be simply laughed away. Coyote is a powerful entity, as heroic and anti-heroic as he is humorous. He is not simply a character in a story but an important player in a variety of complex belief systems.

In Native American cultures "the comedic is often connected to the sacred."[62] "Coyote manifests meaning in so many cultural domains on so many levels" in part because, truly, "all knowledge is integrated"[63] into a greater, complex whole rather than divided into a series of segmented subjects.[64]

William Bright defined Coyote as one of the First People who "occupied the world in ... mythic times" and who is able to "alter [his] shape at will."[65] He is both hero and anti-hero, disaster and miracle, comedic and sacred, creator and destroyer. But, in fact, "in most traditions he does not act as original creator; rather, 'he changes things into the forms they have retained ever since'—he is the creator of" the world as we know it.[66] In other words, Coyote is a major wellspring of human (and American) transformative power; he is the ultimate transformer not only of himself but of the world around him. Coyote is an exceptionally liminal figure, constantly in the threshold of numerous identities, somewhere between the natural and the cultural, hero and anti-hero, just as Ginsberg found himself constantly torn between conventional academic and bohemian, homosexual and socially acceptable, traditional and revolutionary. It is important to note, however, that Coyote is not a "god" or "demiurge" but rather a powerful entity that existed (exists) in a time when these types of actions, tricks, and (mis)adventures were possible.

Coyote is perhaps the most complex of the Native American tricksters as he is the most popular and widespread of them. This lends his identity a peculiar and heightened flexibility, enabling him to take on the powers of both a "rock musician shaman" and "culture-hero/trickster."[67] Though his native cultural importance ranged primarily through the West, Southwest, and Great Plains, he has—like the physical animal coyote[68]—since expanded his terrain through his impressive ability to adapt and survive. He has since become a mythic figure of mahatma-Hollywood proportions in multiple cultures, including "mainstream" popular North American culture from Mark Twain's *Roughing It* ("the coyote is a living, breathing allegory of Want") to Warner Bros.' Wile E. Coyote.[69] Snyder also wrote on this popularity, positing that "would-be coyotes [are] hanging out all over" the country and that he has, perhaps, been able to largely "overshadow the other figures of western North American oral literature ... partly because he has not been kept 'secret.'"[70] However, as with all forms of adaptation, as new things are acquired and integrated so some original aspects may slowly become lost. In this case, some particularly crucial aspects of Coyote's Native identity are being rubbed out in the mainstream.

The Native Peoples that Coyote originally wiled his way around were primarily the Pueblo, Navajo, Crow, Shoshone, Arapaho, Cherokee, Maidu, Cheyenne, Jicarilla Apache, and Nez Perce. And each, of course, possess their own versions and narratives through which he interacts with them and their culture. It is a vital point in understanding Coyote and all tricksters, that one "can never know the complete trickster from hearing one story about him.... Only by meeting the character in a variety of situations, can the listener come to understand his complexity."[71] And this observation extends to aspects of "Howl" as well, given Ginsberg's ability to return to the poem again and again over his life and continuously discover new traits, meanings, and symbols.

To quote Barbara Schutz-Gruber and Barbara Buckley from their *Trickster Tales from Around the World: An Interdisciplinary Guide for Teachers*,

> Although Coyote sees himself as a cool dude, everyone else from listeners to characters, sees him as he really is—superficial. Coyote breaks the rules of society. He barges in uninvited; he does not return hospitality; he offends the Spirits.[72]

And while Schutz-Gruber and Buckley did pin down some important aspects of Coyote, namely his rebellious and often offensive tendencies, I contend that there is nothing "superficial" about him. This aspect of Coyote, this ability to occasionally mask his own cleverness and power behind his own foolishness or mistakes, is akin to the ways in which Ginsberg's stream of consciousness sometimes serves as a stylistic mask for the meticulous and elaborate construction of each and every line of his poetry. This aspect of Coyote, however, also does not seem to be a purposeful attempt to mislead others into believing that he is "superficial" or sans power. This, I proffer, is probably more akin to the misinterpretations Ginsberg suffered through many of his reviews, such as those provided by John J. Miller in the *National Review*, claiming that though he does not have a favorite poem, he does "have a least favorite" in "Howl" as "Howl" "reeks to high heaven" and "blew [him] away with its sheer awfulness ... [and] characteristically wretched lines."[73]

It is clear from these sorts of descriptions that, as Coyote is often mistaken for simply a fool or villain due to his general popularity yet widespread lack of understanding (or even attempt of understanding), Ginsberg also suffers from widespread (and often willful) misunderstanding and fear due to his poetry's surface layer of still-surprising frankness. James Breslin also speaks to this misunderstanding of Ginsberg, explaining that perhaps it is partly due to "his attempt to reassert the romantic role of the poet as prophet" that has "obscured" his "genuine literary talent" in the minds of "those manning the literary armchairs."[74] Neither Coyote nor Ginsberg seem to be cultural figures whose deeper complexities concern many minds within the academies, a sad problem Oliver Harris addresses in his article "Beating the Academy." According to Harris,

> I'm concerned with how to teach the Beats when my colleagues don't care why I teach them. My concern is paradoxical, perverse even, since it makes teaching the Beats always odd. The problem is Beat pedagogy's position within pedagogy itself, ... [given that] what makes Beat pedagogy problematic is the anti-academicism that is generally held to characterize Beat ideology and aesthetic practice.[75]

Beyond this, Harris finds that the Beats knew that this and their own biases would not be quick to dissipate within the academy. Consider, after all, this stanza from "Howl":

> who passed through universities with radiant cool eyes hallucinating
>   Arkansas and Blake-light tragedy among the scholars of war,
> who were expelled from the academies for crazy & publishing obscene
>   odes on the windows of the skull,[76]

wherein Ginsberg deftly illustrates the Beats' general relationships and feelings regarding academies. The Beats purposefully set themselves against traditional academic structures—making their work particularly difficult to teach in a formal academic setting. They (the Beats generally and Ginsberg specifically) wanted nothing of "the essence [to] be lost in translation" as such "essences" have often been lost or misinterpreted throughout the different recorded, (sometimes) censored, and translated versions of Native American myths and narratives.[77]

These are two complex characters, both in constant motion and transformation. Even though "to the younger generations, *chip-chap-tiqulk* [the

Animal People] are improbable stories, ... to the old Indians ... they are accounts of what really happened when the world was very young," and, like the parables and characters of any religion, they change throughout the years.[78] The variability and adaptations of tricksters to the needs of the always-skeptical and questioning younger generations make Coyote, like Ginsberg's "Howl," ghostlike and profoundly relevant in a timeless way. However, given the issues brought up by such definitive statements as those made by Schutz-Gruber and Buckley, it is important to keep in mind the forms of censorship already explored as well as the differences existing between what Coyote and Ginsberg do in their narratives versus how their actions and words are perceived by others.

The issues and propensities for transformation over time also relate directly to the fact that Ginsberg's personal interpretation of Coyote may never be fully explicated or understood, as it is impossible to know where he learned certain stories from, what sources and voices he relied upon, or how those stories transformed for him as a decoder. Take, for example, the Klamath story, "Coyote and the Wren," as told by Chief Eaglewing (Klamath Indian of northern California whose stories were published by Grover Sanderson in 1938).[79]

In "Coyote and the Wren," we find Coyote traveling — as we usually find him traveling — with Wren and others down to a river "to fight the Yurok Klamath Indians."[80] However, before reaching the battle, they braked to eat some acorns. Blue Jay did the cooking, and as he boiled them, there was one acorn that kept floating up to the top. Watching this continuous bobbing up, Coyote came to believe it had to be the only acorn there was. Due to this, Coyote continuously attempted to sneak the acorn out of the pot, but the heat of the water prevented him.[81]

However, when the acorns were finally ready, Blue Jay went to strain them out and accidentally spilt many of them. When the mice traveling with them saw all of the acorns, "their eyes popped out, and all the mice still have popped eyes."[82] And though Coyote tried his best to devour all of the acorns, there were too many even for him. Thus, to this day, this site by the river is littered with little acorn-like stones. When they had all finished eating, Coyote called upon Wren to sing, but Wren refused. Still, Coyote prompted Wren again to sing. "'No,'" Wren replied, "'my song is too powerful, and it will cause a big storm.'"[83] However, at Coyote's continued insistence, Wren finally relented. And, as predicted, as soon as the song began a large storm blew in, blowing so powerfully that it carried

Coyote away, "towards home," which was precisely "what he [had] wanted, so he would not have to go to war."[84]

Evan T. Pritchard, of Mi'kmaq and Celtic descent, explains that in many (primarily older) Native American narratives, the protagonist (in this case, Coyote) takes action in order to "stop a war without violence, just by their wits alone."[85] In his notes regarding this story, Pritchard asserts that we may see Coyote encouraging Wren to sing "in order to prevent a disastrous and unnecessary war"— rightly reminding Pritchard of the era of Ginsberg's "Howl," as he expounds that "much of this reminds [him] of the 1960s in America, where protest singers caused the storm winds of controversy to blow and helped to stop the war in Vietnam."[86]

Consider once again his letter to Gary Snyder in which Ginsberg compares Gregory Corso to Coyote as both a "valuable local genius" and "sonofabitch," possessing the "irreducible orneriness" of Coyote, and the "human stupidity" simultaneous with the "spirit of genius"— that which might convince "Bear or others [to] get so mad at Coyote [that] they [might want] to kill him."[87]

In this letter, Ginsberg provides a glimpse of his understanding of Coyote in 1977. He discusses Gregory Corso as possessing an "element" of Coyote, and, perhaps more importantly, he specifies that this element is inherent to the "social" realm of his person.[88] From this, we may understand that Ginsberg viewed Coyote as a characteristic of social behavior, one involving both "genius" and the aspect "sonofabitch." However, perhaps the more notable characterizing words in this passage are "valuable local," "human stupidity," and "spirit of genius," as these terms demonstrate Ginsberg's understanding of the Coyote trickster specifically as a liminal entity, at once firmly located in a place and yet also existing simultaneously within both the spirit realm and the human realm, simultaneously sacred and profane. Moreover, given that Ginsberg chose to utilize Coyote in this instance to describe the values and pitfalls of another Beat is particularly interesting as it prompts the consideration of other Beats under this purview. Even so, this passage reveals only the smallest of clues into Ginsberg's full understanding and conceptualization of Coyote and the trickster archetype generally. Therefore, for the purposes of this work, it is important to bear in mind that this analysis is at least three times removed, as it is my interpretation of Ginsberg's interpretation of others' interpretations of Coyote.

Of course, this passage also reveals a slight trick of its own, Ginsberg utilizing Coyote to play a rhetorical game with Snyder: "Didn't Bear or others get so mad at Coyote they wanted to kill him?"[89] This may unveil a unique insight into Ginsberg's personal feelings and/or frustrations with Corso at this moment, as one might interpret this question to also include a bit of role-play with Ginsberg and others painted as "Bear or others" brought to the brink of their sanities from dealing with Coyote's constant genius and tomfoolery. Nevertheless, under all of these circumstances Ginsberg does seem to locate the crux of Coyote's being: a liminal spirit-man comprised of both genius and foolishness.

And while it is, of course, impossible to know precisely which story Ginsberg is referring to here, there certainly are plenty of Coyote narratives (many Maidu narratives in particular) published in journals and books he very well may have encountered at Columbia, such as the *Journal of American Folklore*. In 1900, this particular journal published Roland B. Dixon's "Some Coyote Stories from the Maidu Indians of California," which included the Maidu narrative "The Coyote and the Grizzly Bears." This particular story was given "as part of the work of the C.P. Huntington Expedition during the summer of 1899, among the 'Koyoma' or Maidu of the higher Sierra in the vicinity of Genesee and Taylorsville, Plumas County, Cal."[90] Of course, it is also important to note that this expedition was made possible by C.P. Huntington, Leland Stanford, and Charles Crocker who fueled and financed the final pieces of the transcontinental railroad,[91] the "pioneer railroad line ... [that] formed the basis of the gigantic Southern Pacific system."[92] Dixon participated within this expedition and received these narratives (those which were later published in Maidu with English translations [1912][93]) from a man named Tom Young. Young, a part Maidu and part Atsugewi individual, has been called "the last great Maidu storyteller," his "real Indian name" being Hanc'ibyjim.[94]

For the Concow of the Sierra Foothills, as told in Donald Jewell's *Indians of the Feather River* (1987),[95] Coyote holds a complex role (as he usually does) within their culture, as he is both a member of the band of thieves who brought fire to the human realm as well as one of the reasons given by Onkoito (one of the Hero Twins of their sacred narratives) for his leaving the Maidu:

> It is said that Onkoito finally became discouraged. "You are listening too much to *Henyakano*, Old Man Coyote," he said to the people. So the young deity got into a canoe and left, saying that he would return someday when the Indians behaved better.[96]

This relationship seems to suggest,[97] especially considering the great importance of the Hero Twins as those who "went about solving people's problems," that Coyote may be considered a force which, while inventive and with a potential for good, also carries a potential to lure a person away from living as a "good" and cooperative member of society.[98] Eric Josephson, a member of the Konkow Valley Band of Maidu and NAGPRA[99] coordinator, elaborates that "Coyote brought death to us [the Konkow Maidu]," and even compares Coyote's bringing of death to Adam's bringing of death through his fall from grace in the Garden of Eden.[100] He further illuminates this complex relationship by drawing on certain Coyote narratives. In one narrative, Josephson explains, Coyote "tries to take advantage of two young girls swimming in the swimming hole," a narrative that ends with his body washing up in the stream after "they drown him."[101] In other words, "Bad things happen to people like Coyote. Coyote does bad things to other people."[102]

Similarly, Coyote Man (Robert Rathbun[103]), who transcribed many different Maidu narratives in *Sun, Moon, and Stars*, expounds that Coyote's relationship to the Maidu (presumably those of the Sierra Foothills) is exceptionally complex. Of course, the confusion between the different interpretations of Coyote from Maidu community to Maidu community is not surprising, considering that the term *Maidu* is often misused. As Josephson further explains, the word *Maidu* could be compared to *American*.[104] In other words, "Maidu is just a word we [the Maidu tribes] have in common, it means person or people," and while Dixon's texts may refer to Maidu narratives, they are "not written in Konkow" (at least not those of his Maidu texts of 1912) but document narratives of "the Eastern Maidu or Mountain Maidu."[105] It must therefore be borne in mind that even among tribes and communities sharing similar root names such as "Maidu," their narratives and histories are unique and diverse. Thus, the following text is according to Dixon's "The Coyote and the Grizzly Bears" coupled with my own analysis.

> Long ago the Coyote and the Grizzly Bears had a falling out. There were two Bears who had a couple of small birds, called Pitsititi. Whenever the Bears went down to the valley to get berries, they left these two birds at home. Once, while the Bears were away, the Coyote came to the Bears' camp, and asked the two little birds whether the Bears gave them enough to eat. Said the little birds, "No, they do not; we are always hungry." The Coyote then asked whether there was any food in the camp, and the birds told him that there was, the Bears keeping a large supply on hand. Said the Coyote, "If you will show me the food,

I will get up a fine dinner and then we can all eat." The little birds agreed, and the Coyote prepared the food, and all had a great feast. When they were all through, the Coyote took up a small stick from the ground, thrust it into his nose to draw blood, and then with the blood marked a red stripe on the heads of the birds, and said, "When the Bears come back and ask you two who did this, say, 'The Coyote did it.'" Then the Coyote went off down the hill into the valley where the Bears were picking berries, and shouted from the side-hill, "Get out of there! That ground belongs to my grandmother." Then he went back up the hill to his own camp.[106]

This first section is of special interest as it shows a rather unique combination of Coyote's roles as hero and villain, as generous savior and gluttonous thief. While Coyote exploits the hunger and dissatisfaction of a weaker group within the Bears' camp to feed himself, he also is certain to share the bounty of his boldness with this weaker group, these *Pitsititi* birds although he is under no obligation to do so. After all, it seems fair to assume the birds would have blamed Coyote for the thievery automatically had he simply come in, exploited them, eaten his fill, and then left them to starve. The generosity of Coyote in these situations is of great significance as it bars us from assuming only the worst of him and forgetting the deep wisdoms and sacredness he is also constantly capable and representative of. This is of particular interest when considering Ginsberg's (admittedly vague and culturally decontextualized) interpretations of an incident and relationship between Coyote and "Bear."

After all, Ginsberg's letter is referring to his own dualistic frustration and admiration with friend Gregory Corso as he is writing to Snyder attempting to justify why Corso deserves grant[107] money despite him being, apparently, a deeply difficult man to work with. Throughout the letter, Ginsberg cites the excitement and alertness of Naropa student responses to Corso's teaching as signs of his ability to "enrich"[108] his community; however, Ginsberg also mentions several times (in passing) the troublesome nature of Corso's behavior—behavior that Corso also elaborates on within his own letters to Ginsberg.[109] On February 7, 1979, Corso wrote to Ginsberg admitting that he was certain both Ginsberg and Naropa would want him back and teaching "but for [his] behavior," and that, given the chance, he could "blow their minds with how nice [he could] be"—although he also conceded that he continued to find himself succumbing to the occasional "drinky poo."[110] By comparing these trials and actions within Corso to Coyote, Ginsberg keenly *re*contextualized Coyote within the Beat subculture, as an actor and symbol of Corso (at least in this instance), and thereby demonstrates Ginsberg's own ability to not only recognize elements of Coyote but to try and creatively reapply them within his own reality and culture. Of course, it should also be noted that this type of cut-and-dry case of appropriation, at least in relation to Coyote, does not occur within "Howl." In "Howl," Coyote remains a shadow actor and influence. This combination of troublesome behavior with creative teaching abilities is well illustrated throughout the rest of the narrative of "The Coyote and the Grizzly Bears."

> The two Bears came home, and when they saw the birds, asked them who had been there, and painted their heads with red. The two little birds answered that it was the Coyote. The Bears were very angry. They wanted to have their revenge, so they set out for the Coyote's camp. Before they reached it, however, the Coyote had made all his preparations to receive them. He let the fire go out, cluttered up the camp with filth, then lay down beside the fireplace, and blew the ashes up into the air, so that they settled on him as he lay there, and made it appear as if he had not been out of the camp for a long time. He meant to deny everything that the two little birds had said, and claim to have been sick for a long while.[111]

This passage exhibits both Coyote's cunning and creativity as well as his tolerance for behaving badly, selfishly, and with a constant hunger for attention (whether it be good or bad). Here we see Coyote not only being willing but eager to destroy and clutter his own camp "with filth" all for the sake of pissing off those he currently held a grudge against, those with whom he had "had a falling out." Coyote sets a layered trap within this story, desiring to both deceive and earn notoriety for his actions so that the Grizzly Bears might know who invaded their home, painted their birds, and stolen their food. Ginsberg seems to blame Corso for setting up a similarly layered trap between Corso's behaviors, needs, and desire for funding. As Pritchard observed in his reading of a separate Klamath narrative called "Coyote and the Salmon," acting with cunning is of vital importance "when hunting and at war, but ... should not be" utilized when "with our friends and family," as Corso apparently attempted to do with Ginsberg and his allies at Naropa University.[112] Coyote, like Corso, often "learns by doing" learns that due to his behavior while seeming to simultaneously bemuse and exasperate Ginsberg, providing, perhaps, some healing through his own — in this instance — tragic humor.[113] Of course, in this story, it is not Coyote who learns the lesson, but the Bears.

> The Bears on their part had made plans also. Said one, "I will go in after him, while you stay by the smoke-hole outside, and catch him if he tries to escape

by that way." They both carried sharp-pointed digging-sticks. The first Bear went into the hut, and found the Coyote lying by the fireplace, groaning. The Bear asked him what the trouble was, and the Coyote replied, "Oh, I'm sick." To this the Bear said, "I don't believe you. You have been down at my camp, and made trouble there." "No, I haven't," said the Coyote, "I've been sick up here for a long time." "But the birds said that you had been down at the camp, and had marked their heads with red, and eaten up all the food," replied the Bear. The Coyote, however, stoutly denied that he had been to the Bears' camp, and repeated the statement that he had been lying sick in his hut for a long time. "I've been here sick," he said, "and have heard the children playing round outside, but no one has come in to see how I was." At this moment the Bear made a thrust at the Coyote with the sharp stick. The Coyote dodged, crying, as he did so, "Whee." The Bear struck again, but this time the Coyote jumped up through the smoke-hole, and escaped. The other Bear, who was stationed at the smoke-hole, struck at the Coyote as he passed, but missed him.[114]

This is not the first or last time Coyote attempted to trick and trap through a ruse of illness or death (nor the first or last time that his ruse is called out). Even this seems to hold a peculiar redolence of Ginsberg's situation and comparison to Corso, as Corso's suffering (a combination of bad behavior, drinking, marital problems, and no doubt a number of other things) might be perceived as staged to some extent, a cry for attention or expression of greed (whether born of grief or genius selfishness). Thus the Bears, those who have been taken advantage of and had their home camp invaded, find themselves dubious of all tales counter to what they heard and smelled. Whereas Coyote, like Corso, sticks hard and fast to his story, much to the Bears' exasperation and, at least this time, comes out on top with a full belly and recommendation for more funding under his belt.

As soon as he was clear of the hut, the Coyote ran to a big log, where he had hidden his bow and arrows. The Bears followed as fast as they could, crying, "Hurry up, there, hurry up! We'll catch him, and make a quiver out of his skin." The Coyote jumped over the log to where his bow was, and got it and his arrows all ready. He waited for the Bears to jump up on the log. The one that had been at the smoke-hole reached the log first, jumped up on it, and was shot by the Coyote at once. The other Bear came next, and was likewise shot by the Coyote. When he had killed both the Bears, he came out from behind the log, and said, "All people can call me Coyote."[115]

As Gregory Corso is the Coyote in this scenario, we may also see other connections take shape between this narrative and the construction of "Howl," as Ginsberg too, with the publishing of this poem, defeated his

2. Considering Coyote

obscenity suing adversaries and proudly announced, *All people can call me Allen Ginsberg!*

This next Coyote narrative, "Coyote and the White Man," is a Coeur d'Alene story as told by Bingo SiJohn (Coeur d'Alene) (a part of a larger oral history project directed by Rodney Frey [1993, *Me-Y-Mi-Ym* Project]) and also showcases the peculiarities of Coyote's simultaneous generosity and selfish gluttony. For the Coeur d'Alene, Coyote's stories as a whole culminate in a variety of important lessons. Similarly to Pritchard's explanation of Coyote in relation to the Klamath story of "Coyote and the Salmon," it is whenever a person's actions are done in the service or defense of "one's family ... [that] it is appropriate to be the 'Coyote,'" full of cunning and cleverness.[116] However, when these Coyote characteristics are used "against ... one's own family or tribe" then they only lead to defeat and failure.[117] In this particular story, Coyote begins, as usual, in motion until he comes upon a group of animals encircling and frightening a "poor human being."[118] Seeing this, Coyote immediately takes action to rescue the "human being" and frightens all the animals away. Through this ordeal, Coyote and the human being become fast friends, spending a great deal of time living, helping, and eating with each other all through the prosperous summertime. They were thus glad to be friends as "they learned from one another" through their differences, although SiJohn reminds us they are actually quite similar as Coyote — despite being the Coyote — "was a human being too."[119] However, as wintertime approaches, a time when food is less plentiful for foragers such as they are, Coyote — who is "always scheming" — suggests that he and the human play a trick for some quick food.[120] Coyote explains that there is a trading post not too far off and that if only the human being would pretend to sell Coyote to the storeowner for his fur, then they would be able to thieve away a great deal of free food.

The human being happily agrees to this plan, apparently double promising to Coyote that he (or she) will not leave Coyote behind and tied up at the trading post. And so everything seems to go according to plan at first — the storeowner is pleased with Coyote's fur and allows the human being to pick out what foods the human being wants. However, when the time comes to make the escape and free Coyote from his bindings, the human being simply keeps walking, his or her back never facing away from Coyote or Coyote's cries and accusations. And it is not long after that that the storeowner skins Coyote, leaving him cold and dead much to the chagrin of "The Great Animal Spirit" who proceeds to enlist the services of the Fox to correct the situation.¹²¹ And when Fox inquires as to why the Great Animal Spirit continuously saves Coyote's skin 'given Coyote's constant troublemaking, the Great Animal Spirit replies, "Maybe he gets into trouble but he has a good heart and he is generous.'"¹²² And so Fox goes and performs the necessary rituals to return Coyote to life (before bringing forth Badger and Big Bear to help him also restore Coyote's fur for the wintertime). SiJohn goes on to explain that the primary lesson within this story is that we must be able to "trust people, but trust them only so far" and to "always be generous."¹²³

Of course, this story is also valuable for how it highlights both Coyote's endless appetite (which may lead even his "generous" nature to be left out in the cold temporarily given his plan to steal from the storeowner) and the good-natured aspects of Coyote as he went out of his own way to save a complete stranger. He is thus a complex character of both grand generosity as well as blinding want, traversing the boundaries of human/divine/animal as well as those of seemingly contradictory moral standings to exist within a liminal zone of constant reorganization and invention.

And on October 7, 1955, the same day "Howl" became famous at the Six Gallery reading, Gary Snyder stepped up to the stage and performed his Coyote poem: "A Berry Feast." Snyder begins this poem with, "Coyote the Nasty," before tracing out the berry origins of some "bearshit" cooking in the sun, the plight of the bear's wife's bloodied breasts before he announces Coyote, who has come across a rattlesnake, and is "Mating with / humankind."¹²⁴ This poem follows Coyote through the summer dried city"¹²⁵ demonstrating how, as William Bright has interpreted (both Coyote and the poem), Coyote is "a powerful symbol of a viewpoint that looks beyond abstractions and beyond technology to the ultimate value of survival."¹²⁶ Interestingly here, Bright suggests that Coyote is not necessarily, at least entirely, an archetypal figure or poetic, cultural hero-trickster, but is a *viewpoint*, a way of seeing the world through the lens solely of survival.

Survival is, obviously, a deeply significant focus for many Native American storytellers, scholars, and authors; this makes Coyote and his ability to die again and again yet rise with a bolt of laughter and wisdom again and again a particularly apt figure of hope and horror, the twin sides of survival. For example, Joseph Bruchac (Abenaki) frames his entire body of interviews concerning Native American narratives around the concept of survival. In his *Survival This Way: Interviews with American Indian Poets*, he provides a series of compelling interviews, and in his interview with Peter Blue Cloud (Mohawk), he inquires after Blue Cloud's repeated employment of Coyote within his poetry. To this Blue Cloud explains that he actually first heard of Raven on the West Coast, around British Columbia, but began to hear more of Coyote while in California and Oregon. He explains, "with Coyote, you can cover any kind of ground — philosophy, history, make fun of current events," while also professing a great disapproval for what he calls "white shamans" or "Would-be Shamans" — those non–Natives who "aren't writing about themselves" but instead opt for problematic "'retranslations'" of others' stories by filling their poetry with appropriated Native American figures, narratives, and histories.[127]

Blue Cloud presents a series of fascinating Coyote narratives in his anthology, *Elderberry Flute Song: Contemporary Coyote Tales* (2002). He included within this collection "Coyote's Anthro." In this narrative, we are first introduced to an enthusiastic, young (and presumably white) anthropologist, simply referred to as "the anthro." He has just been awarded his doctorate for a dissertation on Coyote and now we find him camping out in the desert, gathering more data for some other study. And, as he is sitting out, considering Coyote, Old Man Coyote startles him — "It couldn't be!" thinks the anthro, "he was a myth!" but Old Man Coyote responds with a simple, "Not always."[128] From here, the hilarity and wisdom only escalates as Old Man Coyote settles down (however briefly) with his anthro for a philosophical chat. While the anthro stumbles over misunderstanding after misunderstanding, Old Man Coyote keeps trying to find new ways of crossing the divide of the anthro's own thickness (perhaps one of the only boundaries Coyote often does not cross). For example, when the anthro inquires as to the "true meaning" of "the Creation myth," Old Man Coyote wisely replies, "If you think Creation's a myth, you just might be in serious trouble."[129] The narrative comes to a climax when Old Man Coyote grows impatient and brings the anthro to a pool of water to teach him how to bounce off the water and hang from the moon in the sky. Singing all the while, Coyote demonstrates and, hanging from the moon, laughs, "And I wasn't even sure I could do it."[130] However, when the anthro tries to mimic Old Man Coyote (as per Old Man Coyote's beckoning), he only sinks in the water. "You know, I thought only us coyotes were silly enough to try things we weren't sure of."[131]

In this narrative, we find Old Man Coyote attempting to cross the boundary from Native tradition, ethic, and understanding into those of the non–Native. However, much as in "reality," there seems to persist an uncrossed borderline drawn of miscommunication and misunderstanding. Even as Old Man Coyote attempts to explain, demonstrate, and teach things to the anthro, the anthro only responds by attempting to interpret the lessons through non–Native lenses and mindsets rather than by stepping outside of them. In this case, it may be that Old Man Coyote also failed to step outside of his own set of stories, symbols, and meanings in his attempt to get the anthro to do likewise. However, it was not Old Man Coyote who began the narrative by professing a great and "professional" understanding of the anthro, and so any misunderstandings of non–Nativeness on his part is not of issue — he is not, in other words, the one proliferating a misunderstood version of another culture under the awning of professionalism, comprehension, and expertise.

Coyote, in other instances, also exists as an entity that is consistently successful and then cyclically foiled by the high gained from each success. This may be observed in the Navajo story, "Coyote and Skunk Kill Game," (as told by Barry Lopez).[132] In this narrative, Coyote recruits Skunk to help him trick a group of prairie dogs and rabbits. He aims to trick them into believing that he is dead so that when Skunk leads them all over to see his corpse in proof, Skunk may then blind them all with his spray, enabling Coyote to pounce on them and catch plenty for his (and now Skunk's as well) next meal. It is a deeply elaborate trap Coyote constructs, and though at first it works, due to his own insatiable hunger the trap ends up caging him as well. Coyote's appetite and ego persuade him to challenge Skunk to a race, knowing that he is much faster than Skunk, to win over *all* of the meat rather than be satisfied with his already ample share. These are trademarks of Coyote's tricksterness: the vanity of success, the underestimation and mistreatment of his peers, the grossness of ambition, and putting the good of the self before the good of the group. And though not all of these trademarks are represented by Ginsberg's "best minds" in "Howl," they are all significant players in "Howl" as a whole. Ginsberg certainly applies the issues arising from the vanity of success to his "best minds," but the rest of the trademarks exhibited in this story are more clearly applied in "Howl" to the entity of Moloch, the demonic representation of America's mainstream society.[133]

But the story is not over yet. Because Skunk is well aware of his speed disadvantage, he demands a short head start of Coyote in order to rush ahead, hide himself, and simply wait for Coyote to pass by before turning back and finishing off all the food for himself. When Coyote first presents the plan to Skunk, he is extremely detailed in how he is to be made to look convincingly dead. He quickly devises a plan to take "slime grass" (resembling maggots) and use it as stuffing in his orifices—nose, ears, "under his tail," et cetera—so that while he floated in the water surrounded by "a pile of driftwood," his death disguise would be complete.[134] Thus, when Skunk went and explained to their prey that Coyote had died, they could be brought to his body and see him stuffed from ears to "his anus" with maggots and be convinced.[135] After all, who would not be convinced of a death upon seeing a body floating motionless and maggot infested in water up to their ears?

Of course, Coyote does not always follow his hero cycle directly into failure so blatantly as in this story. In many instances, he does come away with a prize. He wins only to realize the superfluous nature of winning for winning's sake, revealing his taste for the spotlight and not simply for meat as was the case in "Coyote and Skunk Kill Game." The Jicarilla Apache have a funny story depicting this trait called "Coyote Shows How He Can Lie," (as told by Barry Lopez) in which Coyote comes upon a group of men discussing Coyote's ability and apparent talent for deception and lying. They then ask him to teach them how to do likewise, to lie well and often without getting caught. Coyote complies though only with the stipulation that first he must be reimbursed the amount for which he paid for the gift of deceit: "my best buffalo horse, with a fine bridle."[136] The men, considering a single horse for the ability to lie so well a real bargain, promptly agree and bring him the requested animal.[137]

Of course, through a number of different deceptions, Coyote also manages to procure from them a blanket, saddle, and whip. He then claims he must first test the horse out before he can divulge his secret to the art of lying. He then "rode off a little way," calling back to the men, "'This is the way I lie, I get people to give me horses and blankets and saddles and other fine things'" before simply riding away home.[138] But it's not until he gets home to brag to his wife that he realizes he has no idea of how to care for the animal. So, when he dismounts, it simply returns to its former master, leaving Coyote with nothing but wasted time and the exposure of another trick, though certainly not a broken spirit.[139]

This is one of the most significant and important of Coyote's enduring traits: his unending perseverance despite all pains, failures, and humiliations (even deaths). Coyote to the Jicarilla Apache, however (and according to Morris Edward Opler, a non–Native anthropologist of the mid–1930s), is a figure of "little honor" and whose stories are typically told in a certain sequential order (although this order may vary slightly from storyteller to storyteller as is the way with oral traditions).[140] Coyote is largely considered a dishonorable figure here due to the fact that the majority of stories concerning him involve him acting unwisely and/or dishonestly. Although Coyote does gain some favor for bringing fire to mankind in the Jicarilla Apache tradition, he is still viewed negatively given that even this good deed depended upon Coyote's "theft and the deception of little children."[141] However, it does seem, from others of Opler's own descriptions (especially concerning consternations with mothers-in-law), that Coyote still holds a place within Jicarilla culture beyond simply the negative role, given the joy and relief people may derive from the humorous nature of even Coyote's darker antics.

This particular trait's importance may also be understood by how other cultures have caricatured Coyote, a prominent example being the slapdash Warner Bros. character Wile E. Coyote. In Wile E. Coyote this perseverance and humor seem to be the only traditional and original characteristics they attribute to Coyote and his tricks. This is the sort of "'crazy wisdom'" that Tom Robbins discusses in his article "In Defiance of Gravity: Writing, Wisdom, and the Fabulous Club Gemini."[142] He describes "the archetypal role of the holy fool" as possessing and providing "a kind of *divine* playfulness intended to lighten man's existential burden and promote ... 'the rapture of being alive.'"[143] Holiness and the combination of elements of the divine with the earthly, with humor and pain, are certainly traits all at play within Ginsberg's "Howl" and especially within its "Footnote," and, I argue, within Coyote as well.

While Coyote does tend to take things a step beyond rapture and enter dangerous territory, he has the advantage of immortality and the blessing of never being the best. Manifesting as this revelation, rapture, and divine playfulness, Coyote is reminiscent of other cultures and ideas such as "Zen, Taoist, Sufi, and Tantric teachings" which also focus on these elements.[144] This creates an even clearer avenue for Ginsberg and his rapturous "Footnote" where *everything is Holy*, where we (those so often suffering and considered foolish or grotesque) possess a "wisdom that flouts taboos in order to undermine their power; wisdom that evolves when one, while refusing to avert one's gaze from the sorrows and injustices of the world, insists on joy in spite of everything."[145]

2. Considering Coyote

Coyote also provides examples for learning how to distinguish between joy and greed and the dangers that may lurk in humor. In the Northern Pueblo narrative (as recorded in Richard Erdoes and Alfonso Ortiz's *American Indian Trickster Tales: Myths and Legends*), "Putting a Saddle on Coyote's Back," Coyote illustrates the possible consequences of indulging greed and allowing it to becloud his strongest gift: his cunning. It begins with another trickster, with Rabbit Boy, whom Coyote came upon one day and greeted with a joke: "'You look good enough to eat.'"[146] Rabbit Boy scoffed at the joke though he was secretly unsettled and frantic to escape the trickster's belly. Nevertheless, Coyote pursued him, complimenting him on how "appetizing" he looked.[147] However, quite suddenly, Rabbit Boy revealed that he was just on his way out to "a big feast" with his aunt and her family.[148] At this point, Coyote should have realized the scent of a trap and accepted that a rabbit now is worth two rabbits later. Instead, Coyote, like so many, manages to be both impatient as well as willing to wait for the hope of the larger haul, like a gambler eager for a quick fortune but also willing to sit all night to win it, accepting greed's mask of putative cleverness.[149]

Instead of acknowledging the possible cunning of this fellow trickster, all Coyote could think of was a feast and that a family of rabbits would be far superior to only one. Therefore, he bit at Rabbit Boy's trap without ever realizing the foolhardiness of the one spinning in his head. Rabbit Boy thus invited Coyote to join him for the meal in return for a ride to his aunt's abode. Coyote, desperately pleased with his new and improved prospects, never thought twice about Rabbit Boy's request for a ride or his request to fashion Coyote with a saddle in order to ease the ride — Coyote even provided the bridle himself! Just as Coyote was about to run away with Rabbit Boy, he unwittingly allowed his lusty imagination and ambition to run away with him.[150]

While Coyote gathered the bridle and saddle, Rabbit Boy took for himself "two long, sharp thorns from a thornbush" and made two spurs from them and tucked them secretly "in his fur."[151] When Coyote returned, ready with a saddle and bridle, Rabbit Boy came around instructing Coyote to turn tail so that he might "mount [Coyote] from behind."[152] And with that, Rabbit Boy leapt up and stabbed the spurs hard into Coyote's sides. Coyote cried out against the spurs and ran forward at the excited yowls and taunts of Rabbit Boy. Once they arrived at the feast, despite all of Coyote's protests and struggle, Rabbit Boy managed to dismount and knot the bridle about a nearby tree before Coyote could escape—forcing Coyote to sit hungrily and watch all the rabbits eat the day away.[153]

However, the humiliations did not end there. Once the festivities finished, Rabbit Boy launched himself back onto Coyote's back, determined to ride him back home. Of course, by this time, Coyote was in no mood to run along feebly and so planned to flash right past Rabbit Boy's home and, with the aid of his wife, finally capture and cook Rabbit Boy. However, this plan of vengeance did not succeed as Rabbit Boy managed to zip back into his hole so quickly that Coyote could not catch him. His plans undone and his stomach still empty, Coyote was forced to retreat home with the laughter of Rabbit Boy at his back. Moreover, upon returning home to the questions and concern of his wife at his pitiful state, Coyote ends the story with a single remark: "'Old woman, mind your own business.'"[154]

It is of particular interest that this narrative begins with a disagreement over the use of humor and ends with nearly the same disagreement though with the concerned parties reversed. The narrative gives new meaning to the more modern phrases "getting screwed" and "getting taken for a ride." The narrative possesses a variety of subtle, sexual jokes such as Rabbit Boy tricking Coyote into allowing him to "mount [Coyote] from behind" and stabbing him with a long thorn over and over again.[155] In this way, we may see Coyote, who was originally utilizing humor to close in on Rabbit Boy as prey, being "screwed" or "taken for a ride" by Rabbit Boy who now controls the grander joke, the one he's pulling on Coyote. This narrative thus explores humor as a tool to teach about the threat greed poses to one's dignity and safety as well as the threat posed by arrogance and the unwise use of humor to antagonize.

However, in order to more fully understand the trickster and its influence upon Ginsberg, we must also look at the important sexual element of Coyote, an element that directly intersects with appetite. It is also interesting to note that though "tricksters are ridden by lust ... their hyperactive sexuality almost never results in offspring, the implication being that the stories are about non-procreative creativity"[156] and so we typically find Coyote described as a male entity.[157] This is important because it reveals yet another correlation with Ginsberg as much of Ginsberg's trickster humor and wisdom is derived from sexual jokes about freedoms and rights for homosexuals. We will begin here with a Crow (Apsáalooke)[158] story, retold by Barry Lopez, entitled "Coyote's Member Keeps Talking." The oral history and narratives of the Apsáalooke, according to Rodney Frey, generally "begin with Isáahkawuattee, Old Man Coyote," with most of his actions and journeys signifying him as a "trickster character par excellence," though he retains great significance also as "the creator of the world" (although Frey later explains that for some "the trickster-creator figure of Old Man Coyote is pivotal ... [to the] conception of the spiritual and its agents while for others he is marginal").[159]

Fred Voget elaborates on this, explaining that Coyote, or "Esahcawata or Esakawuete," did not appear or act as the "special creator and mentor of the Crows until they separated from their Hidatsa kin" (which occurred sometime in the early 18th century).[160] Voget also refers to three of the four core trickster traits (although he does not label them thus), consisting of Coyote's ability to undergo "instantaneous change of form," possession of "an insatiable appetite," and tendency for "cunning trickery that often failed."[161] Voget uses these traits to posit that, for the Crow, Old Man Coyote served as both "creator and patron" bringing them both laughter and counsel.[162] This particular narrative, "Coyote's Member Keeps Talking," portrays Coyote as less of a trickster world-creator and more as a trickster trapped by his own wild hungers and who finds himself coerced by his own sexual desires. This narrative thus depicts a situation which, as Voget might agree, encourages great laughter "at the troubles [Coyote has] hatched for himself," pointing to a "tragicomic quality" within Old Man Coyote.[163]

The story begins with Coyote searching for buffalo while on a hunting trip. But once he comes upon them in a small valley, he decides to first take a moment to answer the call of nature before pursuing them. And so, turning his attention to his penis, Coyote addresses it in the following way: "'Hey, my member ... [do] you see that buffalo over there?'"[164] His member promptly replies in the affirmative, but this either does not satisfy Coyote or Coyote is simply and inexplicably unable to hear his penis at first and so he shakes his penis and asks again if it can see the buffalo in the valley. Of course, his penis replies positively once again, reaffirming its sight of the buffalo. But Coyote, apparently still unsatisfied, demands a third time if his penis can see the large bull buffalo roaming about with the others, to which his penis, with some exasperation, cries out, "Yes!"[165]

Still, Coyote presses once more, shaking and commanding his penis to look at the prominent bull. This, however, seems to pull the final straw of his member's patience as it simply and suddenly begins to shout over and over again that *yes, it sees it!* Coyote apparently had not anticipated this reaction because he immediately began working to silence his yelling member. He tried covering it with his hand, he tried "punching [it]," he attempted to "choke it," but nothing worked to quiet the raucous penis.[166] It was not until finally, however momentarily, his penis interrupted its own stream of shouts that Coyote learned of how he might silence it once and for all. His penis offered him this ultimatum, "'I won't quit until you sleep with your mother-in-law,'" before resuming its annoying chant.[167] And so Coyote traveled back to the village where his wife and mother-in-law resided, all the while with his penis chanting so that his wife heard it like some troublesome herald as he approached, prompting her out of their lodge to discover what the matter was. Coyote quickly and frankly explained the situation to his wife, from beginning to end, instructing her to fetch her mother and find out her opinion on the matter of copulating with him for these member-hushing purposes.

Coyote's mother-in-law heeds the call hurriedly and says, "'Well, my son is having a hard time there.... Come right inside.'"[168] With that, Coyote follows her inside where she began to "[sing] a song and seize[s] his member" which alleviates him of its problematic shouting.[169]

This narrative illustrates how even Coyote, a powerful, sacred creator, is helpless to stop his sexual appetites save for indulging them. The story goes into great detail to explain not simply that his mother-in-law complied with his penis's demands but that "she sang a song and seized his member and cured him."[170] And this is what makes this story important for this illustration and comparison. Euro-American folktales, mythologies, and religious texts are hardly lacking in sexual content, but few are as explicit as this taking a penis in hand or stipulations of incest to quell bodily desires too loud for us to simply ignore.

Of course, the stories and the poetry go far beyond these mentions of sex and sexual organs and how they function in relation to power and freedom over the self and others. The Nez Perce story (also according to Lopez) of "Coyote and the Mallard Ducks" exemplifies Coyote's cunning in regard to sex, sexual desire, and the humor involved with them both. The story begins with Coyote traveling (as most of his stories tend to begin) and stumbling upon a group of five, young Mallard Duck girls swimming. It is a story of Coyote's quest to then satisfy his immediate arousal over these girls without them ever knowing what he's up to. Coyote hides himself and then begins to slowly elongate his penis out across the river to where the girls are playing only to discover that his penis floats problematically atop the water.[171]

To address this issue, he reins himself back in and binds his member to a stone in order to weigh it down. Of course, much to his chagrin, his penis simply sinks to the bottom of the river. And so, "with much pain" he reins himself in once more and attaches a smaller stone, which enables him to whisper his penis under the surface of the water and have secret sexual intercourse with the eldest of the Mallard Duck girls.[172] This series of actions speaks clearly to Coyote's perseverance as well as to his heightened sexual nature and proclivity for creating traps. The eldest girl then began making odd noises and movements that her sisters could not understand, so they commenced a search for the cause of her sudden ailment. Upon discovering the intrusive penis, the girls, still presumably uncertain as to what exactly was going on, began pulling at the organ in attempt to free their sister of it.[173]

However, it proved stronger than anticipated, prompting the girls to go so far as to climb out of the river, "[hold] down their older sister and [try] to pull it out that way."[174] But still they were unable to free their sister and, in fact, found some humor in her plight and began laughing. This moment of rape commixed with slapstick humor reveals a duality of life in order to highlight a parallel duality within Coyote, as both a wise and clever figure who can teach compassion, reason, and creativity (such as his ability to quickly problem solve and construct traps) as well as one who often uses those abilities to meet his own, more selfish ends.

Once Coyote "satisfied himself," he called out to the sisters and asked what the problem was, to which they explained as best they understood.[175] Coyote then instructed them to slice the "thing" off using "wire grass."[176] Coyote did the same on his end of the penis so that the elongated middle section fell off into the water and formed into a long "ledge."[177] Of course, since the head of the penis was now still trapped inside of the eldest sister, she very quickly fell ill; Coyote then proceeded to swim up to their camp in order to help, but by the time he made it up to their camp, "the oldest girl was almost dead."[178] The other girls instantly recognized Coyote as a particularly strong medicine man and beseeched him to heal their dying sister. He agreed to heal her but instructed the sisters to seal up every chink and hole in the lodge because he would require absolute privacy in order to complete the process without anyone spying on him and thereby stealing away his medicine.

He then instructed the other sisters to gather about the lodge and "sing a song and keep time on a log with sticks."[179] From there Coyote himself began to sing the words, "'I will stick it back on. I will stick it back on.'"[180] Coyote then entered the lodge, finally alone with the eldest Mallard Duck girl, and then began to recover the end of his penis by reconnecting and having sex with her once more. Once he was finished this second time, the girl was revived, was "cured," and everyone lauded Coyote as one whose medicine was "very powerful."[181]

In this narrative, it is essential to note that it is not the mention of sex or sexual organs that creates the humor. Rather, it is how the people react to the sexual situations as well as the circular notion that the bearer of illness (Coyote and his sexual desire) and the bearer of medicine (Coyote and his sexual desire) are derived from a single source: Coyote. Paradoxical and even dark, uncomfortable humor is found and revealed here in the message that nothing is wholly good or bad, that neither sex nor sexual desire, neither tricksters nor women should be demonized, but viewed with some level of reverence as they proffer unique wisdom for societies. It is the simultaneity of the danger and good making up Coyote's medicine that lends it true power. This idea of reverence and healthy wariness of sexual power is quite normal in many Native American cultures, understanding that all things have their place, their limits, their goods and their bads—especially when it comes to something so human yet supernatural and so deviant yet sagacious as a trickster. The idea of sexual power being considered dangerous is more to do with some Native American cultural beliefs concerning the balance between purity and pollution, that of moderation.

It is the knowledge that too much contact with blood or too much power in sex, such as a pregnancy, may tip the scale into someone else's power or weakness, and so sexual power is something to be revered and respected, not feared or shunned. This embrace is acknowledged (though also abused by) Coyote, just as Ginsberg also makes certain to embrace and acknowledge the lack of reverence and respect so much of mainstream America has for sexuality. This lack of respect may be seen in everything from our unwillingness to educate American children about sexuality to our long history of denial of women's sexuality in general. The embrace of sexuality and sexual humor is thus a particularly important and unique connection existing between Coyote and Ginsberg, two who have been historically misunderstood by mainstream America as simply sexual deviants.

One other important aspect of Coyote is his role as cultural hero and medicine man. As a medicine man, he is able to ameliorate situations such as in the story of the Mallard Ducks and provide wisdom and lessons as he does for the New People once they have been created. But as a medicine man and cultural hero he is also a part of that creation. Coyote creates human beings in many different origin stories that change from tribe to tribe. According to one Miwok origin story, "How People Were Made" (as told by Richard Erdoes and Alfonso Ortiz), Coyote is effectively bullied into work as a creator by Falcon.[182] Coyote does this by first playing dead and preying upon the appetites of others (namely, buzzards and crows), serving as a testament both to his innate ability to set traps as well as his keen understanding of hunger. The vultures come and eat a hole into his backside, which he quickly closes up in order to capture them. After doing so, he charges Falcon with the task of culling the feathers from these birds so that they may plant the feathers at various spots along the earth. These feathers eventually grow into people that look, according to Coyote, just like he and Falcon.

This realization triggers yet another of his main four characteristics into action as Coyote turns to Falcon and explains that they now must each assume a different appearance; they must not share the same visage as the New People. Thus, transformation becomes a major part of the cultural hero, turning him from something like the New People into a creature of fur and the Falcon into a creature of feathers. Already Coyote has set up a precedent not only of the power of his trickster character traits but also of the necessity to set oneself apart from the rest and establish and utilize one's own powers to create, differentiate, and entrap. In this same fashion, Ginsberg worked to craft his own unique voice and celebrate frankness, humor, and triumphant transformation in order to promulgate a need he saw within the American people to break free from the trap of artificial borders, boundaries, and rules—the trap of mainstream society.

In *Legends of the Yosemite Miwok*, Frank Lapena provides another Miwok origin story wherein Coyote again creates the New People through the use of feathers. However, in this version entitled "Yel'-lo-kin, the Man-Eating Giant," Coyote is a much more willing participant and, in fact, is the one who suggests putting in the extra work for the simple sake of creating the New People and a richer, more hospitable world for them. This narrative begins with the villainous Yel'-lo-kin, a gigantic bird who was in the habit of snatching young children and flying off with their heads in his talons "through the hole in the middle of the sky," where he then devours them.[183] Yel'-lo-kin also kidnapped Toad-woman for his wife, who was also aunt to Eagle who was uncle to Coyote. And so, when Eagle is eventually kidnapped as well, Toad-woman explains to him how to go about slaying Yel'-lo-kin. It is not until the moment this killing takes place that Coyote leaps into the sky to retrieve his uncle and becomes witness to the murder.

Coyote approves of the killing, knowing as Eagle did that Yel'-lo-kin had caused them to lose many people due to his appetites. However, when Coyote inquires as to Eagle's intentions with the remains of Yel'-lo-kin, he disapproves of Eagle's suggestion to simply "burn him, so he would not come to life again."[184] In place of this killing or waste of power, Coyote proposes that Eagle allow him to cut away Yel'-lo-kin's wings and "plant the big feathers and grow trees" so that there will be plenty of greenery and sustenance to support "many people"—people he volunteered to make as soon as he finished planting the new trees.[185] From these feathers, Coyote created fields of "flowers," "sugar pines," "blue oaks," and a great variety of things, instructing them "to bear seed every year" in order to produce plenty of food for the people about to be made from the remaining feathers.[186]

These stories together reveal both sides of Coyote at play in the creation of the Miwok peoples, both the inventive teacher as well as the (sometimes slothful) trapper. It must be noted, however, that there are many distinctly different Miwokan dialects, including Lake Miwok, Central Sierra Miwok, Northern Sierra Miwok, Bay Miwok, Plains Miwok, Saclan, and Southern Sierra Miwok; thus it makes sense that origin stories would be so similar as well as so different in various circumstances.

Collectively, Native American narratives and stories such as these are meant to, as Simon J. Ortiz explains, "give a sense of the vastness and depth of Indian cultural life."[187] He further explains that, as a vital element of these narratives, Coyote functions all at once as a "story character, storyteller, and story coming into being" and thus cannot simply be thought of as "animal and motif"—these are too small for his multitudes, too stagnant.[188] By recognizing Coyote as all three elements of the narrative, we may recognize his unique power to continuously come alive in new ways with each retelling of these narratives. And while this realization represents an enormously deep well of culture, literature, and history, it is interesting to note the similarity between this phenomenon in Coyote and that in Ginsberg's "Howl," as it enables him and his readers to continuously discover new elements, themes, lessons, and ideas from this work with each new performance or reading.

The work of authors like Gerald Vizenor helps further illustrate the variety of ways that Coyote and other figures may be continuously rediscovered and come alive yet again in new and different circumstances. Vizenor, a man who has been described by many as a trickster himself, is the author of several books of fiction that utilize "tribal tricksters" in order to "playfully expose verbal ironies as they try to maintain a balance in the complicated terrain of urban America."[189] This not only works to reinvent how the more traditional stories and figures may be perceived and understood in modern settings but also to reinvent the stereotypical perceptions of Native Americans generally and break down problematic rhetorical barriers. In much the same way that it is vital to the understanding of Coyote to recognize him as a complex figure of good, evil, humanity, and supernaturality, so it is vital to dismantle mainstream simplifications or stereotypes of Native Americans and reorient the non–Native understanding or conception of Native Americans so that they may be recognized as *people*. It is a staple of modern Native American literatures to examine the humanity of Native Americans and, through these displays and examinations of humanity (examinations Vizenor often combines with examinations of the trickster archetype), strive to unravel the work of prevailing prejudicial and colonizing rhetoric and perceptions. Perceptions and rhetoric that extend to the insidious, the unwitting, and the outright prejudiced include the infantilization of Native Americans in rhetoric and art such as the children's rhyme, "Ten Little Indians"; the victimization of Native Americans in media and products such as caricatured versions of supposed Native American traditional dress but sold as Halloween costumes; the racialization and stereotyping of the "stoic Indian" as exemplified in the mascot of the Washington, D.C., football team the "Redskins"; the objectification of Native American cultures and identities in turquoise jewelry, media labeling, or in the bizarrely pervasive claim of many non–Natives to be somehow, distantly and with convenient ambiguity, related to a mysterious Indian chief (often of Cherokee, Sioux, or Apache descent); and the stigmatization of Native Americans as either wealthy casino owners or gamblers, degenerate alcoholics, or lazy and impoverished.

Due to all of these remaining challenges and modern misconceptions, we must continue to consider Coyote and other elements of Native life, history, politics, and culture in more critical and complex ways. It is only through such critical and respectful thinking, discourse, and consideration that we may begin to dismantle these schemes of domination and victimization. Ginsberg recognized such a need for a new type of discourse and rhetoric which, for him, manifested in poetry, in poetry such as "Howl."

Part II
Coyote-ing "Howl"

Chapter 3

Space, Place, and Traversing Boundaries

> *The power of liminality lies in its ability to upset the materialistic notion of categorization which so concerned Western naturalists and anthropologists of the nineteenth and early twentieth century.* — Kate Holterhoff

June 1948, early evening

A young, thin man, Allen Ginsberg laid back on his bed alone in East Harlem, with only a window, a book of William Blake, and an erection for company. Having already read Blake more than once, he began masturbating, leaving the poem, "Ah! Sun-flower," grinning off the page and the window eagerly watching him from the wall. However, as Ginsberg began cooling down, the poem rose up, announcing itself as some sort of poltergeist, and appeared to him through "an ancient-sounding voice," a voice "which he took to be Blake's."[1] As if summoned by the poem, by the voice, Ginsberg "looked out his window and saw ... the sign of a Creator," he saw something like a threshold between the values and significances of one world and those of another, a connection to a vast eternity.[2] This was the first of a series of poetic auditory visions Ginsberg experienced as a young man. He later described this sensation to Kerouac as:

> something that we can know if we are able to shoulder the responsibility of destroying our present lives, but it is by its nature so far beneath or above existence as I normally know it that it is of no use except to invoke ... the vague sensation of something dreamlike.[3]

Here Ginsberg recognizes a slip into another dimension or reality as well as the necessity to be able to destroy "our present lives" in order to know this other reality or eternal "something"; he recognizes a keen connection between the horrific, the liminal, the powerful, and the poetic—

a connection most certainly trickster in nature given its irony, boundlessness, and transformative power. By bearing witness of this auditory vision, Ginsberg admits to having experienced inhabiting a truly liminal space, something that is both in motion through time as well as existing on a threshold between at least two different realities, something "vague," "dreamlike," and requiring the utter "destroying" or transforming of one's life. Ginsberg further illuminated this auditory phenomenon in his 1965 interview with Thomas Clark. He explained that what he came to understand from his vision of Blake was simply that poetry "was something basic to human existence ... [and functioned as] a kind of time machine through which he could transmit, Blake could transmit, his basic consciousness and communicate it to somebody else after he was dead."[4] In other words, Ginsberg recognized the potential for poetry to function as both timeless, spatial, in motion, and yet capable of pausing to create new meaning at certain points or *places* along the way (just as Blake's poem paused in its movement through time in the life of Ginsberg). In this way, Ginsberg demonstrates an understanding of poetry as something both continuously moving as well as something capable of creating new places (or, as spatial theorist Yi-Fu Tuan might say, of creating pauses within spaces).

This moment reveals Ginsberg's keen recognition of the fact that arbitrary social boundaries and rhetorical constructs (such as those which prompted the attempted banning of "Howl" as obscene, those that once allowed for separate water fountains for blacks and whites, those that promote the persecution of homosexuals, or even those which label incest a taboo and heterosexual marriage romantic) are deeply engrained components of how people understand the world and, I posit, are part of what gives people a feeling of safety or groundedness in their different realities. These boundaries are part of what enables people to create their own "place" in the world — even if that place is predetermined and quietly, albeit coercively, managed by mainstream society (which is evidenced by the displacement of so many populations and peoples whether literally such as in the case of Native American populations who were forcibly moved to reservations or nonliterally in cases such as that of the ostracization of homosexuals, African Americans, Hispanic Americans, and so on). Thus, it is only with the disruption or destruction of one's self insofar as one's identity pertains to these predetermined realities and boundaries that this new form of "enlightenment" may be achieved. In this shifting across boundaries, Ginsberg believes himself to be "nearer to the ultimate realization" he has always striven for.[5] Such a step toward the liminal, toward the neither-here-nor-there space, illustrates Terrie Waddell's assertion that "meaning is formed in [the] continuous traversing of boundaries where shifting realities interact with each other."[6] The feeling of constant liminality is one shared by both Ginsberg and Coyote as they are both agents of change. This feeling is also clearly exhibited within "Howl" as it is a timeless, liminal *space* at once created and inhabited by Ginsberg, the trickster, and other readers as well as a distinct and significant *place* for Ginsberg and other readers.

This chapter serves as the transitional (or liminal) phase leading into the more direct exploration of Ginsberg's "Howl" through the Native Coyote lens rather than as a continuance in examining the two as pieces of two separate realms. By first briefly and broadly (too briefly and too broadly) comparing the differences and similarities existing between Coyote and "Howl's" relationships with liminality and how liminality functions within the structure of the four core trickster traits outlined earlier, I attempt to lay a clearer foundation for poetic comparison and close readings.

This sense of liminality within both Coyote and "Howl" is founded through the core elements of the trickster, primarily those traits of boundlessness and transformation. Within "Howl," Ginsberg utilizes a menagerie of liminal images, including, "who passed through universities with radiant cool eyes hallucinating / Arkansas and Blake-light tragedy among the scholars of war"; "Pilgrim State's Rockland's and Greystone's foetid halls, bickering with the / echoes of the soul, rocking and rolling in the midnight solitude-bench / dolmen-realms of love"; "who dreamt and made incarnate gaps in Time & Space through images / juxtaposed, and trapped the archangel of the soul between 2 visual / images"; "the madman bum and angel beat in Time, unknown, yet putting down / here what might be left to say in time come after death."[7] These are all examples in one way or another of Ginsberg attempting to capture the motion of a body or soul in transition through poetic exploration, transitioning from one state of understanding reality to another (a transition thus facilitated by the poem itself, by the liminal space of "Howl"). These moments and images all work to enable the poem to transcend itself and to aid its readers in transcending themselves by disrupting their preconceived realities, by challenging them to reconsider what is normal, horrific, humorous, and joyful. The liminality, here, derives from this upset notion of reality, from the disturbances of the self-destruction and madness that Ginsberg speaks of both in relation to his auditory vision and within his poetry, linking a spiritual/psychological type of liminality to a more physical world sense of being in two places at once.

In "Inhabiting the Space between Discourse and Story in Trickster Narratives," Anne Doueihi discusses the necessity of examining Native American tricksters as elements both *in* their stories and as the teller of their trickster stories—the signifier and the signified. She explains that the sacredness of tricksters like Coyote lies partly in their ability to exist "in the *space* between discourse and story," an existence which enables the trickster to create meaning (emphasis added).[8] In other words, trickster narratives are inherently spatial given that the trickster is able to inhabit them in multiple ways and places, existing within the liminal zone (a zone that is settled within the overlap of the discourse ["discursive presentation or narration of events"] and the story ["a sequence of actions or events, conceived as independent of their manifestation in discourse"[9]]).[10] This liminal nature is part of what makes the trickster and Coyote specifically sacred, enabling him to exist simultaneously within a sacred and nonsacred realm, encompassing both wisdom and foolishness or, as Ginsberg might say, being both the "madman bum" and the "angel" who "beat in Time, unknown" to record "here what might be left to say in time come after death."[11]

Doueihi even goes so far as to say that this type or means of sacredness carries within it another layer of the trickster's playful, tricky tendencies as it too represents a trick and a trap, a trickster narrative within a trickster narrative. She explains (in something akin to her own trickster narrative): Traditional non–Native Western methods of examining Native trickster narratives that attempt "to frame the trickster in a context of Western metaphysics and ontology" only end up falling into a trickster joke and trap by, ultimately, mistaking the core of the trickster through this process (as the trickster knew they would misstep and, perhaps, as the trickster may have meant them to).[12] This trap is crafted "by the undecidable coexistence of story and discourse in every trickster narrative" which, while existent within all narratives, is played with and utilized particularly shamelessly by the Native trickster.[13] Past non–Native Western approaches to examining trickster narratives are therefore "already victims of one of the trickster's pranks" as they tend to take the Native trickster narrative as a myth or story only.[14] This lack of recognition of the discursive play inextricable within trickster narratives reveals the snapped trap: the trickster pries its readers and audiences open wide so that they "construct an apparently solid but ultimately illusory reality" from ever deeper and deeper levels of symbol and play, luring them farther and farther away from the trickster's Native origins.[15] These traps make possible a narrative capable of both base or obvious referential meanings as well as a meaning signaling the creation of meaning, one both deep and sacred.[16]

In other words, part of Coyote's sacredness is derived from his ability to play and move stealthily within the various layers of symbol and meaning from culture to culture within himself and his narratives (raising interesting questions regarding even my own analysis here as a new interpreter with a unique cultural lens).

Stephen Prothero also acknowledges this liminal and spatial element within Ginsberg and many others of the Beats' lives and works, explaining that they coped with and expressed "their cultural marginality by living spontaneously" and by acting and performing as "'Zen lunatics' or holy fools."[17] For the Beats, for Ginsberg, "transition was a semipermanent condition," as their goal remained "not to arrive" at any particular point or to cease their endless traveling but to "transform into sacred space" every forgotten or neglected passage and dwelling along their way.[18] In other words, one of Ginsberg's primary poetic goals was to spiritually transform his and others' marginalized places in the world. And his mention of their "cultural marginality" is another important link to the liminal within the Beats and within "Howl." Cultural marginality is a centerpiece, in many ways, to entering a liminal phase or zone as it signals the departure or isolation from one culture that enables one to fully enter a zone of transition and transformation. If one were to remain forever enmeshed within a preliminal zone or culture, then there would be no prompt, reason, or opportunity to enter into a transformative state of liminality. In this way, given "Howl's" suffering both an attempted banning and continued lack of critical examination (despite its general acceptance and inclusion within both high school and college curriculums now), it is fair to posit that not only does "Howl" remain at least in part culturally marginalized, but it also, in turn, remains a site of liminality.

But what does it mean for "Howl" specifically to be a liminal or timeless space or place—for it to be a space or place at all? And how does this connect to its relationship with Coyote? Throughout this chapter, I will be utilizing the concepts of space, place, and liminality in order to transition the separate discussions of "Howl" and Coyote into one larger, combined conversation. And while these concepts are obviously and indelibly interrelated, they also possess stark differences from one another central to our larger understanding of both them and how they may be applied to projects such as this reinterpretation of "Howl."

Arnold Van Gennep, an anthropologist and father of liminal studies, defines liminality through his dissection of ritual as a rite of passage which is broken into three parts: "preliminal rites (rites of separation), liminal rites (rites of transition), and postliminal rites (rites of incorporation)."[19] In other words, liminality is the movement from one state of being to another, a movement through a zone of overlap or transition containing aspects of both pre-rites and post-rites in a wild, mobile, and unknowable combination. "Howl" thus functioned as the liminal rite of passage for Ginsberg as, for Ginsberg both personally and professionally, there is a definite divide between the pre–"Howl," "Howl," and post–"Howl" Ginsbergs. Pre–"Howl" largely represented for Ginsberg the slow rise of recognition that the restricted, poetic worlds of Lionel Trilling and his father were not for him while the post–"Howl" era demonstrates Ginsberg's larger, more confident embrace of himself and his writing. This situating of "Howl" within Ginsberg's lifetime presents the poem as more of a period of liminality for Ginsberg. However, "Howl" moved beyond this surface-level liminality for Ginsberg given its rise from text to performance, treating this relationship between the written and the performed "as a field for experimentation" in and of itself somewhat similar to the practice of "ethnopoetics."[20] Although ethnopoetics more precisely describes the action of translating and transcribing older Native narratives (as many of the traditional stories derive from ancient oral traditions), the notion of a poem's existence between text and performance serving as a "field for experimentation" points to the inherent liminality in poems built for performance, poems like "Howl" (announcing its intentions to perform in its very title).

Victor Turner expands this definition of liminality through his concept of "liminal *personae* ('threshold people')," which are entities that "are neither here nor there; they are betwixt and between the positions assigned and arrayed by law, custom, convention, and [the] ceremonial."[21] In fact, in *The Ritual Process*, Turner explicitly (albeit briefly) includes the Beats and Allen Ginsberg specifically within his discussion of liminality as he

3. Space, Place, and Traversing Boundaries

expands it from a "phase" to a "generic type," such as "social and personality types other than those initiands in a liminal ritual phase and to situations other than the 'betwixt and between' period in a specific ritual process."[22] As Barbara Babcock-Abrahams expounds, Turner extended his definition "to such marginal or liminal phenomena as ritual neophytes, court jesters, and participants in millenarian movements" under the following set of common characteristics: those who "fall in the intersitices of social structure," "are on its margins," or "occupy its lowest rungs"— characteristics, Babcock-Abrahams argues, that in different ways reach directly into the character of the trickster.[23]

Devin Proctor also interestingly contributes to this conversation, explaining that the liminal "categories of understanding and symbols of meaning are no longer assumed. Everything must be tested and proven."[24] In other words, to exist within a liminal space is to lose all tethering grips to what was formerly reality and certainty and to move through a zone of constant reorganization and change. Thus, liminality exists not as a "threshold" in the traditional sense of the term, as this seems to connote more of a line to step across or a doorway to step through. Liminality is more akin to a zone or antechamber of transition and overlap where the reality of the preceding room and the reality of the room yet to be entered intermingle in a reality of constant reorganization and movement. Liminality is an unknowably vast zone where people and ideas simultaneously exist and move about in a confluence of social, cultural, and individual forces, much like the center field of a cosmic Venn diagram. Thus, "liminality" may best be defined as a threshold zone an entity simultaneously inhabits and moves through for an undetermined period of time in which reality is reorganized, enabling the entity to transition from one time/space/reality into another time/space/reality.

"Howl" uniquely exemplifies this mode of existence as a poem which is at once a poem and not a poem (as many critics will tell you), based upon reality and yet the product of many different imagined realities, a work whose meaning continuously shifts from not only reader to reader (including Ginsberg himself) but from year to year as well, as new cultural and political phenomena come to cast their own shadows across the timeless words. Through these sorts of changes and motions, "Howl" becomes not only an example and an instrument of untethering oneself from mainstream realities, but a space for committing the disjuncture as well.

Proctor goes on to state that "through examining our own internal liminal space of the unconscious, we can see a ... risk of transformation as we endeavor to be 'not ourselves,' but also '*not* not ourselves.'"[25] Proctor thus recognizes both the elements of fear and desire existent within liminal spaces. This keenly highlights the struggle within "Howl" to at once boldly face demons and thereby become shameless, powerful, and free while also remaining aware of the intense limitations of a human body, the types of limitations Ginsberg worked to sever with his first and originally unintended public reading while still honoring the beauty or usefulness within even fear itself. This struggle to both escape onself while not wanting to let go of the safe Entirety, however, is something that sets "Howl" and the trickster archetype within Coyote apart as Coyote is an entity who knows no fear of these sorts of transformations— they are, ironically, inherent within his Coyote self, representing both a transition into a new self as well as remaining intrinsically connected to the ancient self. However, to fully understand what it means to examine an "internal liminal space" at all, lines must be drawn between the concepts of "space" and "place."

Yi-Fu Tuan conceptualizes "place as pause" and space, conversely, "as that which allows movement."[26] By these explanations, he means that "place" is what people endow with significance or "value" such as through naming or inhabiting.[27] By "space" he means that which is the opposite of "the security and stability of place"—it is "the openness, freedom, and threat," it is the rush of movement through which only a pause makes "possible for location to be transformed into place."[28] Through these interconnected and cyclical definitions, Tuan provides a framework for looking at both abstract and concrete ideas or examples of both "space" and "place." He provides the rhetoric for examining "Howl" as a poem in motion through time—and as a space, in other words—as well as a poem of socially produced space of cultural contention, freedom, and uncertainty (as exhibited by "Howl's" subjection to an obscenity trial), making its liminality twofold—that of an altered dream/reality state and that of a more physical sense of being in two places at once.

Waddell provides greater illumination on this notion of space through her work with "the process of *intertextuality*" by which "the outer and the inner are negotiated."[29] I, similarly, posit that it is through this movement, this process, that literary and poetic works become spaces. Intertextuality results from the fact that no single text exists in a vacuum. Texts are dependent upon those other texts preceding them to provide place and meaning, to enable readers to engage in "a process of moving between texts" and finding the meaning "which exists between a text and all the other texts to which it refers and relates," disparate stars becoming a constellation.[30] In this way, by locating "Howl" within its historical, poetic, cultural, and trickster contexts, we have already begun to treat it as something with a distinct place and identity of its own. However, "Howl," more than being merely spatial, is also in itself both a space and a creator of space. This characteristic again connects "Howl" to the trickster as the trickster also exists in a liminal reality of space/place creation and inhabitation as exhibited by its immortality, creation of tricks and traps, tendency toward transformation, and inherent boundlessness. As Karl Kerenyi states, the trickster is "the spirit of disorder, the enemy of boundaries."[31]

Of course, Waddell is also in conversation with scholars such as Franca Bellarsi who, rather than films or televised stories, explicitly engages Ginsberg's poetry in a spatial dialogue. In her article "Proxemics and Poetic Discourse: Spatial Relationships in the Work of Allen Ginsberg," while she does not expressly discuss "Howl," she explains that,

> just as the perception of space and its use reflects states of minds that typify a culture, one could argue that the structuring of space in art or literature reflects mental patterns characteristic of the universe that a writer or artist creates in his/her work.[32]

And Ginsberg's poetry in particular, she argues, lends itself to this type of study and the "verbalization of proxemic relationships" as much of his work relates directly to his attempt to recreate the moment of profound revelation he experienced in his auditory Blake vision — it relates to an attempt to expand his consciousness so that one realm might meet another and "release him from the shackles of the empirically visible."[33] In order to examine how Ginsberg translates this perception of space and place into poetry, Bellarsi focuses upon his poems "Psalm IV" and "The Reply," as these directly deal in issues of the divine for Ginsberg.

Unlike Bellarsi, I contend that this spatial transcription of thought and vision for Ginsberg goes beyond those poems of his that focus explicitly or even primarily upon his quest for recapturing this sensation of spiritual revelation. By exploring "Howl" under similar criteria and attempting to understand it as both a space/place and a creator of space/place, we may begin to move beyond the spatial implications of this biographical moment and more into the actions of the poetry itself. For example, when tracing the history and motion of his creative process in "Howl," Ginsberg explained that by draft fourteen, certain verses had taken their time but had finally found "a fitting place by hand" within the larger "Howl" while other verses such as "Moloch whose name is the Mind"[34] continued to drift in search of a "logical sonorous home among the verses."[35] Thus, here in Ginsberg's own annotations of "Howl," he not only discusses it as a space through which verses and ideas may move themselves, but as a space in which verses and ideas actively seek out "homes" for themselves and find their own "fitting places." Ginsberg reveals that not only may "Howl" be liminal and spatial in terms of its content or in terms of its readers and author, but also in terms of the "physical" phrases and verses themselves. "Howl" is a work in three different levels of spatiality: its creators (the author and readers); its own "physical" and "spiritual" makeup (the words, phrases, pages, and the imaginative zone in which those phrases — lent agency by the author — move and seek place); and its content and subject matter (the actual poetic events and depictions of liminality, space/place, and motion).

For Ginsberg, writing poetry, writing "Howl," allowed him glimpses into his deepest, perhaps even most "authentic" sense of self and existence, such as when he "sometimes" felt "in command" when writing, experiencing "a sense of being self-prophetic master of the universe," a man fully aware of his own place in the world.[36] Thomas Clark bears witness to such an inhabitation of poetry from a night spent in a bar in Bristol, watching Ginsberg give a poetry reading. He explains that when he saw Ginsberg perform some of his poetry at one of the bars, he "was struck ... by the way [Ginsberg] seemed to *enter* each of his poems emotionally while reading them, the performance as much a discovery for him as for his audience" (emphasis added).[37] This speaks not only to the nature of poetry as place but also to the liminal nature of Ginsberg existing simultaneously in both the role of reader/decoder and that of author/encoder.

Anne Waldman, perhaps unintentionally, summarized this liminal, trickster complexity sweetly in her article "Premises of Consciousness," wherein she describes "Howl" as "the Outrider."[38] Her observation that the "Outrider rides the edge — parallel to the mainstream, is the shadow to the mainstream, is the consciousness or soul of the mainstream whether the mainstream recognizes its existence or not," stands right in line with the aforementioned concept of "cosmic consciousness" and Coyote as a larger whole.[38] That this trickster Outrider, this "Howl," "rides through the chaos, maintaining a stance of 'negative capability,' but also does not give up that projective drive, or its original identity, which demands that it intervene on the culture," is redolent of the evidences brought forth in Ginsberg's journals and interviews where he openly discusses his hopes for transforming America, of intervening in mainstream American culture through "Howl," tricks, humor, and Coyote-negative capability.[40]

Of course, this all begs the question of how "Howl" can exist as an "Outrider" or entity of permanent liminality when such a thing is, in fact, a paradox. Christine Teresa Mazur explores the nature of "permanent liminality" in relation to horrific literary elements within her thesis, "Gothic Fiction, Liminality, and Popular Culture: Stephen King's 'Grotesque' Social Commentary in 'Salem's Lot." She utilizes the figure of the vampire to explain that the vampire "exists in a permanent state of liminality," despite this being an impossibility (even for a supernatural being), as liminality, by nature, is transitory.[41] If a being or entity were eternally liminal, it would cause liminality to "evolve into another form of structure" rather than exist as a phase of motion between and within multiple structures.[42] Thus, not only does "the vampire state" exist as a *parallel* version of the society it replaces," but it also necessitates destruction (much as Ginsberg called for the destruction of the self after experiencing his auditory vision) before the state or "liminal phase" may be ended and the entity reenter human society or state.[43] Thus, we return to the question, what does it mean to argue that "Howl" exists within a liminal state and as a space of liminality for others/readers? Essentially, for "Howl" to exist as an entity of constant liminality, it must exist, as Waldman suggests it does, as both a parallel version of the society it replaces as well as subject to constant deconstruction by the "external forces" or needs/interpretations/decodings of its readers (and thereby reenter the "human state" with the human reader).[44] As a parallel to society, "Howl" becomes a "safe space" in which Ginsberg and other readers may inhabit and create places/meaning for themselves within, sans fear of persecution, exile, or ridicule. As a subject of constant deconstruction, "Howl" fulfills the needs of readers to decode texts, inhabit the spaces therein, create places and meaning using the instruments of deconstruction (which become the fruits of decoding), and reenter the human state anew from the lessons and places acquired and organized through the liminal space and process of the text in question.

Waldman, however, sheds even more light on the issue by further defining the functions of the Outrider, "Howl," as a kind of shaman, the true spiritual "insider." The shaman travels to zones of light and shadow. The shaman travels to edges of madness and death, and comes back to tell and enact the vivid stories.[45]

These "zones of light and shadow" that "Howl" is moving through, in this case, also seem to mirror almost precisely the zones of liminal space *created* by "Howl" for others to inhabit and move through. Zones such as those referenced by Ginsberg in his 1956 letter to Eberhart, where he explains that poetry such as "Howl" enables one to take "a leap of detachment from the Artificial ... of what is acceptable and normal" and to celebrate the types of "madness" he discusses throughout "the Who section" of Part I of his "Howl."[46] In other words, "Howl" enabled Ginsberg to leap outside the arbitrary bounds of one reality and create his own reality filled with his own values, goals, and guidelines. Ginsberg later wrote of this section of "Howl" that he had "depended on the word 'who' to keep the beat, ... [to] return to and take off from again onto another streak of invention: 'who lit cigarettes in boxcars boxcars boxcars,' continuing to prophesy what [Ginsberg] really knew despite the drear consciousness of the world."[47] And, as Michael McClure confirmed within his own recollections of that first opening, of the Six Gallery performance of "Howl,"

> In all of our memories no one had been so outspoken in poetry before — we had gone beyond a point of no return — and we were ready for it, for a point of no return. None of us wanted to go back to the gray, chill, militaristic silence, to the intellective void — to the land without poetry — to the spiritual drabness,[48]

to the land before "Howl."

Thus Ginsberg traces through "Howl" his "taking off points" or platforms (which suggests that a poem is something in which a person may inventively take off) and explains that the poem is constructed of "streaks of invention," movements and motions of invention depicting forces of motion ("boxcars boxcars boxcars" both referring to a moving locomotive as well as visually simulating the moving train). Beyond this, in his notes Ginsberg draws the explanation back into what is perhaps the single line within "Howl" directly referencing a cultural aspect of many Native American communities — that of the vision of the legendary Vision Quests (another journey, another motion, another moment of "Howl" encompassing and illustrating a spiritual pathway).[49]

This liminality — existing in the merger of place and process, of author and reader — is well exhibited in passages of "Howl" such as this

3. Space, Place, and Traversing Boundaries

one from Part I, where each successive "who" enables Ginsberg to leap outward:

> who howled on their knees in the subway and were dragged off the roof waving genitals and manuscripts.
>
> ...
>
> who blew and were blown by those human seraphim, the sailors, caresses of Atlantic and Caribbean love,
>
> who balled in the morning in the evenings in rosegardens and the grass of public parks and cemeteries scattering their semen freely to whomever come who may,
>
> ...
>
> with the absolute heart of the poem of life butchered out of their own bodies good to eat a thousand years.[50]

Each of these stanzas serves as a place within the space of "Howl," as well as entities that have, according to much of Ginsberg's own rhetoric, sought out these, their own places within "Howl." This makes them simultaneously pauses in the space of "Howl" for readers to inhabit or rest upon as well as movements through "Howl" given their uniquely spatial subject matters. In these stanzas, we may begin to better understand the many spaces and places of "Howl." Here Ginsberg is once again depicting the actions and plights of those "best minds" through illustrations of movement. However, this time, we focus upon not simply locating a general case of the trickster within Ginsberg's language, but upon Ginsberg's use of liminality in order to further elucidate the connections and actions between the two ("Howl" and Coyote). In the first of these stanzas we notice, again (while looking beyond the biographical references to the artistic expressions), the fantastical movement between "the subway" and "the roof" where the best minds appear in either two places at once or as capable of existing on the opposite poles of society—howling deep underground while waving dangerously high above. Each of these stanzas deals in motion and ceaseless journey from the city to the sea to the gardens, parks, and cemeteries—all but the final stanza work with physical, typical "place" locations.

This last stanza-place explores poetry as a projective space sprung from the place of the best minds' bodies. Interestingly, exploring the body as a place in and of itself (as a possessor of spaces—one Large and containing Multitudes) from which poetry may be harvested (however brutally) brings out the trickster in the situation in a number of ways. Not only does this stanza suggest the existence of an insatiable hunger for something intrinsic to us, for something that was inside of us until we decided to tear it out, it also suggests that the means of satisfying that hunger may be more gruesome than lovely. Where others might write their poetry, allow it to "flow" out of their minds and act as transcribers or translators, here the Beats seek something rawer. Thus, they attempt to utilize a barer, more explicit means of producing or pulling poetry out of themselves in order to bring forth the original substance and stuff of Poetry, a tough self-butchery but a sacrifice with its own gluttonous reward.

Kenneth Lincoln addresses these city-space aspects of Ginsberg's poetry within his *Sing with the Heart of a Bear* (although he focuses upon Ginsberg's "A Supermarket in California"). He compares Ginsberg's use of and focus upon city-space where "people imagine the cosmos of their own questionings" with much of Native poetry which, he contends, deals more typically in the non-city landscapes which possess a "country sense of free space," a sense allowing "communities, tribes, clans, for superstition and sorcery and feeling as a part of the natural landscape of magic — something larger than *one-* self."[51] He continues the comparison to this keynote: where Ginsberg worked as a part of "the now, the new" and

"crawl[ed] out of mid–American alley dives to
        Howl!"

Native American poetry, which he calls "the past manifesting the present," and "regenerative traditions," do their work to

        "Listen!"[52]

Much as Tom Spanbauer recognized in his *The Man Who Fell in Love with the Moon*, a primary difference running between Native American and non–Native American poetry lies in their differing senses of time. Non-Native poetry seems primarily concerned with making its voice heard *now* for the sake of the future, concerned with the now and later. On the other end of the spectrum, much of Native poetry chooses to listen more to the voices of others and focus upon understanding the past as a means of understanding the present — one works in a linear time progression and the other in more of a spiraling forward motion through time. However, I would contend that though Ginsberg does often remain primarily concerned with the future of both himself and others, his "Howl" is also a

3. Space, Place, and Traversing Boundaries

working attempt to document and understand his and his Beats' status in the late 1950s (as a group of young people feeling untethered from any semblance of community beyond themselves with increasingly fewer and fewer elders to turn to but for their romanticized and mythologized heroes of the American Self such as Walt Whitman).

This has not only deep implications for the readings and comparisons between Native Coyote narratives and "Howl" but also for the conceptions of space and place existing between the two. Snyder, a studier of both Native and Japanese philosophy (in this way similar to Gerald Vizenor), was certainly learning about these differences during the 1950s and 1960s. And, upon receiving news of the death of Ginsberg's mother, Snyder wrote in return (August 20, 1956) a letter filled with advice, including the suggestion that Ginsberg "take a good look at Indian philosophy sometime" and examine how their shamans, elders, and holy people have been searching out for not just enlightenment and spiritual revelation but also for all those mystical "interior landscapes."[53] This is the same terminology Vizenor would later use for the title of his book *Interior Landscapes: Autobiographical Myths and Metaphors*, in which he explains that his "stories are interior landscapes."[54]

Tim Cresswell interestingly defines "landscape" as "the shape — the material topography — of a piece of land," something that is viewed by humans rather than lived within.[55] This makes landscapes uniquely capable of shifting and transforming through imagination and nostalgia as they may become or begin as internalized mind-spaces and places. In other words, if we are to understand "interior landscapes" as something that may be sought out through spiritual journeys as spiritual places, liminal in their physical humanity and in their presumed dreamlike spirituality, as well as something which enables us to extend, invent, and expand beyond all "exterior" landscapes, we should also consider them as inherently trickster. This trickster notion of "interior landscapes" traveling from mind to mind and story to story is another way in which to begin examining the spaces and places within and created by "Howl."

Take, for example, the following stanzas:

> who dreamt and made incarnate gaps in Time & Space through images juxtaposed, and trapped the archangel of the soul between 2 visual images and joined the elemental verbs and set the noun and dash of consciousness together jumping with sensation of Pater Omnipotens Aeterna Deus[56]

> to recreate the syntax and measure of poor human prose and stand before you speechless and intelligent and shaking with shame, rejected yet confessing out the soul to conform to the rhythm of thought in his naked and endless head,
>
> the madman bum and angel beat in Time, unknown, yet putting down here what might be left to say in time come after death[57]

In these stanzas we may see a number of spatial occurrences including the dreaming and creation of "incarnate gaps in Time & Space," the trapping of "the archangel of the soul between 2 visual images," and the conjoining of spaces through words. Of course, for part of these stanzas, Ginsberg is not only channeling Coyote liminality and spatiality; he is also alluding to Paul Cézanne.

Paul Portugés' article "Allen Ginsberg's Paul Cézanne" expands upon this and speaks directly to the first of these particular stanzas in "Howl." Portugés offers a passage from one of Cézanne's letters that particularly captured Ginsberg's attention in which he describes "his theory of nature portrayal" and explains that he "was attempting to find the 'All-powerful Father, Eternal God' in his art."[58] From this letter and other journals of Ginsberg, Portugés proffers that Ginsberg believed that Cézanne had discovered a means within his art "to go far beneath the surface of reality and bring forth the eternal, the all-powerful from nature," the *Pater Omnipotens Aeterna Deus*.[59] In many ways, these particular stanzas are a show of Ginsberg's appreciation for and work toward "getting close to the eternal in the everyday" via what Cézanne termed the "petite sensation."[60] However, though this passage is undeniably related (if not in dedication) to Cézanne and his work, these notions and explorations combined with the rest of "Howl" also function to better encapsulate the full nature of Coyote.

This passage also reveals an attempt made by Ginsberg (or perhaps by his other "best minds") to create new places for themselves through poetic "images juxtaposed" as well as through the inherently Coyote-ish traps (also composed of poetic images) wherein they capture "the archangel of the soul." And it is here that Ginsberg begins to more explicitly discuss the art of creating spaces and places through poetry, through the "joined elemental verbs and set[ting] the noun and dash of consciousness together"— a space/place creation which he quickly links to the divine, explaining that these creations are brought to life "jumping with sensation of Pater Omnipotens Aeterna Deus." Of course, Ginsberg promptly reveals that this, the first stanza of the series, may also serve as the first phase of pre-liminal rites as it is the second stanza that describes life in the liminal. Ginsberg illustrates that within the liminal, within the second stanza here, you must suddenly "recreate" or reorganize everything all the way down to "the syntax and measure" of life (of prose language in this case). Moreover, it is only after this process of reorganization or recreation that one, as Hyde suggested, can confront "shame" and exit out once more, into the post-liminal, and reenter society. Although, for Ginsberg, this reentry only ironically represents a new state of liminality, that of life within which both "the madman bum and angel" overlap.

But even here, at the very peak of liminality, Ginsberg continues on to further develop this relationship with "the madman bum and angel," which, I argue, is the Coyote within his poem. Consider the following stanzas as they speak to both the liminality and sexuality of Coyote within "Howl."

> who blew and were blown by those human seraphim, the sailors, caresses of Atlantic and Caribbean love,
> who balled in the morning in the evenings in rose-gardens and the grass of public parks and cemeteries scattering their semen freely to whomever come who may[61]

Ginsberg projects several instances of his many interior landscapes, bringing out both a spatial conversation (as may be implied by the notion of landscape) as well as an excursion into the many lands and spaces of the trickster. The physical landscapes of rose gardens, public parks, and cemeteries may be seen enmeshing themselves with the blurry boundaries of the Atlantic and Caribbean, enabling Ginsberg to linger along the poetic liminal beaches where these two interior landscapes— one obsessed with Hart Crane, the other obsessed with Ginsberg's own feelings and trickster tendencies— meet. The nonphysical landscape, those of the interior spaces, highlight the ability of a poem such as "Howl" to become a place where Ginsberg may both explore as well as share his interior landscapes with others.

The connection to Crane here is notable as it not only links "Howl" interestingly to Coyote (through the journeying, constant journeying through the wild spaces of the sea as well as through the sexual connotations of blowing and being blown, not to mention through the wisdom and guidance of an elder poet) but also in how it interestingly links "Howl" to a larger history of non–Native American poetic fascination with Native American poetry. Crane, in certain of his poems, "employed the Indian as a symbol associated with the land and with a new American identity, an expanded consciousness based on a mystical participation in the land's spirit."[62] Of course, Crane's fascination with Native America was largely if not entirely colored by deep and intensely problematic stereotypes and paternalism. For example, in a 1927 letter, Crane explained that his poem "The Bridge" was an attempt to lead the reader "back in time to the pure savage world."[63] This is the type of rhetoric and action Ginsberg protested in his poem "America" where he satirically employs what has been termed "Hollywood Injun English."[64]

In the following stanza, Ginsberg artfully marries trickster concepts of appreciating life through experiences of death, humor, and space/place.

> who plunged themselves under meat trucks looking for an egg,
> ...
> who jumped off the Brooklyn Bridge this actually happened and walked away unknown and forgotten into the ghostly daze of Chinatown soup alleyways & firetrucks, not even one free beer[65]

This place within "Howl" focusing on the place of the Brooklyn Bridge and the way it was used in an attempt to escape into another space and way of being, refers to a moment, a pause, a place within the motion and space of one Naphtali Tuli Kupferberg's lifetime. In the spring of 1945, filled with anger and depression due to World War II (and a number of other problems), a young Kupferberg attempted suicide via leaping off the Manhattan Bridge only to survive and realize his folly, calling out across time and space, "You'll be dead a long long while, & sooner than you imagine. Patience patience, my young, wild, beautiful, damned friends!"[66] However, the dark humor in leaping off a bridge — perhaps the most poignant physical symbol of liminal space — in order to escape the madness of someone else's reality hearkens to that Coyote element of coming to incorporate and face death before life might be better appreciated or understood. However, to threaten death for some semblance of understanding only to end up "walk[ing] away unknown and forgotten into the ghostly daze" suggests that, for the members of Ginsberg's "best minds," they already exist within an in-between space of life and death, in a "*ghostly daze of Chinatown soup alleyways & firetrucks.*" This points to not only finding solace and the power to leap off bridges within poetry but also the recognition of a certain type of marginalization within society, existing in the alleyways rather than in the neighborhoods or workplaces.

The humor exhibits itself in strange and unexpected ways throughout this stanza, working in a unique fashion to enhance the liminality of the moment. Humor is a "generally cooperative venture, not only in face-to-face communication but also across time and space," blurring the responsibilities of the authors and readers, turning them both into creators of a single moment of humor.[67] Ginsberg's humorous intentions are clear here, especially given his admission of intended humor within his own annotations, calling his first-verse reference to the "hysterical" a setting of a "Chaplinesque tone" to combine meaningfully with the "apocryphal burlesque" of "meat trucks" leading into the catch tale of the Brooklyn Bridge business.[68] Where this reference originally applies to the desperate attempt of one young man to escape the horrors of global and societal ills, it also brings into play a number of absurdities. The first level of irony may appear in the attempt itself, given that it is ultimately an effort to commit suicide out of some form of protest against the senseless deaths in the war abroad. Among the other humorous absurdities of the moment, Ginsberg plays up the apparent ability of a failed suicide attempter to simply get up and "walk away" into the buzz and zoom and neon lights of typical city life (revealing, perhaps, another form or means of suicide), although without so much as "one free beer" to show for all the effort. This suggests that, unlike an event of great emotional and physical trauma, this bridge jumping was really more a moment of riskless recklessness, as nothing, at least according to the apparent inattentions of the larger society, was lost or gained in the best mind's survival. In other words, perhaps the best mind should have recognized that, rather than leaping from a bridge for attention, he could have earned at least the guaranteed attentions of a single screaming fire truck had he thought to sweeten the death pot with a few other lives such as in the event of a fire. As Snyder explains in his *The Old Ways*, "Coyote never dies, he gets killed plenty of times, but he always comes back to life again, and then he goes right on traveling."[69]

This is a sentiment surely exhibited by Coyote within the Coyote story, "Coyote and Doña Coyote Ride Up Elk Mountain and We Explain Things to Each Other" (1991) relayed by Webster Kitchell.[70] In this story, there comes a moment during a road trip to Elk Mountain when a large bug smashes messily into the windshield, to which the narrator asserts, "The universe gets its kicks out of being troublesome, difficult, petty, and mean.

"Coyote said, 'Oh, stop it. The universe is not mean.... The universe is magnificently unaware of you.'

"'You'd think differently if you had a windshield,'" the narrator quips.[71] At this moment in the story, not only is humor a more obvious factor (the author having set up a clear instance of recovery and repartee between the narrator and Coyote), but it provides Coyote with an opportunity to reveal his wiser side. Coyote plays the "straight man" here, wisely explaining the awesomeness of the universe ironically through its unawareness of its inhabitants moving (literally in this moment as they drive along) within it. Of course, this story possesses the added layer of the death of the bug. Even as Coyote describes the unawareness of the universe of our lives, the inhabitants of the car remain unaware of the life of the bug, creating a darkly humorous comparison between the life and fate of the bug and the lives and fates of all against the vast purposes and windshield of the universe. In this way, by keenly highlighting the vast unawareness of the universe as well as critiquing the troublesome lack of awareness on the part of human society for others within their own cities and communities, Ginsberg displays both the wit and wisdom of Coyote through this stanza.

All of this ties uniquely into the conversation of space and place as these stanzas and stories both deal in motion and the meeting or overlap of multiple worlds. In the "Howl" stanzas, this overlap comes into play: (1) in the motion of a person "plunging" beneath a meat truck in search of an egg (marrying the times and spaces of death [the presumably dead meat] with those of rebirth and possibility [the presumably undamaged egg]) and (2) the bridge jumper's attempt to leave one realm for another. This jump makes the space between the bridge's lip and the smack of the water's surface the jumper's first liminal crossing into what he assumes will result in his incorporation into a post-liminal space, that of the afterlife. In Kitchell's Coyote story, we find the narrator (presumably a human being) discussing the facts and philosophies of life with the supernatural being, Coyote. This discussion, this meeting of two types of worlds (the natural and the supernatural) within the symbolically liminal realm of the car illustrates both a movement through space as well as a meeting of two spaces.

> who lit cigarettes in boxcars boxcars boxcars rocketing through snow
> toward lonesome farms in grandfather night
>
> ...

> who reappeared on the West Coast investigating the F.B.I. in beards and shorts with big pacifist eyes sexy in their dark skin passing out incomprehensible leaflets
>
> who burned cigarette holes in their arms protesting the narcotic tobacco haze of Capitalism[72]

In these stanzas, we may begin to see once more the peculiar regional connections to the West within "Howl," linking it and its inner places interestingly to the terrain of Old Man Coyote. These references are scattered throughout "Howl" from Ginsberg's trips through Denver with Neal Cassady to this second stanza discussing the goings on of one Joffre Stewart. Stewart, a bold anarchist, came to visit Kenneth Rexroth in San Francisco in 1955 during which time Ginsberg had the pleasure to learn that Stewart was working on "investigating the F.B.I." and who always, apparently, carried with him an ample white sack of various pacifist and anarchist flyers.[73] These stanzas, when considered together and from a liminal standpoint (combining the phrases "reappeared," "boxcars boxcars boxcars," "West Coast," "rocketing through snow toward," and "burned cigarette holes in their arms protesting the narcotic tobacco haze"), create a place of demonstrable Coyote tendencies, of travel, irony, humor, paradoxical violence and pacifism, at once setting and falling victim to different traps.

Liminality is not simply a type of space but a type of zonal movement within an in-between space, a simultaneous space and motion in which places may be created. Here, in these place-stanzas within the wider space of "Howl," we may better understand how places and movements work together to create one another as well as how Ginsberg used "Howl" to create unique places for himself and his feelings. This type of place creation within "Howl" would have been a necessary turn for Ginsberg, as it was for other Beats through their own artistic works, given that the external, non–"Howl" space would refuse them (Beats, homosexuals, Jews, non-whites, non–Christians, and so forth) the room or right to forge their own places therein.

In some ways, the role of "reappeared" may seem obvious in relation to conversations regarding space, place, and movement. However, what is unique about this phrase in particular are the connotations of play and trickery it possesses. "Reappeared," after all, suggests a certain type of apparition, as if Stewart could have simply "poofed" in and out of existence like a phantom or specter. Of course, this essence communicated through the place-defying concept of the phantasmal, unexplained "reappearance" relates cleverly to the ironic notion of "investigating the F.B.I." The irony is showcased by turning the tables on the FBI given that they (at least presumably) pride themselves not only on their investigative abilities but also on their ability to act stealthily, secretively, and be panoptically everywhere — as if they could appear, disappear, and reappear at any moment, anywhere, and at any time. Thus, Ginsberg's playful bending of place and time through the decision of "reappeared" enters his work that much deeper into a humorous, liminal, and inherently Coyote-like space as he reimagines the world through an ironic rather than heroic lens, using wit and poetry to critique the spatial goals and fantasies of those who would paint themselves as heroes and control the country's knowledge and culture if they could. "Howl" thus comes, much as Coyote does, to create and inhabit spaces and places in between the heroic and the villainous, at once ironic, clever, and generous, yet constantly beating forward with his own goals and troublemaking.

As for "boxcars boxcars boxcars," Ginsberg manages to create not only a sense of place (on the train, within the cars moving through the snow) but also a clear sense of motion as the visual representation of the words as well as the audible sound of the line when read aloud create the image of a pounding train's boxcars rushing past you, cutting through trees and precipitations. Trains are a marked motif throughout "Howl" as they represent not only a particular type of romanticized motion (especially westward motion) but also symbolize the harsh and smoggy "progress" of the machine of Moloch. As such, trains in and of themselves keenly embody the concept of liminal space as they are at once made up of places but are also constantly in motion cutting through a variety of overlapping spaces. Due to this, they make for a uniquely appropriate metaphor chugging throughout "Howl" as a poem at once concerned with forward motion while also protesting for a new understanding of progress and freedom. However, what's perhaps most interesting about this passage in connection to Coyote is that within this stanza Ginsberg was channeling Crane's "The Bridge" specifically. In his annotations of "Howl," Ginsberg quotes:

> Hobo-trekkers that forever search
> An empire wilderness of freight and rails.[74]

In this moment of Crane's work, we may see the utilization of the American classic, liminal figure of the "hobo-trekker" hopping from train car to train car searching for work or something larger, something constantly a train car ahead of them. This figure in particular reflects a certain essence of Coyote given that the hobo-trekker is usually gendered male as well as exists constantly and inherently on the move; the hobo-trekker, like Coyote, always begins his story already in motion, as Ginsberg began his story in "Howl," tracing for his readers the peculiar en medias res movements and actions of the best minds.

Through these sorts of winding influences and rhetorical play, the connections of "Howl" to Coyote become clearer and clearer. As Stephen M. Llano asserts in his "Beating Rhetoric: Rhetorical Theory in the Beat Generation," "Ginsberg is the Beat of embodiment" as he "calls attention to the material limits of being an embodied human being" yet simultaneously "using those limits as a source of invention, style, and delivery for his rhetoric."[75] In other words, Ginsberg is the Beat of Blurred Boundaries, of Inverted Limits, of Liminality, challenging the borders and boundaries of his humanity through poetry. Ginsberg calls attention to human limits (limits such as death) only to dismantle them for his own innovative use, much as Coyote constantly plays with his, society's, and nature's bounds for the purposes of teaching new ways of viewing and understanding them, of crossing them and blurring them.

Llano points to these verses in particular,

> Peyote solidities of halls, backyard green tree cemetery
> dawns, wine drunkenness over the rooftops,
> storefront boroughs of teahead joyride neon
> blinking traffic light, sun and moon and tree
> vibrations in the roaring winter dusks of Brooklyn, ashcan rantings and kind king light of mind,[76]

in order to explain that the very "notion of a 'peyote solidity'" through which (1) great bursts of motion occur (flashing from a "backyard green tree cemetery" to "the rooftops" to "storefront boroughs" through traffic, through all manner of earthly "vibrations" and "dusks of Brooklyn"); (2) "the status of the hallucination with reality" blurs; and (3) becomes worlds where the hallucinations and "the visions become solid, there's little out of bounds."[77]

When there is "little out of bounds," the question quickly becomes, what bounds were there to begin with? What constructs or hierarchies or structures are Ginsberg and Coyote putatively disrupting and breaking out of? Hyde addresses this question head-on, positing that it is in fact the cultures of "shame" which these two figures work their ways out of time and again. Hyde cites the Interior Salish (Idaho) story of Coyote and the Sun Lodge where Coyote takes it upon himself one day to become the "'Sun-god'" in which post he proceeds to spy upon everyone's secret and private actions only to loudly announce them to the rest of the world.[78] Due to his inability to keep things to himself or to know when to keep quiet, the people quickly demote him once more, bringing him back to simply Coyote. Through this story, Hyde suggests that Coyote is, in fact, "shameless" as demonstrated by his lack of shame in pointing out the secret affairs of others and as symbolized by his refusal to be silent. Hyde then explains that Ginsberg, like Coyote, possesses or practices a sort of shamelessness given that his poetic works and, I suggest, given that "Howl" specifically have been repeatedly denounced as profane or obscene despite the fact that much of "Howl" is biographical in nature and has been judicially recognized as possessing literary merit.

Hyde explains that in order to become shameless and thereby embrace a certain unique aspect of tricksterhood, one must be able and willing to face their own sense and feelings of shame. For Coyote, this act of facing up to one's shame is demonstrated countless times throughout various narratives (stretching throughout many Native communities) by his ability to make small and grand mistakes yet always return to life ready and willing to make another bold move, try another trick. In Ginsberg's case, Hyde cites familial and societal pressures against Ginsberg's blooming sexuality, mentally ill mother, and befriending of criminals as the primary generators of shame within Ginsberg. These divisions between "deviancy" and "civility" or, at least, "normality" illuminate the spatial nature of propriety and shame, of "spheres of speech and spheres of silence" which become inextricably entangled with cultural divisions between "the sacred and the profane."[79] These divisions suggest that people are able to spatially separate or compartmentalize their world into different sectors or levels of social acceptability, enabling them to at once anchor themselves to certain sets of "givens" or naturalized ideas (such as race, gender, sexuality, what is shameful, what is appropriate, etc.) while simultaneously cutting adrift those who do not feel safely anchored so much as coercively handcuffed (those such as Ginsberg).

Hyde posits that it is this tendency to act shamelessly within Coyote and tricksters generally that may cause some to confuse Coyote as psychopathic; this mistake reveals a deep lack of understanding of Coyote as it suggests that his shamelessness is in some way a defect or deviancy barring him from the other aspects of himself including his role as creator and teacher. To write Coyote off as psychopathic is to deny the sacred aspects of his stories and the wealth of humor laid within his words and actions— it is to attempt to construct a set of limitations about his character in order to fit him into the dominant, mainstream construct of shame or dignity, of hero or villain, when in fact he is often Irony, the Liminal Zone Walker who creates his own spaces and places within a variety of worlds.

Both Ginsberg and "Howl" have suffered similar attempted encasements or entrapments as many critics have decried them over the years as figures which could not possibly be either *poet* or *poem*. This is due to the fact that, like those who would lump Coyote into a simply psychopathic category due to misunderstandings of his multitudes, they allow their preconceived societal spheres of separation to direct their understandings of "poet" and "poem" as well as their understandings of Ginsberg and "Howl." Rather than considering the possibility of a new poetic style or voice, many opt to instead "blame" Ginsberg's drug use, his history in the hospital with Carl Solomon, or any number of other "peculiarities" of his past as justification for their brushing his poetry off as thoughtlessly as they might brush loose hairs from their shoulders, anything to maintain their own borders without pause or reflection upon the necessity or rightness of those borders. That an aspect of another's identity and the worth of their artistic work may be so brutalized by another's concept of shame marks a clear relationship between social divisions or hierarchies and conceptions of what can and cannot be sacred, multitudinous, poetic, or constantly expanding.

And while I agree with Hyde that Ginsberg possesses certain trickster abilities or tendencies I would add that it is through "Howl" specifically that Ginsberg began to truly exercise his burgeoning powers of shameless poetics. By this I mean that "Howl" became a new type of asocial space, perhaps a Beat social space, created by and for Ginsberg—a liminal space where he became free to explore and safely face his own feelings and accusations of shame and shamefulness. Thus, "Howl" came to function as a safe albeit liminal and trickster zone in which Ginsberg could create new places for himself, places of security and shamelessness through which to explore, critique, celebrate, and satirize himself, his friends, his worlds, and the worlds of many others. In these ways, "Howl," like Coyote narratives, becomes not only a poem about spaces, places, and living in liminality but is, in fact, a liminal space in and of itself containing within it a variety of unique places for both Ginsberg and his readers' exploration, decoding, and transition.

In the following sections, these connections and liminalities are further explored in even greater detail, with focus placed upon the explication and analysis of "Howl." However, in order to keep the analysis from degrading into an echo chamber wherein every line and stanza seems to encapsulate or symbolize Coyote, it will be important to note that the entirety of "Howl" is not analyzed here. Rather, only very selected lines and stanzas (although these do comprise a significant portion of the poem) will be discussed in detail. The following chapters are structured upon the four core trickster traits, beginning with appetite, wherein various places and moments within "Howl" are examined through this and each successive lens (i.e., tricks and traps, smearing borderlines, and transformative power).

Chapter 4

"Howl's" Appetite

"Appetite" refers not only to the physical hunger for food or the more decadent hungers for fame, glory, or recognition, but also for the physical hunger for sex, freedom, power, mobility, and spiritual rebirth. As Andrei Codrescu expresses in his reflective essay "'Howl' in Transylvania," Ginsberg's poetry "instantly infected" him with "an irresistible appetite for freedom" and moved thick and phantasmal through the "light-starved minds" of his generation in Transylvania.[1] Beyond even these inspired elements of hunger, Codrescu goes on to credit "Howl" for stirring in him a trickster desire to become and to act "epically, infamously bad" and "test the limits of [his] mind and the far reaches of liberty" — it instilled in him the hunger for transformation, for a new identity, the desire "to become American."[2]

These elements of hunger and appetite within "Howl" are undeniable and borderless in their applicability to the starvation and appetites of its many readers. Ginsberg recognizes and seizes upon this by depicting the sexual, political, spiritual, and intellectual appetites of himself and his contemporaries throughout "Howl"; he offers up metaphors of these urges and pursuits as extensions of that most human (and perhaps most trickster) desire for freedom. It is there in the very first line: "I saw the best minds of my generation destroyed by madness, *starving*, hysterical[3] naked" (emphasis added).[4] How are they starving? How is this hunger a part of their being the best and their being destroyed, of their being hysterical (mad, raving, and hilarious)? How is it a part of their being related to the trickster?

Ginsberg speaks of them fondly, those "angelheaded hipsters" whom he describes as "*burning* for the ancient heavenly connection to the starry dynamo in the machinery of night" (emphasis added).[5] This is a layered sexual moment in the poem, at once discussing a *burning* for an *angel-headed hipster* (a phrase which might encapsulate both the angelic minds of these hipsters as well as pun into the angelic heads of hipster penises, beautiful, brilliant, and orgasmic) and a *burning* for that *ancient heavenly connection* that may dualistically resemble both some moment of divine inspiration or epiphany as well as some heavenly sexual contact or relationship. Doing so, Ginsberg thereby combines the human with the divine, the humorous with the sincere in order to celebrate that negative capability of trickster complexity within the pursuits and trials of these "best minds." But as is the way with the work of poetic geniuses (however renegade or rebellious this one may be), there is always a skeleton supporting the pleasurable flesh of humor and innuendo. For "Howl," this skeleton consists of extreme stylistic and narrative deliberation, wherein Ginsberg creates his own firm cycle of storytelling through the careful reconstruction of Beat history. In this way, Ginsberg provides a queer history of events (both literal and literary) through which to understand the expansion and growth of Beat philosophy and thought. He enacts his own Beat principles and thought processes within his unique retelling of these narrative places,[6] and in this enacting we may see Coyote in action, at play in the hyperbole, at work in the sincere. As it is with Coyote, there is more to the story than the never-ending quest for appetite satisfaction, but the quest itself remains never-ending. Ginsberg elaborates upon this and the peculiar combination of the "hysterical," the humorous, the severe, and the thoroughly planned chaos in the following stanzas:

> who ate fire in paint hotels or drank turpentine in
> Paradise Alley, death, or purgatoried their
> torsos night after night
> with dreams, with drugs, with waking nightmares, al-
> cohol and cock and endless balls[7]

His diction, though masterful in its free-flowing, stream-of-consciousness aesthetic, is carefully made; it is redolent of the finest impromptus in this way, with every word carefully selected and debated for the absolute perfect meaning, perfect length, perfect sound in performance while still working to seem spontaneous and freshly inspired throughout. This is evidenced by the heavily edited and annotated drafts of "Howl" provided in the original draft facsimiles and transcripts of the poem. This evidence of great intentionality and purpose enables close readings and analysis of his style and content to fly with viability and validity. After all,

4. "Howl's" Appetite

if Ginsberg had merely scribbled and abandoned such strings of images without consideration or deeper message, few arguments for any sort of ulterior influences and transformations could be made. Though Ginsberg does go into great detail within his letters and annotations regarding the symbolism and references housed within specific stanzas, these do not imprison the poem from other readings or possible influences (as is evidenced by the many twists and transformations the poem underwent for Ginsberg throughout his life).

Here his verbs—"burning," "ate," and "drank"—all ring powerfully and bluntly in their relation to hunger.[8] This creates a repetition of appetite-driven actions which, naturally, demand to be indulged and which, if not indulged, tend to dig out their own means of fulfillment whether it be legal, socially acceptable, or otherwise.

Within this stanza, Ginsberg mentions a "Paradise Alley" that is likely in reference to "a cold-water-flat courtyard at 501 East 11th Street, NE" in New York where various Beats had bunked over the years, in cramped rooms that were "suffused with the smell of turpentine."[9] The phrase "ate fire" also takes on an entirely new and perhaps more unsettling meaning in the context of the brick-and-mortar history of Paradise Alley as it burned into ruin and eventual demolition in a 1985 fire. Examining these images within their historical context, we may begin to see how they function beyond the more basic sexual puns and enter into their liminal realm of *purgatoried* torsos—with purgatory serving as perhaps the most classical example of a liminal zone. Before the final draft of "Howl," "torsos" had long remained "bodies"—this change, according to Ginsberg, was made for the purposes of improving the "sound and sex" of the moment.[10] But how does this change better signify sex and express sound?

It not only produces greater alliteration (with hard *t* sounds following through purga*t*oried, *t*orsos, nigh*t*, af*t*er, nigh*t*) but also provides readers with a more intimate glimpse into both the heart as well as the sexualized body involved in this circle of wants and decisions. This stanza is, ultimately, about the desires and hungers of many different Beats across various times and places within their lives: the hero of Kerouac's *The Subterraneans* who once lived in Paradise Alley; other Beats coming and going through the small hotels surrounding the Alley; the drugs mentioned likely referring to not only alcohol, cigarettes, and marijuana but also to the "Benzedrine inhalers" commonly supplied by members of Herbert Hunke's crew; and Ginsberg's almost constant "dreams" of becoming sexually involved with a slow succession of men over the years but finding himself and his young torso instead "purgatoried" night after night with only dream-nightmares of the "cock and endless balls"[11] of the sexual and loving relationships he hungered for. In other words, this stanza subtly reflects the many and varied sexual desires and desirers of the best minds of Ginsberg's generation; it speaks of those who were made to feel that their own deep and sacred selves were perversions, feelings that thus plagued them with "waking nightmares," entrapping them within purgatories built of their own desires to fulfill themselves as well as by the pull to meet the desires of others.

Of course, Ginsberg is not a child throwing a fit for sexual gratification in this stanza or through these hunger-driven choices: "burning," "ate," "drank," and "dreams."[12] He is a whole minority, one hungry for real freedoms (such as the freedom to love others and appreciate oneself in one's entirety, to fulfill one's needs and pursue one's happiness). But once his readers realize this, suddenly the joke (the constant play and pun within this more serious subject matter upon sex and sexual desire) seems less of a joke and more of a moral trap that has just been snapped — "cock and endless balls" representing not only the ache for a good time but also stretching into a serious call for gay rights to love, live, work, and philosophize without prejudice or fear.[13] After all, it is with the "dreams," the "drugs," the endurance of "waking nightmares," "alcohol," and "cock and endless balls" by which the "best minds" kept their own torsos purgatoried, tormented, and pulled from all sides. This conflict and confluence of desires, to please and be pleased, trapped as well as freed them during this time of Cold War fear and the rigid restructuring of American propriety, obscenity, and social acceptability.

This tumultuous concoction of physical hungers and desires, combined to communicate deeper spiritual and ethical hungers for America, reveals some of the zest of the trickster. For just as Coyote narratives so often utilize seemingly asocial or amoral behaviors and actions, they are typically utilized for humorous and socially beneficial purposes. For example, reconsider the story of "Coyote's Member Keeps Talking." In this story we not only see Coyote experience the wildness and naturalness of his own sexuality but also see him find himself helpless to assuage the loudness of his sexual desires by any means but by fulfilling them, despite how this fulfillment may counter or affront societal norms and mores (such as the incestuous nature of having sexual relations with one's mother-in-law). In this way, Coyote combines common jokes (such as those at the expense of the mother-in-law and those of the unsatisfied husband) with certain social norms (such as the fact that incest is morally wrong) in order to create a story which both reveals the issue of hunger, tests the moral boundaries of society, and makes these easier to examine and consider through the light and lubricant of laughter. Much as Ginsberg attempts to explain for those "*who ate fire in paint hotels or drank turpentine in Paradise Alley*" or who "*purgatoried their torsos night after night with dreams, with drugs, with waking nightmares, alcohol and cock and endless balls*," so Coyote demonstrates for the good humor of his audience that certain hungers cannot be silenced through anger or sheer will but must be indulged—lest one find oneself losing the humor and ending up purgatoried, alone, and hungry.[14]

What may also be seen within these two stories (that of Coyote and that of Ginsberg's best minds) are the ways that power is renegotiated through stories of humor and hunger. By hunger's very nature, the hungry are the ones wielding less power than those who provide the food or sustenance. In these cases, Coyote is put at the mercy of his mother-in-law as well as at the mercy of his culture's mores to enable him to satiate his needs; Ginsberg and his best minds, similarly, are put at the mercy of not only each other but also of their larger society as mainstream tolerance and acceptance generally dictate what desires may or may not be indulged. However, through the humor within these stanzas and stories, we find these power dynamics turning topsy-turvy. Coyote uses his desire and trickster courage and boundlessness to take control of the situation, look past the traditional borderlines of social normality, and become shameless by facing society and his mother-in-law head-on (pun intended) in asking for what he knows will sustain him. We also find Ginsberg using these stanzas (and all of "Howl") to challenge the shaming boundaries (through which power may be achieved) of society by facing them directly through his confessional, desirous, and commanding rhetoric, all in an attempt to recapture that original moment of vision and satori.[15]

This language is pervasive throughout "Howl" as these hungers proceed unfulfilled or overindulged from stanza to stanza, and from place to place. He elaborates upon his best minds as those,

> who lounged *hungry* and *lonesome* through Houston seeking jazz[16] or *sex or soup*, and followed the brilliant Spaniard to converse about America

> and Eternity, a hopeless task, and so took ship
> to Africa,
>
> ...
>
> who *bit* detectives in the neck and shrieked with delight
> in policecars for committing no crime but their
> own *wild cooking pederasty and intoxication*,[17]
>
> ...
>
> who *copulated ecstatic and insatiate* with a bottle of beer a sweetheart
> a package of cigarettes a candle and fell off the bed, and continued
> along the floor and down the hall and ended fainting on the wall
> with a vision of *ultimate cunt and come* eluding the last *gyzym*[18] of
> consciousness[19] (emphasis added)

Yet again, Ginsberg packs these places tight with strong hunger-related vocabulary. He makes certain his audience is sure of nothing if not the size of these brilliant minds' stomachs. These signifiers of desire and gluttony (as emphasized above), if taken with both the humor and severity with which they were intended, reveal that same humorous gluttony used in many Coyote narratives to unmask and highlight both the panacea for and consequences of societal ills. By using such jocular, exuberant, and hyperbolic lingo as "wild cooking pederasty" rather than simply "sex" (in order to highlight both the inherently wild-natural quality of sexuality as well as to criticize how and what others may label as "perversion"); "intoxication" rather than "drunkenness"; "copulated ecstatic and insatiate" rather than "excited and eager"; "ultimate cunt and come" rather than "vagina and orgasm" or even just "ultimate sex and pleasure"; "gyzym"; and so forth throughout the poem, Ginsberg makes a joke of otherwise violent and/or oppressive mainstream rhetoric regarding sexuality generally.

He boldly underlines the ridiculousness of blaming every ill upon sexual diversity, experimentation, and exploration as well as the ridiculousness of placing such a stigma of evil upon the sexual act and body itself. Coyote also well exhibits these traits and feelings within stories like the Northern Paiute narrative, "How Her Teeth Were Pulled" (as told by Kenneth Lincoln), wherein Coyote saves humankind from a world saddled with a horror of reproductive agony — a world where women's vaginas are filled with teeth. And it takes Coyote's ingenuity and desire for someone, for *him*, to finally discover the solution in simply breaking the teeth out.[20] These traits may also be seen within Coyote through narratives like the aforementioned, "Coyote and the Mallard Ducks," where Coyote plays with the negative sexual notions of taboo and wrongdoing (such as rape) as well as those sexual components of goodness and virtue (by saving the eldest sister's life through further copulation).

Beyond this, however, it may be that Ginsberg did, in some fashion, endorse this type of sexual relationship ("pederasty"), given his membership with the North American Man/Boy Love Association (NAMBLA). He joined NAMBLA in the mid–1980s "as a matter of civil liberties," viewing NAMBLA as "a discussion society not a sex club. I joined NAMBLA in defense of free speech."[21] This is, obviously, not to suggest that Ginsberg was somehow in favor of the victimization or sexual abuse of children, but that he was—as he said—advocating for free speech and open discussion over issues such as the deeply arbitrary legal rulings on age of consent. Moreover, this advocacy delves into the realm of trickster beyond even the desire for sex and questions of socially acceptable sexualities (as Coyote's many tales of incest—attempted and otherwise—well demonstrate) as Ginsberg calls for the *humor* of all things to be brought to the floor so that common sense and civil discussion might prevail:

> A dash of humor, common sense humanity and historical perspective would help discussion of NAMBLA's role.[22]

Sex is something most everyone within the population takes part in at some point in their lives. (Your mother wanted it too, you know.) It is natural and necessary as the vertebra in your spinal cords and the enamel on your teeth. By this fundamental truth, Ginsberg is able to not only employ sex in blatant and humorous ways alike but also to pull from the joke an unmasking of the majority's appetite for a scapegoat, for something to label perverse and then devour. And, of course, Ginsberg never dismisses an opportunity to use examples, issues, and prejudices from his own life and the climate of the encroaching 1960s to display the minorities' vast hunger for their freedoms, for the America that was promised them — the America that had promised them the right to not only life but also to liberty and the pursuit of happiness.

For example, Ginsberg utilized the second stanza of this provided series to play on the continued tropes of sexual desire and hunger to open a window for a trickster from his past to come crawling through: he goes by the name of William "Bill" Cannastra.[23] Ginsberg explains in a note in his annotated facsimile edition of "Howl" that the line concerning the bitten detectives refers to one Bill Cannastra, though, he assures us, the reference is nonliteral (of course, the more one learns about Cannastra the more one may come to question this assurance).²⁴

Of course, we cannot discount some of the simpler or at least more blatant Coyote-connections through his listing of different appetites: for booze, for love, for nicotine/drugs, for seeing/reading/knowing/learning, for sex, for enlightenment. The connection of orgasm-like pleasure with spiritual enlightenment has been recognized by many other religions, including Christianity. St. Teresa was depicted by Renaissance sculptor Gian Lorenzo Bernini in the arms of an angel who looks to have just pierced her with an arrow, as if with divine enlightenment, and she, in response, looks to be in the midst of ultimate ecstasy both spiritual and physical. Sex, thus, is widely recognized as an act which can also be a religious experience; Goldman, in his *Being Jewish,* explains more frankly that some Jews engage in intercourse as a celebration of the Sabbath, a practice which Ginsberg, as a Jew, would have likely been aware of. In this way, this connection between sex and the spiritual functions as another means to ideologically connect Ginsberg and Coyote, to connect "Howl" and Coyote.

Ginsberg's litany of hunger does not stop with simply these beginning stanzas, though. He continues on with the chant,

> who plunged themselves under meat trucks looking for an egg,
>
> ...
>
> who jumped off the Brooklyn Bridge this actually happened and walked
> away unknown and forgotten into the ghostly daze of Chinatown
> soup alleyways & firetrucks, not even one free beer
>
> ...
>
> with the absolute heart of the poem of life butchered out of their own
> bodies good to eat a thousand years.²⁵

The first line quoted here depicts a Coyote-ridiculous sort of desperation. It describes a hunger so deep that in one's drive to satiate it one misses the prize by donning a pair of blinders, just as Coyote did in the "Skunk Kill Game" story. Why continue searching and fighting when you have already found sustenance? Perhaps because you have never been allowed to taste the finer meats and thus, as Ginsberg appears to argue, might as well be unaware of them, such as the freedom to marry or walk down the street without fear. The second stanza offers a real trick for "even one free beer," reminiscent of when Coyote challenged Skunk to that extra race for his share of the booty. The act of leaping off a bridge and walking off alone

4. "Howl's" Appetite

in the ghostly daze and sirens all to simply complain about the lack of a free beer is as if to say, *well, I went to all that trouble for nothing!* All that trouble of acting as if your life was worth a beer to someone, that trouble of setting a trap for someone's charity or humanity for all the food or beer they could spare, only to end up empty-handed.

He sets this trap for others while simultaneously falling victim to his own trap by misunderstanding the value of himself and the beer rather than actually doing something constructive for the drink. In this same fashion, Coyote could have simply accepted his share and been satisfied with what was already his or gone off in hunt of some other animal or even Skunk himself rather than try an elaborate trick to race Skunk out of his fair share. Of course, this is also a joke on Ginsberg's part. Here the drink is the satirical parallel of a reality hungry for compassion, for a wake-up call of some kind to a shared humanity. Through the humor of complaining over a beer, Ginsberg highlights the severity of cultural starvation.

The last stanza, though, suggests a slightly different type of hunger, one that is twofold, liminal in its ability to represent both an evil and a sacrifice. As a sacrifice, this passage might be reminiscent of the Miwok origin story, "How People Were Made" (as told by Richard Erdoes and Alfonso Ortiz), wherein Coyote makes a sacrifice of himself by playing dead in an effort to lure the crows and buzzards into eating a hole in him, a hole he then quickly closes up to capture them and cull their feathers— the chosen instrument for the creation of humankind.[26] In a similar sense, we find here the "best minds" willing to have holes eaten into them so that a piece of their own bodies might be culled and utilized for the benefit of the world, "good to eat a thousand years."

Of course, on the other hand, this passage also suggests a significantly more foolish and ruinous hunger often demonstrated by Coyote but not typically — at least here according to Ginsberg — by those *best minds*. Here Ginsberg also could be describing the salivating mouths of an intolerant American mainstream, illustrating a hunger Ginsberg further addresses in Part II of "Howl" (though by then he begins calling them out more blatantly as the pagan deity, "Moloch," gluttonous for the lives of children and, by symbolic extension, the Future). This Moloch hunger describes that of the United States' desperation to keep everything safely, safely the same. It is the apparent media hunger to make sure everyone's "American" dream remains singular, controllable, and identical; it is what Ginsberg seemed to view as the homogenous nightmare with an appetite for outliers, minorities, and individuals.

And, as Ginsberg keeps saying, there is nothing wrong with the traditional "American" dream or that lifestyle so long as it's not expected of or forced upon everyone else. There is nothing wrong with it so long as one person's ideal and comfort does not become the "pure machinery" of our "stunned governments" (as Ginsberg states in Part II), unable to change or adapt and thus, ultimately, unable to sustain or grow.[27] Of course, this backfiring of the American media trick to convince us there is only one real American way of being (heterosexual, white, preferably Protestant, etc.) is a fact easily seen in the booming divorce rates and gross increase of impoverished and malnourished children. This is similar to the constant antics and rampant greed which lead Coyote so consistently to find himself empty-handed or even worse off than he was at the start.

Due to the American mainstream culture's possession of this desire to assimilate, Ginsberg likewise imposed the nickname "Moloch" upon it. Thus, for his Part II, he focuses more upon the selfish aspects of Coyote, equating these darker tricks with the United States by the name of Moloch. In this way, Coyote's trickster nature comes through in "Howl" in both shades of cultural hero and gluttonous villain. This is intrinsic to Ginsberg's keen sense and awareness of negative capability and the ability of humans to contain multiple contradictions. Moloch is a nickname symbolizing the desire to consume every other culture and perspective whether through commercialization, adversarial establishment rhetoric, or forced absorption via imaginary rules and boundaries (such as the silent "requirement" that one speak English in the United States). Essentially, here, America becomes not a symbol of freedom but an altar upon which other cultures must sacrifice their heritages and traditions in hopes of appeasing this Moloch that Ginsberg sees the country, the ideal, becoming.

It is important to also note here that though this is a tactical switch from the more endearing Dennis the Menace type of trickster as exampled by his "best minds" to the negative example of the deviled trickster through this "Moloch," it remains tied up in the scope of many Native American trickster narratives specifically. The trickster is a character not wholly good or evil, just as no culture may be called wholly right or wrong, and so it may be utilized just as malleably as human beings to discuss the ills, hopes, and benefits of every way of life.

4. "Howl's" Appetite

> What sphinx of cement and aluminum bashed open
> their skulls and ate up their brains and imagination?[28]

The above stanza is in reference to Ginsberg's Moloch, the hateful, fearmongering America, with an appetite he describes as sated only by consuming "their"—those "best minds"—"brains and imagination." The Moloch United States is licking its chops for the ingenuity and creativity of its own citizens, for those things which it itself claims to encourage, prize, and cultivate within its citizens. However, beyond this declaration is the violent description of the actual hunger itself. This hunger apparently exists to devour itself, an act economists have already recognized in their own, kinder terms, what Austrian economist Joseph Schumpeter called *creative destruction* (a cycle of necessary destruction in order to make room for more creation), and which Coyote also demonstrates again and again as he lives to trick and trap, only to find himself constantly caught up in those tricks (live by the sword, die by the sword). But Ginsberg assembles his own apt description of this creative destruction as a "sphinx of cement and aluminum."

He constructs this monument of symbols of our modern urbanization to reveal it as an often fruitless achievement, much akin to Coyote's winning the buffalo horse only to realize he could do nothing with it in "Coyote Shows How He Can Lie." What's more, Ginsberg's comparison also highlights that it is an achievement built on the backs and exploitation of so many Americans whose hopes for freedom were perverted for this illusionary political and industrial gain. Ginsberg elaborates upon this devilish version of urbanization with "Moloch whose blood is running money"; "demonic industries!"; "invincible mad houses!"; and "granite cocks!"[29] All these descriptors attempt to explain how our concrete world and mindsets suck the function and meaning out of our constructions and government.

Ginsberg uses these bombastic and magniloquent exclamations to reveal how this creative destruction has taken the hope and progress out of our cities, hospitals, and governments. He thus unveils the inherent redefinition of who is labeled and mocked as "crazy" and who has demonized the industries that are Jenga-blocked up and up in the name of a more efficient world, a world where the reproductive, pleasurable, and religious purpose of our sexual organs, gifts, and necessities are petrified. These are not simply metaphors for the countless skyscrapers of America but caveats against allowing society to turn to the tranquilizing gradualism of cold stone instead of joining the more dangerous, more courageous political and communal movements for a healthier, more flexible, more survivable future.

Ginsberg compares the construction of this gaping-mouth U.S. to the slave constructions of Egypt. This American sphinx is a symbol of American gluttony, of a trickster's appetite that exists to eat and eat until it eventually turns upon itself and devours its own people, resulting in either rebellion or extinction; it will inevitably, Ginsberg warns, turn and consume itself much as the construction of Egyptian pyramids and monuments resulted in the subsequent death of thousands. Ginsberg elaborates upon this cannibalism and the trickster-cycle nature of it, as he continues the chant:

> Moloch whose breast is *a cannibal dynamo!* ...
> Moloch whose fate is a cloud of sexless hydrogen!
> Moloch whose name is the Mind![30] [emphasis added]

Not only does he utilize the actual phrase "cannibal dynamo" to characterize this appetite, but he also references the "cloud of sexless hydrogen," the hydrogen bomb, a weapon pioneered by the United States—a weapon, Ginsberg implies, that is hungry for our own destruction. After all, what is the purpose of creating a bomb more powerful than the atomic bomb if not to satiate a poorly veiled hunger for power, fear, and destruction? The only true comfort anyone seemed to hope to take from these weapons was that they kept everyone in line, not via diplomacy, but through a thick caking of the fear radiating from the assurance of *mutual* total destruction. For Ginsberg, this weapon represents only the hunger for blood and power the American nation apparently possesses, utilizes, and indulges.

He couples this with the declaration, "Moloch whose name is the Mind!" highlighting that on both a national and individual level, it is our own hunger, invented and fueled by our own minds and media beliefs, that is destroying us, turning us against each other and ourselves. This functions similarly to Coyote in his own trickster narratives as a form of pedagogy, as a means of utilizing the trickster dynamic in order to teach others about the dangers of certain behaviors, beliefs, and desires. In this way, this instance may not reveal another personification of the trickster specifically, but employs the same methods found in trickster narratives utilized for the same communicative and pedagogical purposes. For example, reconsider the Coeur d'Alene narrative (as told by Bingo SiJohn [Coeur d'Alene]) of "Coyote and the White Man," where Coyote demonstrates a lesson in generosity and trust through his thieving and misplaced friendship. In this narrative, Coyote begins as a heroic figure, saving another from being attacked, only to fall to the "Moloch" of his mind by succumbing to greed and the foolish decision to trust this stranger who so quickly supported Coyote's ideas to steal and glut.

As for Part III of the epic, Ginsberg moves from discussing broadly the "best minds" to the gluttonous Moloch, to, finally, Carl Solomon (to whom the poem is dedicated). Carl Solomon is a poet and friend of Ginsberg's whom Ginsberg met while they were both institutionalized at Columbia Presbyterian Psychiatric Institute. Ginsberg thus creates the "I'm with you in Rockland[31]" chant as a promise of community in love, insanity, and strife with Solomon. As such, this part lends itself more keenly to the other elements of the trickster quad and so will be examined throughout the next three sections.

Chapter 5
A Trick and a Trap

    Tricksters and traps fit together like pen and paper, lending each other purpose, practice, meaning, and voice. According to several Native American creation stories (spanning across a variety of tribal and community boundaries), it is left up to Coyote, a trickster, to teach human beings (still new to the world) the best practices for how to live, how to dance, hunt, and so forth. These duties fall upon Coyote for many reasons, preeminent among them being that it is simply the art of a trickster's tricky nature that he serves both as a culture hero and as an entity of seemingly immoral or, at least, taboo actions, all of which culminates into a livelier, more adaptable, and more durable world for us.[1]

    Ginsberg's "Howl" often displays this style of teaching, creating, cooking, and stirring up trouble. Ginsberg himself also became a victim of trouble (both of and not of his own making) while becoming a cultural hero somewhere along the way. Both Coyote and Ginsberg assume this role and mischief in order to trick people into facing the type of cultural traditions Shirley Jackson best displayed in "The Lottery," those traditions which we accept because they have "always" been accepted, ideas we tolerate because they have seen some immeasurable "improvement," hatreds we maintain because maintaining fear is a simpler task than facing it.

    In "Howl," Ginsberg addresses these problems by describing the trickster, "seemingly asocial actions" of himself and his "best minds":

> who lit cigarettes in boxcars boxcars boxcars rocketing through snow
>   toward lonesome farms in grandfather night
>
> ...
>
> who reappeared on the West Coast investigating the F.B.I. in beards and
>   shorts with big pacifist eyes sexy in their dark skin passing out
>   incomprehensible leaflets

5. A Trick and a Trap

...
who burned cigarette holes in their arms protesting the narcotic tobacco haze of Capitalism[2]

These actions—"investigating the F.B.I.," "passing out incomprehensible leaflets," lighting up cigarette after cigarette, playing patron to a product he later dresses up as a symbol for the United States' deadly addiction to super-materialist capitalism — are all forms of classic trickster tricks and traps, turning systems of knowing and being, of ruling and restricting topsy-turvy in order to ask them if they are actually even necessary at all. For example, in the second stanza here, Ginsberg is referring (as aforementioned) literally to the actions of the (seemingly) paranoid Joffre Stewart. Ginsberg also plays with preconceived notions regarding the uses of pacifism and protest, as the "incomprehensible leaflets" not only reflect on literally incomprehensible materials but also present a critique of those poets, writers, and protestors remaining so far on the fringe, so entrenched in their own worlds and mysteries that they forgot how to make their wisdoms, information, and teachings available and valuable to others, to those who might actually benefit from their insights and imaginations. This is a value Ginsberg certainly sought to demonstrate within his own writing by employing as frank and honest a language as possible. Blue Cloud also attempts to highlight this value within Coyote through his "Coyote's Anthro," in which Coyote attempts to explain things to a non–Native "anthro" in as plain a language as possible (though these attempts still leave the "anthro" falling rather short of full comprehension).

The cigarette protests serve as an especially solid example of a trap that the tricksters not only recognize and use as a form of protest against hyper-consumerism and the establishment, but one which they also ironically fall victim to mid-protest. After all, by purchasing the cigarettes with which to protest in the first place, they also inherently support the tobacco industry, supporting "the narcotic tobacco haze of Capitalism," and also (obviously) only end up burning themselves. This type of trick is a protest against the hypocritical norm, against the passive and "painless" morphine-like haze of financial cushions, gated communities, and concentric circle upon concentric circle of segregated space. And it is all accomplished with the paradoxical, humorous echo of Coyote, working to at once teach people a new way of living in the burgeoning new world of 1960s United States while also working against the protestors in bleak, ironic, and humorous ways.

Part II : Coyote-ing "Howl"

  These stanzas are particularly interesting when considering the possible influences of Coyote from their mention of the West Coast specifically to the focus upon trapping the American trappers (the F.B.I.) to self-mutilation (the cigarette burns) for the purposes of satisfying needs, gaining freedoms, creating new social realities, and tricking others. Take, for example, the aforementioned Miwok creation story of "How People Were Made," wherein Coyote plays dead and preys upon the appetites of others (namely, of the buzzards and crows) in order to both satiate his own hunger as well as acquire materials for creating the New People. The vultures and buzzards all come to gather about his "dead" body, but when they begin to devour his backside, Coyote quickly springs "back" to life and closes up the hole around them, trapping them inside himself. It is only after this episode of self-mutilation, confusion, entrapment, and self-satisfaction that Coyote turns the situation into a creation narrative, enlisting the aid of Falcon to harvest the feathers from his prey and plant them about the earth, thereby transforming them into the New People and illuminating the larger goals and purposes of his otherwise baffling, dark, and rather funny actions.

  I have already examined this next stanza (below) under the scope of the trickster's liminality and appetite, but it also very well — as much of this poem does — incorporates many of the traits inherent within the tricks and traps sector of Coyote's tricksterhood, of "Howl's" tricksterhood. For this stanza, along with a clear twist of hunger, also depicts a trap much like that of the cigarettes.

> who bit detectives in the neck and shrieked with delight
> in policecars for committing no crime but their
> own wild cooking pederasty and intoxication[3]

It is a trap set for our abuses and abusers of authority by making a mockery of an actual lawful exercise of that authority. And in the mix is yet another example of falling victim to one's own trap: committing the crime of assault in order to be arrested for committing no crime but intoxication (and, perhaps, some dabbling in nonheteronormative sexual practices, so often considered criminal). Of course, even while these tricks seem ridiculous (thus allowing us to find the humor within them), they still manage to communicate important ideas about how to live, how lives should be allowed to be lived, and how social intolerances and ignorant views wrongly interpret the other possible ways and flexibilities of life. These instructions, lessons, and advice should ring bells of familiarity as they

5. A Trick and a Trap

are extremely similar to Coyote's role as culture hero and teacher of the new human beings.

However, this stanza also provides another possible, perhaps more devious trick: though we may quickly accept the more obvious interpretation — that Cannastra has been wrongfully arrested — Ginsberg is never actually clear here about whether or not it is Cannastra or the detectives who did the tracking, tricking, trapping, and arresting. After all, given the circumstances, who is to say whether or not it isn't the detectives who are trapped in the police car with a devilishly hungry Cannastra?

The next stanza strikingly resembles yet another Coyote story.

> who scribbled all night rocking and rolling over lofty incantations which in the yellow morning were stanzas of gibberish[4]

A Coyote narrative reflected in this stanza may be that explaining how Coyote got his power of cunning (this story actually varies greatly from translator to translator but is usually ascribed to the Karok tribe and sometimes refers to how Coyote attempted to wile Dog and Wolf out of the choicest hunting bow).[5] Coyote received this power, vital to his trickster nature, by attempting to stay awake all night long so that when morning came (on the day of the distribution of powers) he would be the first in line to receive his power. By being first in line, he hoped to be appointed the greatest power. However, because he is Coyote, when he began to grow tired, rather than simply going to sleep as his neighbors did, he tried to prop open his eyes with sticks. Of course, when he inevitably did fall asleep, the sticks stabbed right through his eyelids and locked them shut. And so, Coyote ended up sleeping straight through the entire power-giving ceremony with the sticks through his eyes. This meant he was left with no power at all. However, when the power-granting entity witnessed how pitiful Coyote was down in the dirt, being mocked by all his fellow creatures, he or she granted Coyote the power of cunning out of pity so that Coyote might keep himself afloat amid all his other more obviously powerful neighbors. In this way, Coyote became cunning by acting foolish and greedy, by becoming the outcast, "other," and mocked.

This is in many ways reflected within this stanza through Ginsberg's lamenting that a night filled with fervent work only ended up costing him a good night's sleep, waking up from what seemed like a brilliant plan only to find "gibberish," to find that all the powers he had dreamed of had been taken. Similar to Coyote finding himself worse for wear and last in line for trying to be clever and stay up all night, Ginsberg agonizes for the potential morning work lost due to a supposedly magical night full of progress that only truly yielded him nothing, nothing but sticks through his eyes.

However, if we further consider this moment, it becomes apparent that the moral of this story and the idea expressed in Ginsberg's stanza, share something much subtler, something to suggest that perhaps Coyote had a bit of cunning and his own powerful bow to begin with. They share an oxymoronic quality, a *tricky* quality, one might say. After all, though Ginsberg recognizes that many of the poetic lines written by himself and by his peers were, in fact (as many of his critics claimed), "gibberish," he does not actually say whether or not those are the same lines he has here published or if they were edited out as so many others were. He never actually lets us know whether or not we are reading the "gibberish" or the inspired, and in this question mark we may find not only a clever chuckle, but also a fantastic new idea about how we define these terms of "gibberish" and "profound" or of "lofty incantations" and "lofty prevarications." This asks us whether we define these terms and assumptions for ourselves or if we instead look self-consciously to our neighbor to see if they know the "answer" or agree with ours. This is seconded by the correlating mystery within Coyote's story as it is also never asked whether or not Coyote's goal to attain the greatest power was or was not achieved in the end. After all, when it comes straight down to it, did not the tortoise win the race because he was cleverer than the hare, thus making cunning a more valuable trait than any amount of speed or strength?

This next stanza is also a clear example of Ginsberg's exercise of trickster wisdom as he openly recognizes the need to rebel against the modern shackles of invisible social forces and pressures such as the imaginary boundary of time ("their watches").

> who threw their watches off the roof to cast their ballot for Eternity
> outside of Time, & alarm clocks fell on their heads every day for the next decade[6]

This portrays a series of tricks and traps beginning with the casting of a ballot within a dreamed election, one the "best minds" apparently believe they could actually win, one where they become their own representatives throughout Eternity and thereby escape the imaginary constraints of mainstream reality. Of course, this is all only to have that mainstream reality come raining down upon them in the most tragic of wake-up calls,

5. A Trick and a Trap

whether it means they continued to be berated by and entrapped within another's reality "for [that] next decade" or if they were forced to become a participant in the nine-to-five machine.

Of course, this troublemaking moment of casting ballots through rejections of an old framework (a rejection of one reality) is also a rather humorous one. The image of vigorous misfits littering wristwatches upon the street — an action whose symbolism would surely be lost upon any poor passersby below being pelted by watches — paints a comical picture, just as, Ginsberg may argue, our dependency upon invisible and man-made laws such as time or prejudice or entitlement is comical. This joke, this protest, is an attempt to wake us up before our alarm clocks start blaring; it is an attempt to wake us up to a new kind of day where, like Coyote, the tricks of time and schedules do not apply to us — time and schedules which may suggest a lunch meeting is important and a march for a neighbor's freedom an imposition upon our precious time. This type of trick and trap is thus also redolent of one Maidu creation narrative (relayed by Roland B. Dixon), where Coyote gets bored with the perfection of the way life was in the beginning. So, for his own entertainment and accruement of power, Coyote took it upon himself to introduce the New People to competition and death in the form of a foot race. However, during this foot race, his son begins to take the lead only to be bitten fatally by a rattlesnake, becoming the first death and, consequently, wringing from Coyote the first tears as well.[7] In this way, Coyote attempts to create a new reality within a preexisting one, one which he openly rejects, only to find himself at the losing end of this proposed change.[8]

> Moloch! Solitude! Filth! Ugliness! Ashcans and unobtainable dollars!
>
> ...
>
> Moloch whose name is the Mind![9]

This Moloch in and of itself is representative of a trap the United States has set for itself and continues to set for all who confuse it for its tempting bait of "America." This confusion stands in every exclamation Ginsberg here employs; his cry, "unobtainable dollars!" is perhaps the clearest example, with its acknowledgment of both America's promise of wealth, the presence and actuality of its wealth, and its unobtainable nature — a carrot that might be an American dream or simply smoke puffed out by Moloch. Coyote and his greed for constantly more is a severity typically depicted through a humorous parable. But Ginsberg here makes a temporary switch of humors in Part II of "Howl," from humor built of frankness, sexuality, and youthful charm to humor laced and edged with this biting sort of anger.

Ginsberg here forces America, whose constant cheer has always been the transforming of teeming huddled masses into happy, successful, and wealthy neighbors, to face the reality of the traps it has fallen into: the traps of hypocrisy, greed, and prejudice, of prevaricating rhetoric and slogans unveiled by this ironic, clarion poetry. It's a reality that, if you manage to overlook all the suffering involved (as most humor depends upon the presence of victims), is actually quite humorous in its own ridiculousness and conspicuousness. Here Ginsberg displays a self-destructive type of humor (a humor that is often difficult to acknowledge simply because of its body count) in clear, black ink. As Mark Doty observed in his article, "Human Seraphim: 'Howl,' Sex, and Holiness," this is a "vision of a juggernaut for holiness," of "transcendent wild boys versus spirit-crushing monolithic Moloch ... [that] might be a bit hard to take were 'Howl' not so exuberantly funny."[10] This reaches back to Lawrence Gross and his article "The Comic Vision of Anishinaabe Culture and Religion," in which he discusses the thick and long-understood relationship many Native Americans have nurtured between humor and healing, between humor and survival.

And it's a humor Ginsberg employs to underline the fault of every individual refusing to acknowledge that the United States is just a place, just like the government is just a thing, not some evil phantom. It takes people; it takes many individuals to give these things their goods and ills, their actions and infamies. He recognizes this specificity in "Moloch whose name is the Mind!" a moment meant to remind his readers there is no looming entity to point to and blame but that it is within ourselves and our own apathies that Moloch finds voice and power. Thus, it is Moloch that allows these nobler institutions and ideas to sour into ineffectuality and evil. And this is where the humor lies, where the Coyote mistakes and tricks pop up again: that we have and continue to trick ourselves into believing in these entities such as time and the government without ever pausing to recognize our roles in them and their power.

"Moloch whose name is the Mind!" he exclaims. And in this exclamation, Ginsberg calls us all out as individuals to remind us that we set our own traps, that we trick ourselves within our own minds. Through all of these imaginary issues and excuses we provide to justify our actions and beliefs, Ginsberg reveals that we make ourselves the butt of our own joke and that, absolutely, we are being laughed at.

> I'm with you in Rockland
> > where you laugh at this invisible humor
>
> ...
>
> I'm with you in Rockland
> > where the faculties of the skull no longer admit
> > the worms of the senses
>
> ...
>
> I'm with you in Rockland
> > where you accuse your doctors of insanity[11]

The brain here, "no longer admit[ting] the worms of the senses," reflects that perhaps what we normally define as sensibilities are actually the excuses and rules of a greedy and prejudicial society. These false wormy senses may give time its power over Eternity and give Moloch the name of the Mind. No one wants to admit the ugliness of being sensible when being hypocritical and laughable gets us what we want. And this is precisely what Ginsberg is getting at as he discusses Rockland; he is explaining that the madhouse may be nationwide while the tricked masses lock up the sane voices for disagreeing with them. In this same way, Ginsberg reflects on the tools and labels, such as the label of "madhouse" upon Rockland, which are often used to keep the worms of the senses from working their way through people's brains and realizing the sides and possibilities of stories. This is also precisely what Coyote counted on in the Jicarilla Apache narrative, "Coyote Shows How He Can Lie" (Lopez), where he depended upon the people being too distracted and beclouded by their own mad desires to "admit the worms of the senses."

Then again, Rockland is also used as a place where Ginsberg's past (and present) ensnarement may be clearly reflected upon.

> I'm with you in Rockland
> > where we hug and kiss the United States under
> > our bedsheets the United States that coughs all
> > night and won't let us sleep[12]

Once again we find the sexual aspect of his and Coyote's humor rearing its head. Ginsberg here compares our mistaken trust in the United States to be its promised America to a person we take to bed for a lover, expecting them to be healthy and loving as they have assured us they are, only to find ourselves ultimately unable to enjoy even the freedom and comforts of our own beds because of their secret discomforts and ailments. It is a moment that, in a film or book, would be quite funny as most sexual mishaps and surprises are. But here we also find a jagged tooth poking out from the grinning lips as this sexual mishap cannot be fixed by a simple breakup, checkup, and number change. This mishap carries its own infections, as when Coyote came to realize his tricks and competitiveness had resulted in the death of his only child.

Chapter 6

Smearing Borderlines

...in the middle of Coyote Nowhere. — Jack Kerouac

    This corner of the trickster quadrilateral holds particularly tight hands with the next and last corner: the rule of transformative capability. This characteristic pertains primarily to the trickster's ability to move between our world and the next as well as between identities. It is also invaluable insofar as understanding and incorporating humor into the Coyote narratives as well as into Ginsberg's poetry. Hyde explores this connection in the introduction of his *Trickster Makes This World*. He points out that, for traditional and ancient cultures, the act of wandering aimlessly or constantly was considered abnormal or deviant, a sign of trouble. Thus, there is an extra element of humor within most Coyote narratives as he is constantly traveling and moving at the beginning of his adventures. This follows throughout much of Ginsberg's poetry and especially throughout the entirety of "Howl," as he leaps from city to city, from country to country, from reality to reality within the breath of a stanza. This also comes from a time in modern America when, despite the respected travels of businessmen and soldiers, the movements of teenagers, college students, and minorities were often frowned upon. The 1950s were a time when hitchhiking proliferated and yet began to earn its own stigma as the method of transport favored by criminals and delinquents, mainstream establishment terms that would have certainly applied to Ginsberg at the time as a young gay man.

    For "Howl," however, there is a wider range to this characteristic as Ginsberg employs this boundlessness and mobility in every way from the malleability of reality itself; to distinguishing between America as an idea and America as a place and America as a body of people; to demonstrating the smearing of poetic stylistic borders, religious borders, time-perspective borders, all the way to the most basic of American borders: culture. As Raskin observed in the preface of his *American Scream*, "Howl" helped change the world "by collapsing cultural boundaries at the height of the Cold War and by encouraging cultural rebellion around the world."[1] However, these new border crossings are still, I find, applicable to the trickster and his humors because it is often the trickster's connection with or ability to understand the world from a borderless perspective that gives him such great power and, often, what also sets him up to fail as he tends to either get carried away with or openly abuse this power.

This next stanza also speaks to the notion of "Howl's" boundlessness:

> angelheaded hipsters burning for the ancient heavenly connection to the starry dynamo in the machinery of night[2]

If we strip this stanza of poetic beauty and arrange it into a more linear form, we find ourselves looking at more than simply a hunger for sex or freedom but also at a hunger for this trickster trait of travel. This "burning for the ancient heavenly connection" suggests that some road, some path or relationship once well traveled, is now blocked from us. However, it remains open to the trickster who, like Prometheus, stole fire for the new human beings but who, unlike Prometheus, was not shackled away as a result. Coyote kept free despite the thievery, revealing his unique ability to blur boundaries not only between realms but also between right and wrong, acceptable and unacceptable, rule and guideline. But for us, who readily impose boundaries upon others and ourselves, we would have even the very best of minds blocked from these ancient pathways and connections. Here we find at the very start an urge for action and movement along with a loud pang of hunger. In his annotations, Ginsberg explains that this moment between "the starry dynamo" and "the machinery of night" is derived in part from a Dylan Thomas poem working with the duo of Nature and Machinery, a connection which interestingly illuminates this moment with another glimpse into the many liminal zones of "Howl." By highlighting the peculiar oppositions often superimposed upon Nature and Machinery, here Ginsberg relays the possibility of a new reality, of a new way of existing within both of these spaces and places without the bloody sacrifice of either.

These next few stanzas, however, explore more the idea of travel (from place to place, from thought to thought) and what this may mean from a trickster's point of view insofar as blurring the edges of things and seeing to the other side (and, in some cases, as smearing away the sides entirely).

> who passed through universities with radiant cool eyes
> > hallucinating Arkansas and Blake-light tragedy
> > among the scholars of war
>
> ...
>
> incomparable blind streets of shuddering cloud and
> > lightning in the mind leaping toward poles of
> > Canada & Paterson, illuminating all the motionless world of Time between[3]

More than the mention of streets and lightning smacking through the clouds, what's perhaps most fascinating about the first couple of stanzas here is the treatment of "hallucinating Arkansas and Blake-light tragedy" and "the mind leaping toward poles of Canada & Paterson." Both of these moments examine a particular connection between things typically segregated in the whitestream mindset such as geography, poetry, and hallucination. In thinking on the geography of these stanzas, Ginsberg rewrites the maps by not only resituating the poles of the globe (to Canada and Paterson, New Jersey, where he grew up) but by also locating Arkansas and Blake's tragedy on the same plane, all threaded together through the ecstasies, nuttiness, and complexities of Ginsberg's hallucinations and quests for new visions. This is all compounded, of course, by his nod toward the mind's capability to both enable such imagined realities and cartographies as well as to *leap*, to move itself from one understanding to another in a both desperate and exuberant fashion if given the space and time. From here, Ginsberg has opened his own door to enter into that great "motionless" boundary of Time once more, that which stands against all travelers not trickster in nature. As David Turnbull explains, citing "'us and them,' 'then and now'" as examples of highly problematic and false boundaries,

> The trickster warns us to be wary of such boundaries and divides. The trickster is also a performer and should remind us that history telling is also a performance; we in the academic West make too much of representation and neglect the performative side of knowledge making and knowing the world.[4]

However, even as he writes the words, Turnbull does not enact their message — through his use of "we," "us," and "the academic West," he has clearly drawn a map of "us and them, then and now," illustrating a world divided wherein Native Americans are not members of the West, where there is a possible East and West on a spherical body, where the so-called West is academic and, by default, the East is somehow nonacademic. Ginsberg recognized, like the trickster, these ways that people trapped themselves daily through the endlessly powerful and trickster tool of language. And in this stanza, this blurring of boundaries and rewriting of maps (both spatial and temporal) reveals a trickster attempt on Ginsberg's part to traverse a preconceived boundary and bring his readers with him.

This blurring of compartmentalized understandings of space, philosophy, and existence is very much in keeping with the trickster behavior of twisting and rearranging understandings of being and space to fit his own purposes and journeys, as Blue Cloud illustrated within "Coyote's Anthro." The mention of Blake in this stanza is of particular importance due to the significant moment in Ginsberg's youth when he claims that he was visited by the bodiless voice of the Romantic poet (as discussed in "Space, Place, and Traversing Boundaries"). He was so affected, so moved that he apparently ran onto his building's fire escape and yawped, "'I've seen God!'" to which the ladies neighboring him "slammed the window shut"; this event also caused his father, Louis Ginsberg, to fear for his son's mental health (especially given how Ginsberg's mother, Naomi, suffered from schizophrenia).[5] This moment deeply moved Ginsberg and drove him throughout much of his life to attempt to replicate the vision through various travels, drugs, and meditative means.

This search for vision, however, is quite dissimilar from most traditional Native American vision quests. According to Jack Utter's *American Indians: Answers to Today's Questions*, vision quests changed markedly from community to community; some quests occur at puberty while other groups' visions may require multiple quests throughout a lifetime, and most tended to be accompanied by intense fasting, seclusion, and even "self-inflicted pain."[6] For some, these visions were to "guide ... personal growth and success," while others may take shape as an "animal guide who might teach a special song ... instructions, or describe a power-giving fetish."[7] In these ways, Ginsberg's auditory vision is exceptionally different from how many understand and perceive traditional Native American visions or vision quests, though both hold significant spiritual meaning, both prompt or are prompted by intensive, personal journeys, and both provided something special and powerful for the one receiving the vision. Coyote, interestingly, was also regarded by some Native groups as an almost shamanic being, "a top visionary," due to his supernatural nature and ability to travel between "the visible and invisible worlds."[8]

This connection also plugs neatly into Ellen Rosenberg's assessment of how many Native groups view "all knowledge as integrated" (although not all is considered "public domain"), of working to understand the world as a complex whole rather than as a Rubik's cube filled with segments and separations, or "universities" and "academies" in Ginsberg's case.[9] This suggests, perhaps, that those institutions meant for learning and supposed broadening of horizons may themselves be transforming into nothing more than another gridded and regimented victim of those he viewed as the destroyers and oppressors of those "best minds," into institutions reproducing prejudices, power dynamics, and racism.[10] It is certainly a Coyote move to prefer the idea of diffusing into oneself an entire library rather than facing the segmentation of single book after single book, to attempt and desire to absorb the world as a whole. After all, Coyote's logic is often one colored by a multitude of possibilities, cultures, and understandings, as is demonstrated in Blue Cloud's "Coyote's Anthro" as Coyote attempts to traverse cultural boundaries as well as those of ignorance and histories of misinterpretation and presumption in an effort to illuminate for the "anthro" a wider horizon.

Of course, beyond this blurring of imaginary boundaries such as time and writing styles, Coyote's boundlessness also extends to physical understandings of place whether it be moving from a river to a mountain or from the heavens to the earth (from the greater, deified spirits to the human beings). Ginsberg touches on this quality, this flexibility of space and endless journey, especially in his mentions of Arkansas, Canada, and Paterson (which doubles as both William Carlos Williams' poem "Paterson" and Ginsberg's New Jersey hometown). Coyote is often found in the middle of journeys—journeys that often do not "end" (if they, in fact, possess endings) where Coyote originally intended or hoped, just as Ginsberg's stanzas often end in loops, mishap, or paradox. Both Coyote and Ginsberg reveal through mishap and trickster freedom that no matter how crafty the plan, no matter how clear a shortcut may seem, one can always end up lost (however temporarily), for better or for worse.

This sort of smearing, enabling repetitive and transformative travel both physically and spiritually, is evidenced throughout "Howl," all while still incorporating the Coyote humor and vitality from the journey as he writes,

> Peyote solidities of halls, backyard green tree cemetery
> dawns, wine drunkenness over the rooftops,
> storefront boroughs of teahead joyride neon
> blinking traffic light, sun and moon and tree
> vibrations in the roaring winter dusks of Brook-
> lyn, ashcan rantings and kind king light of mind[11]

Within this stanza, as in many, Ginsberg calls on his own experimentations with drugs (peyote, marijuana, and benzedrine) to highlight the concept of deconstructing boundaries (between sober reality and drug-induced reality, between one perspective and another). He does this in order to also discuss the blurring of different, more physical boundaries such as those standing between hallways and cemeteries, street traffic and rooftops, between humanity and base animality.

In his journals (compiled by Gordon Ball), specifically his entry on April 17, 1952, Ginsberg goes into great detail about his experience with peyote, discussing how it affected him and how, as stated here, it flurried the "solidities" of things. Specifically, it blurred the solidities of the "halls," of the walls separating him from the rest of the world, of its "dawns," its "sun and moon and tree vibrations." Peyote (along with marijuana, considering that "teahead" is Beat slang for "pothead"), in this way, helped him reconsider the supposedly gridded and mapped world about him. Of course, this recreational use of peyote would be viewed as sacrilegious by those Native Americans who employ it for religious purposes. However, it stands nonetheless as an excellent example of Coyote trickster behavior; it is an abuse of sacred gifts in order to discover or create something new, something to feed his own desires and hunger for yet another vision. This is evidenced by Coyote's abuse of his possession of competition and death (within the Maidu creation narrative relayed by Dixon), a possession he brought to the new human beings for his own pleasure. He ends up losing his own son (who became the first to die) due to the introduction of death, but he justifies the loss by acknowledging the good he contributed, knowing that an eminent death would foster in the new people a greater appreciation of life (as well as greater levels of innovation and curiosity, a motivation to learn and make changes).

Similarly, following this trickster tradition, the discoveries and benefits of peyote for Ginsberg came at both detrimental and beneficial costs. It was detrimental to Ginsberg's professional reputation — both as an abuser of sacred elements as well as an abuser of hallucinogenic drugs (though in the Beat community specifically, this may have been more beneficial to a reputation than detrimental)—as well as by the simpler dangers he subjected himself to by indulging in a momentary drug use without any real knowledge of how it might affect him. As we may now understand from my sampling of Coyote narratives, Coyote also often engaged in risky behavior in order to acquire that immediate new prize or gratification, much the same way as Ginsberg's drug use only benefited him and his own desire for more experiences, pleasure, and vision.

Moving from this more tangential discussion of the putative borderlines between life and death, harm and benefit, this stanza itself speaks directly to the phantasmal nature of these borderlines. Ginsberg goes straight to the point by juxtaposing "cemetery" with "green" and "dawns," juxtaposing a symbol of death with new days, fresh life, in order to highlight their obvious intersections (after all, a cemetery is often a plot of comparatively greener and livelier ground than those we pave over and turn to roads or sidewalks). Ginsberg also directly questions cultural and socioeconomic borders by juxtaposing "ashcan rantings" (which suggests poor or street folk gathered and angry about a burnt-out trashcan fire) with "kind king light of mind." This suggests that the borders between darkness and light, poverty and wealth, powerlessness and power, may all be pure imagination—fictitious borders we have all agreed to accept and work around rather than ignore and create our own maps around. After all, Coyote makes these transitions and journeys all the time; as a trickster, he is constantly shifting from destitution or hunger into the creative, wealthy hero (and vice versa).

This stanza also gets at the particularly fascinating and important borderline standing between hallucination and "reality." It is only after the hallucinatory help of peyote, "wine drunkenness," and "tea" (marijuana) that Ginsberg begins to question further boundaries and solidities of what we commonly accept as reality. Moreover, by his simple description of reality through these hallucinatory experiences, he creates an alternate reality. By this creation, he reveals the truth that we all experience reality in different ways and so there is no ultimate border/boundary of reality standing between us and hallucination. After all, who can say that Ginsberg's descriptions in this stanza are not true to reality when environments, moods, and perceptions are in constant change and motion? In this way, Ginsberg takes on the great borderline of "reality" and proposes alternatives, proposes "Howl." Coyote does this constantly. Simply by reading or hearing a Coyote narrative, readers are already accepting a reality outside of the whitestream, with different terms and rules where Old Man Coyote exists and acts upon a different version of the world (a version which, though obviously different, remains peculiarly synonymous and interchangeable with that world which we each individually inhabit). Consider, again, how Old Man Coyote, within Blue Cloud's narrative, bends the spaces between the moon upon the water and the moon within the sky, how he attempts to get the "anthro" to bend his perception of the world as well.

The mind is constantly seeking to impose order upon the general chaos of the world. People seek out and convince themselves of patterns and differences which may only be false, pointless, or detrimental correlations. Ginsberg speaks to this issue in "Howl" by recognizing the mind at once as brilliant, holy, the "kind king light" as well as simultaneously "Moloch" (as he exclaims later, "Moloch whose name is the Mind").[12] Our minds become our own greatest enemies as well as our greatest prize and creative tool, things which we would normally differentiate with a borderline. Where does this line fall between creative force and destructive force? Both Ginsberg's "Howl" and Coyote the trickster seem to suggest that, perhaps, there isn't one at all.

Ginsberg continues on in this fashion by next discussing his encounter with the drug benzedrine in the following stanza:

> who chained themselves to subways for the endless
>   ride from Battery to holy Bronx on benzedrine
> until the noise of wheels and children brought
>   them down shuddering mouth-wracked and
> battered bleak of brain all drained of brilliance
>   in the drear light of Zoo[13]

As mentioned, this stanza concerns itself more with his benzedrine use (and attempted acquiring of morphine) and brings to light another aspect of the boundary issue: the collision course. Ginsberg offers us a graphic image of those brilliant minds charging forward like a battering ram and how their own restless need for movement, spiritual revelation, and freedom (symbolized in their subway train "endless ride") also acted as the machine of their destruction (one eerily redolent of Cannastra's subway decapitation). Their mechanic momentum turned on them, ramming them into Zoo-like cages rather than into a new beatific paradise of "endless" journey such as those Coyote wanders. But here, where these poor souls believed so deeply in the endless ride that they physically attached themselves to this means of under- and above-ground transportation, they only ended up slamming headfirst into the bars and angry borders put up by broader society. Where they were expecting to subway, drug, and poetic-barrel into a new, freer sort of civilization, they instead found themselves drowned out by the roar of their own train (as many took things too far or not far enough)—the same train meant to fuel them forward into rehabilitative, jubilant change, of constantly moving futures. But these symbols, traditionally signifying a future, change, or forward motion, have here become the catalysts sending the brilliant minds straight into the cages (a human "Zoo") for the comfort of the non– and anti–Beat onlookers, hypnotized by their own rhetoric and media to automatically erect such borders and cages between themselves and the "Outriders," the rebellious; between themselves and the aberrant; between themselves and change.

These types of social and cultural boundaries imposed upon people are phenomena widely discussed by cultural/sociological theorists like Henri Lefebvre who posited in his *The Production of Space* that social processes create spaces (and, I would add, also create fences to segment those spaces) which then reciprocate by reinforcing and reproducing those social processes. This process, in many ways, can slow cultural growth by insulating cultural members or agents from those other members desperate and hungry for a more fluid landscape and mode of thinking. As Lefebvre observed, knowledge and cultural assumptions are all a means for the ruling class to maintain hegemony, creating borders and rules where there were none, drawing a line between "a knowledge which serves power and a form of knowing which refuses to acknowledge power."[14] Thus, the trickster characteristic of boundary denial also becomes an active refusal to acknowledge the establishment's power, a clear intention of Ginsberg's "Howl."

Ginsberg turns this thin borderline on its head not only in this stanza (an attempt to defy the power of mainstream society knowledge by railroading through it with their new and brilliant minds) but throughout "Howl." Ginsberg took his establishment-acquired literature work from Columbia University and used that knowledge not to simply move into traditional poetics or law as was expected of him, but to turn against the powers which laid these expectations (the beginnings of borders, blocking possibilities) upon him. He speaks to this directly by accusing the establishment powers of possessing Molochian proclivities, of laying borders upon what you are allowed to feel, think, and say (a possession and accusation they lived up to and brought to fruition in the ensuing obscenity trials—another attempt at laying another boundary: what you are and are not allowed to print and say, where the "line" lies between the obscene and the literary, the obscene and the sexual, the beautiful even). Many modern authors, such as Stephen King, now explore as Ginsberg did these thin places in reality, these things "in a way ... comical; in another way, sad; in another, frankly horrible."[15] And it is these thin places where Coyote flies in and out, revealing the simple truth that perhaps "reality" is not simply a thin curtain to pass through, but nonexistent altogether.

Coyote as an entity speaks to the falsity of these socially and culturally created boundaries simply by his ability to cross into application in Beat culture as well as through his origins within Native American cultures. Coyote as a trickster is able to adapt to changing situations and times at the drop of a hat as it benefits him. This means that, as it benefits him, he is able to simply deny the power of conventional knowledge and understanding in pursuit of his own knowledge, realities, and ends. He is often able to slip into one reality and apply his own rules to change the game entirely. This may be seen not only in his role as cultural hero who brought dance, hunting, and competition to the new people, but in his role as the original trapper and enabler of sexual intercourse.

According to a Northern Paiute version of "How Her Teeth Were Pulled" (as told by Kenneth Lincoln and Jarold Ramsey), originally "women's cunts had teeth in them"; this premise creates many rather obvious problems for conducting productive intercourse.[16] But then one night, Coyote decided to change the rules for his own pleasure, to challenge this painful reality, by taking a "lava pestle / to bed with a mean woman / and hammer hammer crunch crunch ayi ayi / all night long."[17] In other words, Coyote "fixed" the vagina and brought sex to the world by saving the lives of all the sexual inventors, all because he was able to, not only through his transformative powers but through his ability to see beyond boundaries (cultural, spatial, and otherwise) and discover how to work around said boundaries for the betterment of all. There is also a deep and important element of humor in this narrative that ought not go without mention as it is, as Lincoln explains, an "off-color creation" representing how jokes and humor in such sacred stories were utilized "to integrate the tribes" and "free [their] deepest fears."[18] Here again we may see a smearing of the boundaries between humor, survival, and destruction. Without this traversing of conventional boundaries, of examining a problem or situation from a new vantage point, there would not only no longer exist the soul of humor but there would no longer exist the soul of human adaptability and invention. For example, instead of simply attempting to find new types of sex to have with these toothy-cunted women as many men undoubtedly did, Coyote decided to try and change the women themselves—looking beyond a seeming fact of life to recognize something changeable, to realize the possibility and option of another reality (an undoubtedly brighter reality of vaginas sans fangs).

From here Ginsberg transitions into the discussion of physical boundary crossings rather than cultural ones through stanzas like the following,

> who wandered around and around at midnight in the
>   railroad yard wondering where to go, and went,
>   leaving no broken hearts,
> who lit cigarettes in boxcars boxcars boxcars racketing
>   through snow toward lonesome farms in grandfather night[19]

These stanzas depict a variety of smeared boundaries, beginning in motion (as Coyote so often does) at midnight, at the crucial borderline between yesterday and today, within a "railroad yard," a here-or-there threshold, often symbolic of the liminal, enabling one to traverse any number of physical borderlines. Here, the "best minds" seem to choose a train propelling toward some "lonesome farms" in the middle of wintertime, in the moment of the seasonal calendar in which stories and Coyote narratives are told, at the cusp of a new year. Beyond even these thresholds and boundaries considered and successfully crossed by these "best minds," Ginsberg also slips into "grandfather night" as if to suggest that the final border they will cross is that into age and death (which, hopefully, shall recycle itself into a new birth and day).

This locomotive motif ties Ginsberg very tightly to the trickster archetype. The train image serves as a symbol for freedom, travel, power, progress, and artist-mischief[20] as well as for the industrial monster, a creator of boundaries as much as it tracks through them. This train is reminiscent of the train that crashed the best minds into the Zoo cages, another promise of progress against a reality of imprisonment by the proverbial "machine." Here, however, the bodies wandering in the railroad yard are so surrounded by paths with predestined locations that they cannot decide where to go. We can only assume that the boxcars boxcars boxcars they hopped onto sped them toward some desired unknown rather than simply another snow-cold city.

Either way, the train both enabled them to move from city to farm, over every borderline on the map, while also deciding for them where that physical part of the journey would go. In this way, the brilliant minds actually differ from the trickster Coyote who is often able to journey where other beings cannot, off the train tracks, if you will. However, in this same fashion, "Howl" uses this relationship between Coyote and the best minds to highlight its own ability to move outside those trains to an undisclosed "end" or destination. "Howl" by its very poetic nature encompasses more of Coyote's boundary-crossing characteristic than any train ride across the countryside because it continues even today to spiral in every different and undetermined direction without losing itself or wearing away its wheels.

In Part II of "Howl," Ginsberg experiments with several borderlines we do not normally consider. Here we find an elaborated discussion of those lines drawn between a multitude of subjects: humor and horror, the spiritual and the worshipped, the world and our perceptions of it, the wealth of the world and the wealth of the mind, what is valuable and what is valued, between sex, love, and loneliness, between Heaven and our man-made (mis)understandings of it, between the natural, the supernatural, and the man-made imitations of both. Take these stanzas below, for example; each one of them expresses at least one of these separations and connections, the Pangaea of existence.

> Moloch whose love is endless oil and stone! Moloch
>   whose soul is electricity and banks! Moloch
>   whose poverty is the specter of genius! Moloch
>   whose fate is a cloud of sexless hydrogen!
>   Moloch whose name is the Mind!
>
> Moloch in whom I sit lonely! Moloch in whom I dream
>   Angels! Crazy in Moloch! Cocksucker in
>   Moloch! Lacklove and manless in Moloch![21]

Phrases like "whose poverty is the specter of genius," "whose fate is a cloud of sexless hydrogen," "Moloch whose name is the Mind," highlight the particularly thin boundaries between creative progress/invention and constant destruction. After all, when your more ingenious citizens are plagued by the specter of poverty (assumedly because of their genius), you

6. Smearing Borderlines

know your country has crossed the boundary from progress to Moloch. This is easier to see in Coyote, perhaps, as Coyote makes this transition constantly between creative thinker and destructive force of hunger. But this is the largest shift within "Howl," where we may realize that same Coyote characteristics not only apply to Ginsberg's best minds but also, perhaps, to all of America as well in how the monstrous Moloch embodies many of the darker aspects of Coyote's trickster identity.

The entirety of this next stanza stands as an argument against these boundaries society fabricates and silently agrees to adhere to and that have, according to Ginsberg, transitioned us into a world and realm of Moloch.

> Moloch! Moloch! Robot apartments! invisible suburbs! skeleton treasuries! blind capitals! demonic industries! spectral nations! invincible mad houses! granite cocks! monstrous bombs![22]

"Robot apartments," "invisible suburbs," and "granite cocks" are all violent unmaskings of delusions Ginsberg accuses us of holding dear. These realities never applied to Coyote, however, as a trickster and symbol of a different reality altogether. However, this is also true of men such as Ginsberg who (much like Coyote suddenly deciding to detooth the vagina) determined that these constraints no longer applied to him or the Beat generation. Apartments, suburbs, and social classes all serve as examples of confinements or even those red lines we put up between ourselves and others. Whether done physically such as where we choose to build our homes (and beside whom we elect to build them), or ideologically, such as defining oneself as a heterosexual or homosexual, the bars seem cemented down in permanent place.

The struggle against these confinements is well exampled by both Native American tricksters as well as some Native American cultures in general. The boundaries drawn on land and sexuality were introduced not as acceptable societal constructs but were imposed upon many Native communities as assimilative and destructive forces by an imperial power. These borders in no way apply to the trickster (then or now) as they did not originally apply to many Native American communities. In many of these cultures, traditionally, most expressions of sexuality were acceptable so long as they were not incestuous or harmful to the community. Also, many Native Americans did not share a European concept of land ownership (although this is not to discount the numerous wars and disputes between tribes over questions of land). But these are generalizations which do not necessarily apply to every tribe and nation, and generalizations are the devils that lead to terms like "cherohonkee" and "wigger." It's best to keep in mind that though many Native Americans did not practice land ownership as the first European settlers understood it, when a nomadic group came a-hunting through where a more agricultural tribe had settled, violence often ensued.

"Howl" continues on with,

> They broke their backs lifting Moloch to Heaven! Pavements, trees, radios, tons! lifting the city to Heaven which exists and is everywhere about us![23]

This stanza takes the argument a step further by moving to more religious grounds, exploring the malleability of the boundary standing between this world and the next just as the trickster Coyote does time and time again. However, as Ginsberg notes, our attempts to build John Winthrop's "city upon a hill" have failed miserably; many peoples' hopes of the ideal America have crunched under the weight of our modern golden calves of wealth and hydrogen bombs. This is trickster ironic, as Ginsberg points out, in that there was no need to place extra weight on any back at all as the Heaven we sought to reach "exists and is everywhere about us!" In other words, there was no border past which we needed to lift the city. A classic trickster trap if ever there was one, the spreading of fear and strife in order to gain paradise only to miss out on the paradise which already exists about us.

This next stanza delves into something even shadier.

> Real holy laughter in the river! They saw it all! the wild eyes! the holy yells! They bade farewell! They jumped off the roof! to solitude! waving! carrying flowers! Down to the river! into the street![24]

Keeping the holiness in mind, the sacredness of moving between Heaven and Earth, Ginsberg also offers up the image of a river. This symbol, like the train, he comes back to again and again. Water, rivers, rain, and oceans have been symbolic of the holy or sacred for centuries. They have become a prominent and important motif throughout "American" literature whether it be the crazed oceanic voyage of the *Pequot* or the raft rides of Huckleberry Finn down the Mississippi. Then Ginsberg goes so far as to compare the more traditionally romantic river journeys to moving

6. Smearing Borderlines

out into the streets. This is perhaps prescient of the near-future LGBTQ slogan, "Out of the closets and into the streets," however more generally Ginsberg most likely intended it. After all, he was not simply an advocate for gay rights, but an American who was disenchanted with "America" as a whole. He therefore redefines "river" as "street," romanticizing the journey, the march, and the fight, much the same way as Coyote redefines the world to better match his expectations and preferences, shifting our conceptions of spaces and peoples' places within them. Ginsberg does this for some of the same reasons Coyote had for teaching people how to hunt and dance. He wanted to bring forward a new way of doing things, of thinking and talking about things.

And from here, from these journeys across cultures, continents, and identities, Ginsberg makes the transition into the third and final part of "Howl." Part III of "Howl" is, by its very nature, a smearing of borderlines, as it depends upon the repeated chant of "I'm with you in Rockland / where...."[25] Here Ginsberg discusses not only the blurring of distances with letters, poetry, camaraderie, and love, but also the blurring of distances between the physical place Rockland and the symbol that it has become. This is a symbol Ginsberg elaborates upon with every advancing line, where Rockland, the mental institution, switches constantly back and forth between a prison for those who dared challenge societal norms and a hospital for those afflicted and thus unable to comply with those societal norms. Rockland, in this way, becomes much more than simply a mental institution; it becomes a symbol of the incomprehensible prison, challenging us to decide if we have actually provided for the mentally ill or if we have simply locked up a different version of sanity because we could not reconcile it with our own preconceptions. Coyote constantly wanders between these borders in his back-and-forth with wisdom and foolishness, allowing his cleverness at times to entrap him.

> I'm with you in Rockland
>> where fifty more shocks will never return your
>> soul to its body again from its pilgrimage to a
>> cross in the void[26]

This is a prime example of how Ginsberg utilized the reputation of Rockland's status as a mental institution in order to highlight the stark borderline between a religious journey and an unhealthy break from "reality." Ginsberg had had many negative encounters with mental institutions beyond his own brief institutionalization, the most prominent event likely being when he committed his own mother (a schizophrenic) to Pilgrim State Hospital and when he later made the decision to allow the doctors to lobotomize her. This became something of a specter within Ginsberg's life and part of the impetus for his later work *Kaddish*, which he dedicated to his mother, Naomi Ginsberg.

The rhetoric he employs in this stanza to describe a patient undergoing shock treatments borders on the romantic, no doubt due to a mixture of these personal experiences. He suggests here that our understanding of the line drawn between sanity and insanity is hardly fair or accurate given that some whom we subject to such intensive physical treatments may not be insane but have simply offered up their souls to a pilgrimage or quest of their own. In this way, Ginsberg relays to us the innumerable possibilities of the wandering mind and spirit, which we cannot account for in our commonly held and stonier conceptions of how sanity and religious fervor should function in an individual. He suggests here that the boundaries crossed by some of these "best minds" stretch beyond the point of return, beyond what any outsider understands. This is an idea that follows well with Coyote who is often depicted mid-journey, traveling somewhere that, often, other beings are unable to go, whether it be another territory or another plane (heavenly or earthly). Coyote rarely stops to explain himself or justify his wandering to his wife, friends, or any other medicine men along the way; he simply keeps a move on, embodying the need for motion, embodying constant liminal reorganization.

Chapter 7

Transformations: Madman Bum and Angel

This final aspect of the trickster quadrilateral is one of the trickiest to explain. Being Coyote, he is able to make the rather obvious transformation from the more animalistic to the human and vice versa (though this does not exclude the possibility for Coyote to encapsulate them both simultaneously), but, being a trickster, he is also constantly switching identities from medicine man to lusty fool and vice versa (a transformation well exampled in the aforementioned story of "Coyote and the Mallard Ducks"). Essentially, this characteristic stands as his most paradoxical and, as such, probably his most powerful trickster trait. This sometimes tragic, sometimes hilarious paradox is well defined by Russ McDonald through his study of the works of William Shakespeare, "The Language of Tragedy." McDonald proposes that "the sources of human greatness and the sources of human failure are identical," poles that the trickster knows intimately well and constantly shimmies between.[1] This, arguably and ironically, is the trickster's most definitive trait.

This is the trait Vizenor often focuses upon in his works involving tricksters. In Vizenor's *Earthdivers*, for example, he builds his stories upon "tribal tricksters and recast culture heroes" who "dive into unknown urban places ... to create a new consciousness of coexistence."[2]

This mercurial craze runs thickly throughout "Howl," where Ginsberg employs this craze to further elucidate the larger, more complex transformation of America from a freedom ideal and dream to a Moloch — a dark altar upon which other cultures are forced to sacrifice their heritages and traditions (and vice versa). Ginsberg does this in order to discuss the transformations of institutions and thinkers into asylums and submissive cogs, to discuss the transformative power of language itself, its malleability and tendency to change as well as its ability to be solidified and thus require shaking up, breaking up. Language's true face, as Ginsberg seemed to see it, is one of complete and constant transformation, dependent upon the conflicts and manipulations of personal and popular perception.

We may find brief close-ups of these trickster transformations in verses such as these:

> who passed through universities with radiant cool eyes hallucinating
>   Arkansas and Blake-light tragedy among the scholars of war,
> who were expelled from the academies for crazy & publishing obscene
>   odes on the windows of the skull[3]

These verses comment on the transformation of "universities" with their "scholars of war" to "academies" that expel those scholars and best minds for experimentation and exploration (sexual, intellectual, and otherwise). There is a clever subtlety lying within the definitions of "university" and "academy" Ginsberg artfully capitalizes upon. A place of the highest standard and level of liberal arts learning (the university) has in this poem been transformed (or, perhaps, in this case, as many of the anti-academy Beats seemed to believe, *curdled*) into a place of specialized advancement beneath a body of education/administrative authorities who have the power to standardize achievement and ideas under the purview of established opinion generally accepted as truth (the academy). Ginsberg is giving us another look at the trickster transformations that occur subtly and constantly all around, so quietly that we may not even notice the difference at first. This sort of difference, this little tweak between a *university* and an *academy*, is just the sort of hairline separation that McDonald referred to in his paradox, the freedom of education turning in on itself as the educated begin to fear it and its ability to disrupt structures of power, the same sort of souring that Coyote experiences when he jerks quickly and quietly from guru to fool, starting out on the right foot only to end up tripping over it with the other.

Ginsberg then presents moments such as in this next stanza, exemplifying a different, less accusatory though still doom-spirited sort of transformative power.[4]

> Pilgrim State's Rockland's and Greystone's foetid halls, bickering with the
>   echoes of the soul, rocking and rolling in the midnight solitude-bench
>   dolmen-realms of love, dream of life a nightmare, bodies turned to
>   stone as heavy as the moon[5]

7. Transformations

This stanza is chock full of heady transformative (and boundary-underlining) moments such as "rocking and rolling" to "midnight solitude," "dream" to "life" to "nightmare" very quickly, like finger snapping, then "bodies" to "stone" to "moon," celestial, cold, and close yet still untouchable, unattainable. Ginsberg presents us with contradiction after contradiction in quick succession all the while emphasizing their tricky, eerie similarities.

This deep integration of trickster characteristics discusses the transformation of the best minds locked up in madhouses, transformed by the "foetid halls" of Rockland from active individuals to frozen bodies weighted by their own isolation. Through "Howl," Ginsberg illustrates the transformation from active to apathetic by transubstantiating mobile, lively flesh bodies into intolerant, immoveable stone. He also plays with the idea of "heavy" by juxtaposing heavy earthly stoniness with the heaviness of the cold and isolation of the floating moon (heavy stone anchored down by its nature, a floating moon seeming light but in truth moored by its own loneliness). Thus he describes not only the transformation of others within the institutions as either enlightened or entrapped but also reveals society's ability to transform others—to transform them from a person with a different opinion to a person suffering insanity, from a friend to an exile.

These stanzas seem to see the world in such a way as Coyote might twist things for his own ends, turning things as simple as word definitions on their heads. Ginsberg transforms language here from a communicator to a weapon, accusing society in Part II and revealing the consequences of its intolerances in Part III. He turns the larger elements, such as our physical understanding of nature and reality, around by comparing an apathetic or defeated body to a stone statue. He reveals a transformation within American society and within some of those best minds from angel to madman bum, from living body to stone cocoon, and in doing so reveals his own trickster transformation from "obscene" fool to ultra-wise unmasker of deceptions.

> who dreamt and made incarnate gaps in Time & Space through images
>   juxtaposed, and trapped the archangel of the soul between 2 visual
>   images and joined the elemental verbs and set the noun and dash of
>   consciousness together jumping with sensation of Pater Omnipotens
>   Aeterna Deus
>
> to recreate the syntax and measure of poor human prose and stand before
>   you speechless and intelligent and shaking with shame, rejected yet

> confessing out the soul to conform to the rhythm of thought in his naked and endless head,
> the madman bum and angel beat in Time, unknown, yet putting down here what might be left to say in time come after death[6]

These stanzas parallel the aforementioned (Erdoes and Ortiz) Miwok narrative "How People Were Made," in which Coyote is at first resistant to the idea of creating human beings simply because he had the power to create them, as he found it exhausting work to create so much. Here Ginsberg relates to this reluctance to transform from a being capable of creation and creativity to a being who actually utilizes that ability to create. He takes what he has learned concretely from artists like Cézanne and applies it in such a way as to invoke the wisdom of the trickster, taking a version of reality and unveiling a new way of communicating that version, of exploring it. Ginsberg traces the trickster transformation of language from one reality or interpretation to another, holding up a lamp to the next type of trickster transformation. This Promethean transformation in Coyote takes shape in his own switch from a creature of leisure and pleasure to a teacher of others. Ginsberg attempts to make this type of transformation throughout "Howl" and with especial clarity in these particular stanzas. Ginsberg attempts to reveal in this moment the possibility of transformation as well as the reality of "supernatural phenomena," of some deeper and timeless part of existence.[7]

Coyote, as a natural-born manipulator of language, presents prime examples of how language can both liberate people to worship and communicate as well as be used to entrap people in lies and misunderstandings. Consider, for instance, the Jicarilla Apache narrative, "Coyote Shows How He Can Lie" (as relayed by Lopez). Coyote proves he can bend language so well through his trickery that he even ends up tricking himself, riding off on his bounty of horse and saddle without seeming to realize or remember that he has no idea how to keep or care for the animal. And, considering these stanzas, perhaps Ginsberg would propose that the "sources" of McDonald's paradox, the identical sources of human greatness and failing, are simply that creature Language, forever sliding between construction and destruction, divine and earthly, a dimension all its own.

There also exists the even subtler transformation within the best minds themselves as they seem to, as aforementioned, go through a peculiar rite of passage within these stanzas. They seem to transform from dreamers of language and archangelic souls to nervous kids on small stages full of shame and fear of absolute rejection before blooming into a "madman bum and angel" (another likeness of the medicine man and the fool) just trying to create something to teach the future people (the New People) even after they have gone. In other words, they want to write something, Ginsberg wants to write something, that is both timeless and yet ever changing to fit and address the needs of each new generation — a poem with the longevity of writing and the flexibility and potential of orality. This transformation, from the feverish writing frenzy to the knee-knocking performance, is where Coyote takes what he has attained, some new power or gift or idea, and employs it. Though often unsuccessful, he always comes away with something learned and something to build upon for himself and for others, usually leaving him more restless or aggravated than humble or grateful. But we do also see Coyote embarrassed and humbled at certain points, such as in the Northern Pueblo narrative (relayed by Erdoes and Ortiz), "Putting a Saddle on Coyote's Back," when Coyote is so worked up over his failures with Rabbit Boy that all he can manage to grumble to his wife is, "'Old woman, mind your own business.'"[8]

In a similar fashion, Ginsberg builds "Howl" into a state of constant transition, riding waves of confidence and humility as he moves from Part I into Part II, transforming the poem itself as the goals, tone, and chant all change in an instant.

Part II is really a mass unveiling of what Ginsberg perceives to be America's grand and terrible transformation from the dream America into the devilish Moloch as the chant of the *"best minds" who* transforms into the awful cry of *Moloch! Moloch! Moloch!* The poem itself undergoes a transformation of tone and purpose as it moves from an outcry on the part of those persecuted minds to an accusatory shout against the demon responsible for their suffering.

> Moloch the incomprehensible prison! Moloch the crossbone soulless jailhouse and Congress of sorrows! Moloch whose buildings are judgment! Moloch the vast stone of war! Moloch the stunned governments![9]

This stanza is only one out of many examples throughout Part II where Ginsberg lists off all the various and terrible transformations he believes the innards of the dreamed America have undergone. It is no longer a "land of the free" but an "incomprehensible prison," which is a trickster statement all on its own. One might wonder how a person may become imprisoned if they cannot even conceive of the bars that cage them. Ginsberg uses this to reveal a nation no longer of justice and proactive government for the people but one "whose buildings are judgment"; one rested upon a foundation of endless war; one filled with empty death, cages, and "stunned," sorrowful governments. Ginsberg uses this to describe a world that seems to have transformed into something perhaps more trapped than trickster. However, these instances of becoming consumed by "judgment," by "war," and by "sorrows" may still be easily traced through Coyote. After all, it was Coyote who rushed to judge Skunk for a fool willing to bet away his dinner only moments after Coyote had worked to pull off a trap with him. It was Coyote who happily waged vengeful war with the Grizzly Bears even though he could have gotten away with stealing their food without them ever knowing the culprit's identity. And it was Coyote who wept the world's first tears over his only child's death after he took such fun from introducing competition and finiteness to humankind.

And as for the third and final part of "Howl" before its glorious "Footnote," Ginsberg reveals another transformative turn for the poem as it moves from its passionate shout to a reassuring letter. A letter wherein Ginsberg does his best to assure the world (through his reassurances to the poet Carl Solomon) that even in the midst of this great and sudden isolation and pain, we are not alone in the dark.

In these next few stanzas, we may see several trickster transformations:

> I'm with you in Rockland
> > where you pun on the bodies of your nurses the harpies of the Bronx
>
> I'm with you in Rockland
> > where you scream in a straightjacket that you're losing the game of the actual pingpong of the abyss
>
> I'm with you in Rockland
> > where you bang on the catatonic piano the soul is innocent and immortal it should never die ungodly in an armed madhouse[10]

These stanzas speak to many different transformations and changes including the transformation of humor and language ("pun") into a weapon; "nurses" into "harpies" (hideous female bodies in twisted deformity with birds' bodies, ready and waiting to rip men limb from limb); the "abyss" into a potentially defeatable opponent in a game of "pingpong"; and, finally, that transformation of an "immortal" (the innocent soul) into something finite. All of these hyperbolic transformations form stanzas that achieve a dark hilarity, the type of humor we might derive from watching

7. Transformations

Coyote die during some other backfiring trick such as in Bingo SiJohn's "Coyote and the White Man."

Ginsberg continues on in Rockland with this transformative pattern:

I'm with you in Rockland
    where we wake up electrified out of the coma by our own souls'
    airplanes roaring over the roof they've come to drop angelic bombs
    the hospital illuminates itself imaginary walls collapse   O skinny
    legions run outside   O starry-spangled shocks of mercy the eternal
    war is here   O victory forget your underwear we're free[11]

The phrase "imaginary walls collapse" echoes just another checkmark in the trickster category, illustrating the destruction of boundaries—boundaries that never existed to begin with but were merely social constructions we have naturalized through our prejudicial language and misunderstandings. Beyond this, Ginsberg also addresses the trickster talent for transformation and resilience in a more positive direction. He demonstrates this through his exuberant "wake up electrified out of the coma by our own souls' airplanes." He is describing a bright transformation within the self, a sudden return to life from the deadened stone to a warm body capable of motion and change. Most importantly, Ginsberg prophesizes the transformation of the American people from the zombies of Moloch back into bodies electrified by hope and life. This transformation also extends to the hospital as it "illuminates itself," suddenly morphing back into its original purpose and identity as a *hospital* rather than a madhouse.

And it is this action that highlights "Howl" as a trickster, functioning similarly to Coyote as a transformer not only of himself but of those around him. This is especially clear in stories like one Maidu creation story, as relayed by Roland Dixon within his *Maidu Myths*, in which Coyote gets bored with the perfection of the way life was in the beginning. Thus, for his own entertainment and accruement of power, Coyote takes it upon himself to introduce the New People to competition and death. Thus, Coyote transforms not only himself and his own ways of viewing the world and his desires but also the people around him, forcing them to fear and think of the future and to progress by making life finite.[12] In this way, both Coyote and "Howl" work to transform the people around them by forcing them to acknowledge the harsher aspects of life and to utilize them for the progression and spice of life rather than becoming imprisoned by them. I also contend that the motives of Coyote and of

Part II : Coyote-ing "Howl"

"Howl" in these circumstances are not as different as one might expect. Coyote introduces these harsher parts of life in order to make things more interesting and liberating for himself and his own antics. Similarly, the purposes of "Howl" in this instance may also be partly to antagonize the culture of Moloch and to encourage the mainstream to face these aspects of life Ginsberg enjoys. Both Coyote and "Howl" are seeking liberation for themselves and others, attempting to do so by forcibly transforming the world and its viewpoints as they see fit.

However, Ginsberg seems to take things a step further through the entirety of "Howl" by seeking a transformation of the American people to become the *American* people. This transformation we do not even recognize as something that *could* be because we already believe it to be so. Ginsberg essentially charges his fellow Americans with the task of becoming who they claim to be as Americans instead of as the Molochians they have allowed themselves to become through complacency, hostility, and intolerance.

In these final verses, Ginsberg relates the transformation of quiet reassurance into something much more celebratory and triumphant.

> I'm with you in Rockland
> in my dreams you walk dripping from a sea-journey on the highway
> across America in tears to the door of my cottage in the Western night[13]

Ginsberg's movements through the poem transform and roll in robust orchestral sweeps, keeping the paradoxes churning throughout to keep readers on their toes and wondering why they are laughing. "I'm with you in Rockland in my dreams" presents a physical neighboring transforming into one of dreams, from Ginsberg being with Solomon to Solomon becoming the journeyer to see Ginsberg over the American highways that have also experienced transformation from rugged and ruled streets to lawless, tear-mingled seas.

This wet-clay malleability of time and space is absolutely in keeping with many Native American trickster traditions as Coyote constantly traveled to new lands where others could not follow, constantly resurrected himself after death and mutilation, and constantly started the narratives over in yet another medias res. Of course, Coyote is often then proven by the indigenous of new lands to be a fool for presuming to understand their ways, though without ever losing or compromising his status as a culture hero. This in itself is the kind of transformation discussed by Ginsberg — the arrogant, often apologetic kid transforming into something of a culture

7. Transformations

hero himself, the taboo poem transforming into a promulgation of hope for all who have felt and suffered persecution.

Entire books, such as Jason Shinder's *The Poem That Changed America: "Howl" Fifty Years Later*, have been dedicated to the exploration of just this transformation which "Howl" sparked around the globe. In many ways, this seems to be the central goal of "Howl" itself, a poem written by a lonely and disenfranchised youth for the benefit and hope of the lonely and disenfranchised of the world. "Howl," though originally written without the intention of being published, represents a transformation within Ginsberg himself and his hopes of transforming others like him into something more hopeful and of transforming those unlike him into something more curious, something more tolerant and accepting.

Epilogue

*Poets are damned but they are not blind, they see with
the eyes of the angels.* — William Carlos Williams

In Franca Bellarsi's aforementioned article, "Proxemics and Poetic Discourse," she argues for a spatial reading of Ginsberg's poetry. However, she also steps forward from this contention to suggest that these types of studies challenge the critical claims that Ginsberg's poetry "has little aesthetic merit" and that critics only need look "for the tools" around them in order to begin appreciating this truly unique and culturally important poem.[1] I similarly contend that "Howl" and the full body of Ginsberg's poetry must be more thoroughly explored in order to be more fully appreciated for the positive cultural impacts it has had upon the American literary tradition. After all, Ginsberg has already been accepted by and cited as a significant influence on several notable Native American authors and artists today including Sherman Alexie, Paula Gunn Allen, and James Luna. "Howl," as I have attempted to reveal, is a poetic stew with many as yet unidentified ingredients (such as its newly identified connections to the Native American Coyote). This particular epic, if nothing else, is an attempt to reconsider the way America is and could be (in relation to not only itself but to the rest of the world as well); it is an attempt to reorganize America's web of identities and possibilities.

However, scholarly examinations of the works of Ginsberg remain sorely lacking in number compared with those myriad works dedicated to examining his life. This is not to disparage or downplay the cultural importance of these other works, but merely to call attention to the gaps remaining in this body of literature. Take, for example, Stephen Prothero's article "On the Holy Road: The Beat Movement as Spiritual Protest."

Prothero here discusses less of the poetry itself and more of the Beat movement in religious terms. Where I aim at enhancing the current state of literary exploration in Beat writing, he aims primarily to illustrate that "the beats were spiritual protestors as well as literary innovators and ought, therefore, to be viewed at least as minor characters in the drama of American religion."[2] This is certainly a vital conversation, especially when it comes to further understanding and analyzing Beat texts themselves, yet his work remains primarily concerned with the Beats' actions, spirituality, and trials outside of their literatures. In this way, Prothero, while contributing meaningfully to the body of Beat literature, does not significantly ground his work in poetic or literary analysis despite his recognition of their being "literary innovators."

Similarly, Paul Portugés' "Allen Ginsberg's Paul Cézanne and the Pater Omnipotens Aeterna Deus" examines Ginsberg's writing through the influence of the painter Paul Cézanne. He primarily discusses the development of Ginsberg's "theory of composition" through Cézanne's similar painterly theories. Portugés focuses on Cézanne's influences upon Ginsberg's ideas concerning time, timelessness, and means of utilizing art to explore new ways of perceiving and explaining the world. And while this conversation is especially valuable when considering the aforementioned spatial qualities of "Howl" as well as my utilization of a nonchronological interpretation of "Howl," Portugés does not provide an analytical study of any specific texts of Ginsberg's through this established lens beyond the idea and line of "Pater Omnipotens Aeterna Deus." Beyond this, Portugés is also able to secure his argument solidly upon the written explanation of Ginsberg himself, who journaled as well as spoke publicly quite often in regard to his own poetry and influences. In this way, Portugés' analysis differs most keenly from the analysis and purpose of this study. His work in comparing Ginsberg and Cézanne is based upon Ginsberg's own admission of Cézanne's influence upon his poetry and is not heavily reliant upon poetic textual analysis. Thus Portugés' work is akin to an elaboration or exploration of a preexisting fact whereas this work is more concerned with pursuing new possible influences within Ginsberg's poetry.

John Lardas' *The Bop Apocalypse: The Religious Visions of Kerouac, Ginsberg, and Burroughs* also does not discuss Ginsberg's specific poetic works in significant depth. Lardas' work is perhaps better in conversation with Prothero's work as he traces the religious biographies of the three title-role writers. He approaches these Beats from a variety of religious perspectives, incorporating a vibrant breadth of history and poetic influences (though he does not mention Native Americans or Native American cultures, literatures, or religions among these influences). He focuses predominantly upon the influential voice of the German philosopher Oswald Spengler (another influence conceded by Ginsberg himself). Lardas' primary obstacle, as Nancy Grace points out in her "Seeking the Spirit of the Beat," lies in his attempt to tackle too many religious perspectives within one study; this rush of influences and perspectives causes him to become too involved with the historical and cultural aspects of the research to fully "use the historical tool to probe the fiction."[3]

This work, however, has been an attempt to utilize the histories and cultures surrounding Ginsberg and "Howl" to expressly probe the poetry itself rather than to unveil some new piece of Ginsberg's person or politics. Of course, I am not the first to begin to take up this type of work with Ginsberg's poetry. Jonah Raskin's *American Scream*, though it is a history of the Beats, incorporates comparatively significant explication and attention to elements and lines from "Howl" specifically. In *Sing with the Heart of a Bear*, Kenneth Lincoln not only describes Ginsberg as a "trickster of great talent" but also goes on to examine sections of "A Supermarket in California" in comparison with an Ojibwa song. This is not to mention, of course, all of Ginsberg's own work at dissecting and explaining his poetry both in informal letters as well as in formal volumes.

"Howl" possesses a plethora of trickster symbolism and characteristics that speak to the muddled and paradoxical complexities of humanity and the traps we set for ourselves. "Howl" then, true to its trickster elements, moves beyond these broad connections to also touch on the dangers we risk when we fail or refuse to acknowledge these complexities, when we act as Blue Cloud's "anthro" and stubbornly keep ourselves segregated from the ethics, philosophies, and perspectives of others. From its own lamentations and violent passages to suffering the violence of an obscenity trial, "Howl" illustrates a valiant effort to reveal that the emperor is not, in fact, wearing any clothes, that our careful societal, ethical, and prejudicial boundaries are truly without ground but for that which we give them, for which we may be simply too afraid or embarrassed to acknowledge. Through his poetry and its Coyote tricks, Ginsberg explains that we must turn from our "incomprehensible prisons" of prejudice, disrespect, violence, and discrimination before we may embrace the humor and wider possibilities of life with each other. These prisons, by definition, do not exist as iron bars physically caging us, but by our own social constructions of fearing and even hating others and their traditions in an effort to somehow reinforce or define our own. With the use of appetites, transformative power, a tricky sense of humor, and a blatant disregard for boundaries (sexual and otherwise) mortared by the hyperbolic, Ginsberg has revealed in "Howl" the face of the evils we have and continue to unleash upon ourselves.

"Howl" thus functions as a poetic attempt to catapult thoughts into action, inspiring others not only to reconsider the role of poetry in their lives but also their own roles in the world. Just as Coyote functions as both a fool and medicine man, so "Howl" represents a paradoxical dose of foolishness and wisdom. "Howl" itself has come to serve as a kind of medicine for many different individuals over the years. According to Carl Waldman's *Dictionary of Native American Terminology*, the term *medicine* is best defined as "power inherent in the universe ... [or, more specifically, as an] object or substance that effects change or healing."[4] Not unlike how Coyote works as a medicine man, an entity capable of channeling such medicine, "Howl" may also be perceived as a particular medicine channeled by Ginsberg into poetic words for the betterment of the world. And in "reality," all of this work serves to simply explain that this case study does not go far enough into the multitudes of "Howl," Ginsberg, or Coyote. These are all ideas and subjects in need of significantly more diverse and thorough exploration.

Of course, it is not only in "Howl" that we may find these Native American trickster influences. Nor have all the potential influences of Native American cultures yet been fully explored within "Howl." However, beyond simply the context of Ginsberg's poetry, Native American cultures and literatures remain a largely unappreciated, underutilized, and almost willfully misunderstood and misrepresented source of American history, literature, and knowledge. This is not to suggest that the body of my interpretations and attempts to understand are without fault or misunderstanding themselves, but that they were made in an effort to explore these themes, narratives, and ideas with the utmost respect, open-mindedness, and honesty.

While my thesis remains tied up in the connections between "Howl" and Coyote, what is truly important is that we keep talking and reconsidering others and new actors in our writing and in attempting to understand our intertwining histories. Native Americans' rich histories, cultures, and narratives—trickster and otherwise—should be more fully explored and considered (as permitted and accepted by Native American communities) for their value to the North American literary canon and to the illumination of the more complex depths of American history. These are not stories or poems or prayers of savage or deviant people looking to scandalize; these are stories, poems, prayers, ideas, ways of living, and versions of reality that all work to explain how we may come to be more comfortable, respectful, and understanding of ourselves, our neighbors, and different ways of being and thinking. With such a force compelling us into lives of deep self-reflection, how could we not then look upon our neighbors and bestow them with dignity? By challenging and coming to terms with our own beliefs and preconceptions first, by bypassing those trickster traps of simplistic dogmas and prevaricating rhetoric, we may be able to approach each other with fewer accusations or fears and, instead, with many, many more questions.

One of the underlying purposes of arts and religions is to give people a better sense of themselves in relation to creation and the holy cosmos, allowing them to lead lives of greater harmony, peace, and celebratory, victorious love with neighbors of all faults and wisdoms. Ginsberg's poetry and kaleidoscope of religious and cultural influences are an attempt at creating a new type of sacred environment, a place where a trickster such as Coyote may thrive in all of his complexities and multitudes. But it does seem, for now, that we remain more caught up in our own traps (such as these modern notions of "post-racial societies" or the older notions of "golden ages") than we are open to recognizing the wisdoms that may come from a laugh, a poem, or a different perspective.

Chapter Notes

Preface

1. Tom Spanbauer, *The Man Who Fell in Love with the Moon* (New York: Grove, 1991), 7.
2. Ibid.
3. Gary Snyder, "Foreword," in *The Maidu Indian Myths and Stories of Hanc'ibyjim*, ed. and tran. by William Shipley (Berkeley: Heyday, 1991), viii.
4. Ellen Rosenberg, "Native American Coyote Trickster Tales and Cycles," in *Fools and Jesters in Literature, Art, and History: A Bio-Bibliographical Sourcebook*, ed. by Vicki Janik (Westport: Greenwood, 1998), 157.
5. Ann Charters, *The Portable Beat Reader* (New York: Penguin, 1992), 61.
6. Allen Ginsberg and Richard Eberhart, *To Eberhart from Ginsberg* (Lincoln: Penmaen, 1976), 13.
7. James Luna, interview by Katherine Mead, *via telephone*, August 14, 2011.
8. Simon J. Ortiz, "Towards a National Indian Literature: Cultural Authenticity in Nationalism," *MELUS* 8, no. 2 (1981): 8.
9. Joy Harjo, "The Story of All Our Survival," in *Survival This Way: Interviews with American Indian Poets*, ed. and interviewed by Joseph Bruchac (Tuscon: Sun Tracks and The University of Arizona Press, 1987), 92.
10. Silko, in fact, singled out Gary Snyder as one of two writers in particular (the other being [Oliver] Peter La Farge) for what she believed to be a "cultural arrogance in presuming to write from a standpoint of superior knowledge concerning Indian worldviews and spirituality" (Hobson 1). Hobson, on the other hand, throws Snyder a bit more slack, stating that he continues to disagree, at least in part, "with her harsh judgments of Snyder" (though he certainly agrees with her assessment of Peter La Farge) (Hobson 1).
11. Geary Hobson, "The Rise of the White Shaman: Twenty-Five Years Later," *Studies in American Indian Literatures*, Series 2, 14, no. 2/3 (2002): 1.
12. Edmund White, introduction to *Spontaneous Mind*, Allen Ginsberg (New York: HarperCollins, 2001), xii.
13. Edmund White, *The Farewell Symphony* (New York: Vintage, 1997), 341–342.
14. Fran Lebowitz, *Public Speaking*, DVD, Dir. Martin Scorsese (2010; New York: HBO Documentary Films, 2010), documentary film.
15. Craig Womack, *Art as Performance, Story as Criticism: Reflections on Native Literary Aesthetics* (Norman: University of Oklahoma Press, 2009), 104.

Introduction

1. These traits have also been identified and expanded upon by other scholars as well, including the six characteristics discussed by William J. Hynes in "Mapping the Characteristics of Mythic Tricksters: A Heuristic Guide" and the *thirty-two* characteristics outlined by Barbara Babcock in her article, "'A Tolerated Margin of Mess': The Trickster and His Tales Reconsidered." Hynes highlights six core characteristics: "the fundamentally ambiguous and anomalous personality"; "deceiver/trick-player"; "shape-shifter"; "situation-inverter"; "messenger/imitator of the gods"; and "sacred/lewd bricoleur" (Hynes 34). He argues that these six traits create a heuristic guide to the trickster though I would suggest that these six are also incorporated into the four, perhaps broader categories outlined by Leeming and Page.

Notes. Introduction

2. Terrie Waddell. *Wild/Lives: Trickster, Place, and Liminality on Screen* (New York: Routledge, 2010), xiii.

3. William J. Hynes, "Mapping the Characteristics of Mythic Tricksters: A Heuristic Guide," in *Mythical Trickster Figures: Contours, Contexts, and Criticisms*, ed. William J. Hynes and William G. Doty (London: University of Alabama Press, 1993), 34.

4. Allen Ginsberg, "It's a Vast Trap!" in *On the Poetry of Ginsberg*, ed. Lewis Hyde (Ann Arbor: University of Michigan Press, 1984), 78.

5. Daniel Morley Johnson, "(Re)Nationalizing Naanabozho," in *Troubling Tricksters: Revisioning Critical Conversation*, ed. Deanna Reder and Linda M. Morra (Waterloo: Wilfrid Laurier University Press, 2010), 202.

6. Steven Heine, *Bargainin' for Salvation: Bob Dylan, A Zen Master?* (New York and London: Continuum International, 2009), 22.

7. Ibid.

8. Ibid., 2.

9. Ibid., 3.

10. Allen Ginsberg, "Howl," in *Collected Poems 1947–1997* (New York: HarperCollins, 2006) 139.

11. Cathy Ruiz's poem (2007), "Coyote, the Trickster, Comes to the Zen Buddhist Monastery and I Realize his Buddha Nature," is an interesting example of this "Zen Buddhist Coyote" phenomenon. ("Buddha nature," at least according to Ruiz, essentially means "one's true nature" [Ruiz 41].) In this poem, she depicts her narrator as one attempting to focus and meditate at a Buddhist monastery but is continuously interrupted by Coyote who leaps out from behind monks, inquires about the narrator's sex fantasies, and, eventually, wins the narrator over, at least "halfway" (41). A poem that both interestingly connects Coyote more intimately with Zen Buddhism as well as highlights the differences between Coyote's means of attaining illumination and those of the Buddhist monks.

12. Richard Slotkin, *Gunfighter Nation: Myth of the Frontier in Twentieth-Century America* (Norman: University of Oklahoma Press, 1998), 5.

13. Gregory E. Smoak, "Review: *The Mythology of Native North America* by David Leeming; Jake Page," *American Indian Quarterly* 22, no. 4 (1998): 513.

14. Jonathan Goldberg and Madhavi Menon, "Queering History," *Modern Language Association* (2005): 1616.

15. Ibid.

16. Leslie McCall, "The Complexity of Intersectionality," *Signs* (2005): 1771–1774.

17. Ibid., 1774, qtd. Bonnie Thornton Dill (2002).

18. Tom Robbins, "In Defiance of Gravity," *Harper's Magazine*, September 2004, 58.

19. Gary Snyder, e-mail message to author, January 30, 2010.

20. Anne Waldman, "Premises of Consciousness," in *The Poem That Changed America: "Howl" Fifty Years Later*, ed. Jason Shinder (New York: Farrar, Straus and Giroux, 2006), 266.

21. Ibid.

22. David M. Jones and Brian L. Molyneaux, *The Illustrated Encyclopedia of American Indian Mythologies: Legends, Gods, and Spirits of North, Central, and South America* (London: Lorenz Books, Anness, 2009), 12.

23. Ibid.

24. Adrienne Rich, "The Hermit's Scream," *Modern Language Association* 108, no. 5 (1993): 1157–164, http://www.jstor.org.proxygw.wrlc.org/stable/pdfplus/462992.pdf?acceptTC=true.

25. Andrei Codrescu, "'Howl' in Transylvania," in *The Poem That Changed America: "Howl" Fifty Years Later*, ed. Jason Shinder (New York: Farrar, Straus and Giroux, 2006), 54.

26. Mark Doty, "Human Seraphim: 'Howl,' Sex, and Holiness," in *The Poem That Changed America: "Howl" Fifty Years Later*, ed. Jason Shinder (New York: Farrar, Straus and Giroux, 2006), 14.

27. Perhaps the most notable example of this occurred in 1984 when Diana Trilling, wife of Lionel Trilling (one of Ginsberg's former professors at Columbia with whom he shared a tumultuous relationship), took Ginsberg's ironic dedication of his poem "The Lion for Real" to her husband to actually mean that "the poem was *about* her husband," describing the poem as following: it was about a lion in the room with the poet, a lion who was hungry but refused to eat him; I heard it as a passionate love poem" (Genter 24 and Trilling qtd. in Genter 24). Due to this rather painful misinterpretation, "Ginsberg was deeply offended by [her] 'rather ugly mistake,'" stating that her criticism was "'rather self-smug & bitchy & all balled up psychologically'" (Genter 24 and Ginsberg qtd. in Genter 24). Although, I would contend that this was another example of the types of poetic traps Ginsberg occa-

sionally set, waiting for his moment to snap the trigger and tear down one of those traditional academic authorities with their own academia.

28. Stephen Prothero, "On the Holy Road: The Beat Movement as Spiritual Protest," *The Harvard Theological Review* 84, no. 2 (1991): 205.

29. Allen Ginsberg qtd. in Jonah Raskin, *American Scream*, 73.

30. Although, this is not to imply that Ginsberg wrote for any particular audience but for, perhaps, himself. Ginsberg's desire for recognition and acclaim does not extend into gross commercialism but likely stems from his constantly being ignored or discouraged by professors and others during his college years at Columbia (not to mention from the feeling of general repression or even oppression from the larger American mainstream culture as a gay, Jewish man).

31. Nancy M. Grace, "Seeking the Spirit of Beat: The Call for Interdisciplinary Scholarship," *Contemporary Literature* 43, no. 4 (2002): 812.

32. Allen Ginsberg qtd. in Jonah Raskin, *American Scream*, 73.

33. Nancy M. Grace, "Seeking the Spirit of Beat: The Call for Interdisciplinary Scholarship," *Contemporary Literature* 43, no. 4 (2002): 820.

34. Tom Robbins, "In Defiance of Gravity," *Harper's Magazine*, September 2004, 59.

35. For further reference, see articles like Barbra A. Meek's "And the Injun Goes 'How!': Representations of American Indian English in White Public Space."

36. This Latin phrase translates to "Father Omnipotent Eternal God."

37. Allen Ginsberg, "Howl," in *Collected Poems*, 138–139.

Chapter 1

1. Allen Ginsberg and Jack Kerouac, *Jack Kerouac and Allen Ginsberg: The Letters*, ed. Bill Morgan and David Stanford (New York: Viking, 2010), 154.

2. Timothy Patrick McCarthy and John McMillian, Ed. *Protest Nation: Words that Inspired a Century of American Radicalism* (New York: New Press, 2010), 54.

3. Allen Ginsberg qtd. in Milton Viorst, *Fire in the Streets: America in the 1960s* (New York: Simon & Schuster, 1980), 55.

4. Allen Ginsberg, foreword to *The Beat Book: Writings from the Beat Generation*, ed. Anne Waldman (Boston: Shambhala, 2007), xiii.

5. Allen Ginsberg, *Howl & Other Poems*, xvi.

6. Allen Ginsberg, "A Definition of the Beat Generation," in *Deliberate Prose*, ed. Bill Morgan (New York: HarperCollins, 2000), 239.

7. Lawrence W. Gross, "The Comic Vision of Anishinaabe Culture and Religion" *American Indian Quarterly* 26, no. 3 (2002): 447.

8. Ibid., 437.

9. Tom Robbins, "In Defiance of Gravity," *Harper's Magazine*, 59.

10. Ibid., 58.

11. Ibid.

12. Lofton conducted the interview "at the home of *Washington Times* columnist Suzanne Fields" and later (1999) explained that from this interview he'd hoped "to confront him [Allen Ginsberg] with the Truth of God's Word" (Ginsberg and Lofton, 469).

13. Allen Ginsberg, interview by John Lofton, "The Puritan and the Profligate" in *Chronicles: A Magazine of American Culture*, reprinted *Harper's Magazine:* "When Worlds Collide," (New York: January 1990), 13.

14. Ibid.

15. Ibid.

16. Ibid.

17. Ibid., 14.

18. Allen Ginsberg qtd. in Jonah Raskin, *American Scream: Allen Ginsberg's Howl and the Making of the Beat Generation* (Berkeley and Los Angeles: Regents of the University of California, 2004), xx.

19. Ibid.

20. Ibid.

21. Jonah Raskin, *American Scream: Allen Ginsberg's Howl and the Making of the Beat Generation* (Berkeley and Los Angeles: Regents of the University of California, 2004), xx.

22. Allen Ginsberg, interview by John Lofton, "The Puritan and the Profligate,"or "When Worlds Collide" from *Harper's Magazine*, 18.

23. Ibid., 18–19.

24. In 1888, Dr. Richard Bucke "was elected President of the Psychological Section of the British Medical Association" before getting elected, two years later, "President of the American Medico–Psychological Association" (Acklom qtd. in Bucke, Introduction). Of course, these achievements were hardly

valuable to him in comparison to his experiences in 1867 and 1872. Eighteen hundred sixty-seven marked the year when he first heard verses of Whitman's poetry that "opened a door in his mind," much as they pervaded and impacted Allen Ginsberg (Acklom qtd. in Bucke, introduction). However, his experience in 1872 was more akin to Ginsberg's famous auditory hallucination of William Blake. In 1872, Bucke "experienced Illumination," which lit up within him like "a flame-colored cloud" before settling into "a sense of exultation," "an intellectual illumination" that charged into his mind "one momentary lightning-flash of the Brahmic Splendor" (Acklom qtd. in Bucke, introduction).

25. Richard Maurice Bucke, *Cosmic Consciousness: A Study in the Evolution of the Human Mind* (original 1901), (New York: Arkana, 1991), 1.

26. Ibid., 3.

27. Allen Ginsberg, interview by John Lofton, "The Puritan and the Profligate," or "When Worlds Collide" from *Harper's Magazine*, 18.

28. Ibid., 19.

29. Ibid.

30. Jonah Raskin, *American Scream*, xxv.

31. Ed Folsom, "The Walt Whitman Encyclopedia: Native Americans [Indians]." *The Walt Whitman Archive*, 31 July 1998. 2011. http://www.whitmanarchive.org/criticism/current/encyclopedia/entry_34.html.

32. Ibid.

33. Allen Ginsberg, *Indian Journals* (San Francisco: Dave Haselwood and City Lights, 1970), 10.

34. Ibid., 9.

35. Ellen Rosenberg, "Native American Coyote Trickster Tales and Cycles," in *Fools and Jesters in Literature, Art, and History: A Bio-Bibliographical Sourcebook*, ed. Vicki Janik (Westport: Greenwood, 1998), 157.

36. Bill Morgan, *I Celebrate Myself: The Somewhat Private Life of Allen Ginsberg* (New York: Penguin, 2006), 103.

37. Ibid.

38. Ginsberg actually spelled his name "Hendrix" in the letter, but Hendrick was a rather influential artist coming out of California at the time. He helped initiate and plan the Six Gallery gathering.

39. Allen Ginsberg, "Letter to John Allen Ryan," in *Beat Down to Your Soul: What Was the Beat Generation?*, ed. Ann Charters (New York: Penguin, 2001), 207.

40. Ibid.

41. Ibid.

42. Ibid.

43. Bill Morgan, *I Celebrate Myself: The Somewhat Private Life of Allen Ginsberg* (New York: Penguin, 2006), 103.

44. James Luna, interview by Katherine Mead, *via telephone*, August 14, 2011.

45. Allen Ginsberg, *Spontaneous Mind: Selected Interviews, 1958–1996*, ed. David Carter (New York: HarperCollins, 2001), 429.

46. Ibid., 428.

47. Janet Campbell Hale, "Claire," in *Reckonings: Contemporary Short Fiction by Native American Women*, ed. Hertha D. Sweet Wong, Lauren Stuart Muller, and Jana Sequoya Magdaleno (New York: Oxford University Press, 2008), 103.

48. Ari Goldman, *Being Jewish* (New York: Simon & Schuster, 2000), 27.

49. Ibid., 28.

50. James Luna, interview by Katherine Mead, *via telephone*, August 14, 2011.

51. Tyler Hoffman, *American Poetry in Performance: From Walt Whitman to Hip Hop* (Ann Arbor: University of Michigan Press, 2011), 18–19.

52. Robert Bednar (professor) in discussion with the author, Fall 2010.

53. Raj Chandarlapaty, *The Beat Generation and Counterculture: Paul Bowles, William S. Burroughs, Jack Kerouac* (New York: Peter Lang, 2009), 157.

54. Bill Morgan, *I Celebrate Myself: The Somewhat Private Life of Allen Ginsberg* (New York: Penguin, 2006), 208.

55. Ginsberg did not actually meet Snyder until 1955 when he came to San Francisco. He was introduced to Snyder by poet Kenneth Rexroth who was famous for his literary salons. However, given Ginsberg's preexisting network of friends, he was likely aware of Snyder and his work before actually meeting him. Thus, because of how these friendships grew out of salon-like meetings and networks, it's entirely possible if not simply likely that Ginsberg was already clued in to bits of Native American mythology long before the completion of "Howl."

56. Allen Ginsberg, "Letter to John Allen Ryan," in *Beat Down to Your Soul*, ed. Anne Charters, 207.

57. Gary Snyder and Allen Ginsberg, *The Selected Letters of Allen Ginsberg and Gary Snyder*, ed. Bill Morgan (Berkeley: Counterpoint, 2009), 17.

58. Gary Snyder, *Myths and Texts* (New York: New Directions, 1978), vii.

Notes. Chapter 1

59. Gary Snyder and Allen Ginsberg, *The Selected Letters of Allen Ginsberg and Gary Snyder*, ed. Bill Morgan, 87–88.

60. Anne MacNaughton, "'Taos Pueblo' reading features poetry," *Santa Fe New Mexican* (Taos Pueblo, NM), Oct. 12, 1990.

61. John Knoll, "Reconnecting to the spiritual muse," *Santa Fe New Mexican*, Aug. 12, 1988.

62. Gary Snyder and Allen Ginsberg, *The Selected Letters of Allen Ginsberg and Gary Snyder*, ed. Bill Morgan, 106.

63. Ibid., 135.

64. Bill Morgan, "Footnote no. 139," in *The Selected Letters of Allen Ginsberg and Gary Snyder*, ed. Bill Morgan (Berkeley: Counterpoint, 2009), 135.

65. Allen Ginsberg and Gary Snyder, *The Selected Letters of Allen Ginsberg and Gary Snyder*, ed. Bill Morgan, 134.

66. "Maidu People," *City of Roseville, California: Parks & Recreation*, accessed March 21, 2012, http://www.roseville.ca.us/parks/parks_n_facilities/facilities/maidu_indian_museum/maidu_people.asp.

67. Gary Snyder and Allen Ginsberg, *The Selected Letters of Allen Ginsberg and Gary Snyder*, ed. Bill Morgan, 192–193.

68. Allen Ginsberg and Gary Snyder, *The Selected Letters of Allen Ginsberg and Gary Snyder*, ed. Bill Morgan, 194–195.

69. Allen Ginsberg and Jack Kerouac, *Jack Kerouac and Allen Ginsberg: The Letters* (New York: Viking, 2010), ed. Bill Morgan and David Stanford, 149.

70. Allan Johnston, "Consumption, Addiction, Vision, Energy: Political Economies and Utopian Visions in the Writings of the Beat Generation," *College Literature* 32, no. 2 (2005): 104.

71. Ibid.

72. Allen Ginsberg, *Journals: Early Fifties and Sixties*, ed. Gordon Ball (New York: Grove Press, 1977), 4.

73. Peyote is a type of small cactus native to southern Texas and Mexico. The tops or buttons of these cacti are harvested and then ground for consumption; it is also widely considered one of the safest natural hallucinogens (Dotinga). The drug is used in some branches of the Native American Church (NAC). When the drug is used in Native American religious practices, it is with the careful emotional support and safety of the other members of the church and not employed for mere recreational purposes. In fact, "non-religious consumption of peyote is considered by NAC members to be a very serious sacrilege" (Utter 152). This drug, harvested from the land, is another example of how the physical landscape is not compartmentalized out of many Native American religions but exists as a fully interwoven element.

74. Jeremy Isaacs, Interview with Allen Ginsberg, *Face to Face with Allen Ginsberg* (BBC Two, Face to Face, England), television program, 1995.

75. Allen Ginsberg, "Howl," *Collected Poems*, 136.

76. Jeremy Isaacs, Interview with Allen Ginsberg, *Face to Face with Allen Ginsberg* (BBC Two, Face to Face, England), television program, 1995.

77. The trickster (especially Coyote) is often referred to as a culture hero.

78. Jeremy Isaacs, Interview with Allen Ginsberg, *Face to Face with Allen Ginsberg* (BBC Two, Face to Face, England), television program, 1995.

79. Lewis Hyde, *Trickster Makes This World: Mischief, Myth, and Art* (New York: North Point, 1998), 301.

80. Dylan, a friend of Ginsberg's, well recognized and admired the employment of trickster humor and wisdom within Ginsberg's works.

81. Allen Ginsberg, "Howl," *Collected Poems*, 137.

82. Ibid.

83. Allen Ginsberg and Richard Eberhart, *To Eberhart from Ginsberg*, 12.

84. James Breslin, "Allen Ginsberg: The Origins of 'Howl' and 'Kaddish'" *The Iowa Review* 8, no. 2 (1977): 84–85.

85. Allen Ginsberg, "Howl," *Collected Poems*, 136, 139.

86. Allen Ginsberg, "Footnote to Howl," in *Collected Poems, 1947–1997*, 142.

87. These studies possibly helped lead Snyder into his work as an environmentalist, producing works such as his *Earth House Hold* (1969) and *A Place in Space: Ethics, Aesthetics, and Watersheds* (1995), which discusses not only his fascination with ecology but also the world's growing fascination with technology and how this reworks our typical ideas about environment and community.

88. This notion of becoming trapped by one's own ideas, biases, and misperceptions is not only reminiscent of the trickster Coyote's behavior in a variety of narratives but also of Ginsberg's appreciation for William

Blake in his poem "London": "In every cry of every Man, / In every Infant's cry of fear, / In every voice: in every ban, / The mind-forg'd manacles I hear."

89. Lawrence W. Gross, "The Comic Vision of Anishinaabe Culture and Religion" *American Indian Quarterly* 26, no. 3 (2002): 439.

90. John W. Bowers, Donovan J. Ochs, Richard J. Jensen, and David P. Schulz, *The Rhetoric of Agitation and Control* (Long Grove: Waveland, 2010), 10.

91. Mahadev L. Apte, "Humor," in *Folklore, Cultural Performances, and Popular Entertainments*, ed. Richard Bauman (New York: Oxford University Press, 1992), 75.

92. Briefly, a *regional religion* may be defined as "the religion of a relatively small and self-contained place within a larger political, social, and geographical unit [where] the common experience of the land merges with the history and interaction of peoples to yield a distinctive religious expression" (Albanese 346). Many Native American religions are inextricably tied up in their landscapes and physical environments. Many Native American tribes have specific myths and origin stories linking them physically to the land they traditionally inhabited. A Passamaquoddy creation story exemplifies this, describing how they originated from ash trees. The legendary Glooskap shot arrows into the ash trees and released the Passamaquoddy into the world, hence giving them an avenue for experiencing and celebrating a significant and spiritual connection to ash trees. This type of regionalism gives the land a deeply engrained sacredness to some Native American religions; this also makes the coerced uprooting and reservation exile of so many Native Americans especially despicable. This is particularly so, given, as Gross states in his "Cultural Sovereignty and Native American Hermeneutics in the Interpretations of the Sacred Stories of the Anishinaabe," that "it is a generally accepted proposition that there is little to no significant difference between the culture of a given Indian nation and its religion" (127).

93. Lawrence W. Gross, "The Comic Vision of Anishinaabe Culture and Religion," 437.

94 Ibid., 444–445.

95. Although, of course, Ginsberg's humor has since been recognized by many of the American literary and cultural establishment — after all, much of his work comes up under Amazon.com's heading: "Books, Humor & Entertainment, Allen Ginsberg."

96. Allen Ginsberg and Richard Eberhart, *To Eberhart from Ginsberg*, 11.

97. Stephen Prothero, "On the Holy Road: The Beat Movement as Spiritual Protest," *The Harvard Theological Review* 84, no. 2 (1991): 206.

98. Ibid.

99. Lawrence W. Gross, "The Comic Vision of Anishinaabe Culture and Religion," 452.

100. It is important to also not confuse Ginsberg's Judaism with his religious beliefs as his family and, at one time, he as well, were atheists (Ostriker 28).

101. Lawrence W. Gross, "The Comic Vision of Anishinaabe Culture and Religion," 439.

102. Jeanne Campbell Reesman, *Trickster Lives: Culture and Myth in American Fiction* (Athens: University of Georgia Press, 2001), 6.

103. Lawrence W. Gross, "The Comic Vision of Anishinaabe Culture and Religion," 446.

104. Ibid.

105. Jonah Raskin, *American Scream*, 5.

106. Ibid.

107. Anne Waldman, "Premises of Consciousness," in *The Poem That Changed America: "Howl" Fifty Years Later*, ed. Jason Shinder (New York: Farrar, Straus and Giroux, 2006), 269.

108. Ibid.

109. Nancy J. Peters, "Milestones of Literary Censorship," in *Howl on Trial: The Battle for Free Expression*, ed. Bill Morgan and Nancy J. Peters (San Francisco, CA: City Lights, 2006), 5.

110. Ibid., qtd. in Morgan and Peters, xi.

111. The "Roth standard" comes from the Supreme Court case *Roth v. United States* (1957). Book dealer Samuel Roth was "prosecuted in New York for distributing magazines [such] as *American Aphrodite*," a conviction upheld by the Supreme Court (Peters 11). It also provided the opportunity for Justice William J. Brennan, Jr., to decide "that obscenity was not protected by the First Amendment but that literature was" (Peters 11). This decision meant that "the test of obscenity now became 'whether to the average person, applying contemporary standards, the dominant theme of the material taken as a whole appeals to the prurient interest'"; it was decided just "two months before *Howl*

was tried," providing the ACLU with some meaty precedence at *Howl*'s trial (Peters 11).
112. Ibid., 11.
113. Ibid., qtd. in Morgan and Peters, 197.
114. Allen Ginsberg, *Howl, 50th Anniversary Edition: Original Draft Facsimile* (New York: Harper Perennial, 2006), 111.
115. Ibid.
116. (McWhorter qtd. in) Mourning Dove, *Coyote Stories* (Lincoln: University of Nebraska Press, 1990), 234.
117. Alanna Kathleen Brown, "The Evolution of Mourning Dove's Coyote Stories," *Studies in American Indian Literatures* 2, 4, no. 2/3 (1992): 161.
118. Ibid.
119. (McWhorter qtd. in) Mourning Dove, *Coyote Stories* (Lincoln: University of Nebraska Press, 1990), 233.
120. Ibid., 235.
121. Lawrence W. Gross, "The Comic Vision of Anishinaabe Culture and Religion," 447.
122. Ibid.

Chapter 2

1. Barry Holstun Lopez, *Giving Birth to Thunder, Sleeping with His Daughter: Coyote Builds North America* (New York: Avon Books, 1977), xv.
2. Franchot Ballinger and Gerald Vizenor, "Sacred Reversals: Trickster in Gerald Vizenor's *Earthdivers: Tribal Narratives on Mixed Descent*," *American Indian Quarterly* 9, no. 1 (1985): 55.
3. Gary Snyder, *The Old Ways* (San Francisco: City Lights, 1977), 67.
4. Ibid., 69.
5. "Definitions of Folklore," *Journal of Folklore Research* 33, no. 3 (1996): 256, 260, 261.
6. Alan Dundes, "The Study of Folklore in Literature and Culture: Identification and Interpretation," *The Journal of American Folklore* 78, no. 308 (1965): 136.
7. Barre Toelken, "The Yellowman Tapes, 1966–1997," *The Journal of American Folklore* 111, no. 442 (1998): 381.
8. Sharon R. Sherman, "Who Owns Culture and Who Decides? Ethics, Film Methodology, and Intangible Cultural Heritage Protection," *Western Folklore* 67, no. 2/3 (2008): 226.

9. Toelken also, ultimately, decided to destroy the audio recordings of Yellowman's narratives as well.
10. Ibid., 227.
11. Katrina Schimmoeller Peiffer, *Coyote at Large: Humor in American Nature Writing* (Salt Lake City: University of Utah Press, 2000), 5.
12. Daniel Morley Johnson, "(Re) Nationalizing Naanabozho: Anishinaabe Sacred Stories, Nationalist Literary Criticism, and Scholarly Responsibility," in *Troubling Tricksters: Revisioning Critical Conversations*, ed. Deanna Reder and Linda M. Morra, 199–220 (Waterloo: Wilfrid Laurier University Press, 2010), 202.
13. Gary Snyder, *The Old Ways* (San Francisco: City Lights, 1977), 69.
14. I utilize the term "whitestream" as it is defined within Daniel Morley Johnson's "(Re)Nationalizing Naanabozho": this term is used "when referring to the North American mainstream, in order to underscore the reality that the dominant/dominating culture (that is, the self-appointed 'mainstream') remains inextricably linked to whiteness" (Johnson 216).
15. Judith Leggatt, "Quincentennial Trickster Poetics: Lenore Keeshig-Tobias's 'Trickster Beyond 1992: Our Relationship' (1992) and Annhart Baker's 'Coyote Columbus Café' (1994)," in *Troubling Tricksters: Revisioning Critical Conversations*, ed. Deanna Reder and Linda M. Morra, 221–238 (Waterloo: Wilfrid Laurier University Press, 2010), 223.
16. Ibid.
17. Ibid.
18. Gerald Vizenor and A. Robert Lee, *Postindian Conversations* (Charlottesville: University of Nebraska Press, 1999), 90.
19. Heather Ponchetti Daly, "Fractured Relations at Home: The 1953 Termination Act's Effect on Tribal Relations throughout Southern California Indian Country," *American Indian Quarterly* 33, no. 4 (2009): 429.
20. Peter La Farge is a folksinger whose claim to Native ancestry proved false. He also worked with Johnny Cash and later went on with him to New York where they familiarized themselves with the Beat scene.
21. Antonino D'Ambrosio, *A Heartbeat and a Guitar* (New York: Nation Books, 2009), 26–27.
22. Troy Johnson, Duane Champagne, and Joane Nagel, "American Indian Activism and Transformation: Lessons from Alcatraz,"

in *Contemporary Native American Political Issues*, ed. Troy R. Johnson (Walnut Creek: AltaMira, 1999), 286.

23. Ibid., 29–30.

24. In the 1950s, most media associated the color lavender with homosexuality rather than the pink of today, as pink primarily connoted Communist sympathizing (Johnson 216).

25. The Mattachine Society was the "first national organization ... dedicated to bringing about social and political change for gay men and lesbians" (Streitmatter qtd. in Gross et al. 457).

26. Stephen J. Whitfield, *The Culture of the Cold War (The American Moment)* (Baltimore: Johns Hopkins University Press, 1991), 21.

27. Ibid., 22.

28. In 1924, Native Americans were granted U.S. citizenship through the Indian Veterans of World War I Act and the Snyder Act although this citizenship was only recognized on the national level as the U.S. Constitution "permitted franchisement on the state level to be determined at the discretion of the states" (Martin and Chiodo 2). This led to many Native Americans being denied citizenship at the state level, leaving them with varying levels of enfranchisement, a wound only salted by the fact that many of them had been forcibly reallocated to those same states now denying their rights to citizenship (Martin and Chiodo 2).

29. House Concurrent Resolution 108 (qtd. in) Antonino D'Ambrosio, *A Heartbeat and a Guitar* (New York: Nation Books, 2009), 30.

30. Jeffrey D. Schultz, Kerry Haynie, Anne McCulloch, and Andrew Aoki, "House Concurrent Resolution 108," in *Encyclopedia of Minorities in American Politics: Hispanics and Native Americans, Vol. 2* (Phoenix: Oryx, 2000), 629.

31. Nathan Brooks, *Indian Self-Determination and Education Assistance Act Contracts and* Cherokee Nation of Oklahoma v. Leavitt: *Agency Discretion to Fund Contract Support Costs* (Washington: UNT Digital Library. Web. February 25, 2011), 1.

32. Michael D. McNally, *Ojibwe Singers: Hymns, Grief, and a Native Culture in Motion* (New York: Oxford University Press, Inc., 2000), 45.

33. Hertha D. Sweent Wong, Lauren Stuart Muller, and Jana Sequoya Magdaleno, ed., *Reckonings: Contemporary Short Fiction by Native American Women* (New York: Oxford University Press, 2008), 103.

34. Ekkehart Malotki, *Gullible Coyote, Una'ihu: A Bilingual Collection of Hopi Coyote Stories* (Tucson: University of Arizona Press, 1985), 19.

35. Ibid., 8.

36. Ibid.

37. Ibid., 20.

38. Ibid., 11.

39. *Discover Navajo: The Official Navajo Nation Visitor Guide, Navajo Nation Tourism Department*, 2008. Accessed on 9 Aug. 2011, www.discovernavajo.com/.

40. Jay Miller, introduction to *Coyote Stories*, ed. Heister Dean Guie with notes by L.V. McWhorter (Lincoln: University of Nebraska Press, 1990), x.

41. Mourning Dove, *Coyote Stories*, ed. Heister Dean Guie (Lincoln: University of Nebraska Press, 1990), 7.

42. Paul Radin, *The Trickster: A Study in American Indian Mythology* (New York: Schocken, 1956), xxiii.

43. Lewis Hyde, *Trickster Makes This World: Mischief, Myth, and Art* (New York: North Point, 1998), 10, 19, 14.

44. Ibid., 11.

45. David Leeming and Jake Page, *The Mythology of Native North America* (Norman: University of Oklahoma Press, 1998), 47.

46. Ellen Rosenberg, "Native American Coyote Trickster Tales and Cycles," 157.

47. Vine Deloria Jr., *For This Land: Writings on Religion in America* (New York: Routledge, 1999), 132.

48. Ibid.

49. Barry Holstun Lopez, *Giving Birth to Thunder, Sleeping with His Daughter: Coyote Builds North America* (New York: Avon, 1977), xv.

50. Lewis Hyde, *Trickster Makes This World*, 8.

51. David M. Jones and Brian L. Molyneaux, *The Illustrated Encyclopedia of American Indian Mythologies*, 31.

52. David Leeming and Jake Page, *The Mythology of Native North America*, 46.

53. Ibid., 48.

54. Allen Ginsberg qtd. in Jonah Raskin, *American Scream*, xxii.

55. Gary Snyder, *Back on the Fire: Essays* (Berkeley: Counterpoint, 2007), 113.

56. Ibid.

57. Ibid.

58. Jonah Raskin, *American Scream*, xxii.

59. David Leeming and Jake Page, *The Mythology of Native North America*, 47.
60. Richard Erdoes and Alfonso Ortiz, *American Indian Trickster Tales: Myths and Legends* (New York: Viking, 1998), xiii–xiv.
61. Duane Niatum, *Harper's Anthology of Twentieth Century Native American Poetry* (New York: Harper & Row, 1988), xxix–xxx.
62. Ellen Rosenberg, "Native American Coyote Trickster Tales and Cycles," 157.
63. Ibid.
64. In many Native American cultures, all the different aspects of life and understanding are not compartmentalized and separated out, in the same way the broader, "mainstream" non–Native U.S. culture tends to do—separating science from religion, history from literature, art from math, health from happiness, etc. Instead, many Native American cultures strive to understand the world from a fully integrated perspective. Branching from this is the issue of labeling, such as the application of the label "sexualized" to these literatures and cultures. These tricksters and these myths are not "sexualized" but rather simply express no fear or shame in employing and discussing nature, sex, humor, humanness, and the supernatural altogether in order to practice culture, learn about and explain the world and peoples' place within themselves, their community, their environment, and the chaos of life.
65. William Bright, *A Coyote Reader* (Los Angeles: University of California Press, 1993), 20.
66. Ibid., 21.
67. Gary Snyder, *Back on the Fire*, 112.
68. Coyotes once lived primarily in the western regions of North America. But as more and more people have come to settle down in their native habitats, they have been forced to adapt and expand, spreading from the west to cover the eastern half of the country as well, making it all the way to Florida by the 1970s. This migration actually began in the 1960s, their own revolutionary march on and for America, their America. They can live and survive in almost every type of habitat except those most intensely urbanized (though there was a recent report of a coyote tromping through downtown Manhattan). They are able to figure out even the most elaborate traps and dangers, learn how to avoid them, and work around them for food and shelter. An incredibly savvy and independent hunter, they are still working up the rungs for their own American Dream, from poor victim to sweet beneficiary, often living off people's little toy dogs, cats, and garbage in areas where mice, rabbits, fruits, and foxes become too scarce. (Florida Fish and Wildlife Conservations Commission)
69. Mark Twain, *Roughing It*. 1886. (New York: New American Library, 1962), 49.
70. Gary Snyder, *Back on the Fire*, 114.
71. Barbara G. Schutz-Gruber and Barbara Frates Buckley, *Trickster Tales from Around the World: An Interdisciplinary Guide for Teachers* (Michigan: Schutz-Gruber, 1991), 3.
72. Ibid.
73. John J. Miller, *The General Grubbiness of Allen Ginsberg* (The National Review Online. 14 Sept. 2006. Web. 4 July 2011), http://www.nationalreview.com/articles/218704/general-grubbiness-allen-ginsberg/john-j-miller.
74. James Breslin, "Allen Ginsberg: The Origins of 'Howl' and 'Kaddish'," *The Iowa Review* 8, no. 2 (1977): 83.
75. Oliver Harris, "Beating the Academy," *College Literature* 27, no. 1 (2000): 213–214.
76. Allen Ginsberg, "Howl," *Collected Poems*, 134.
77. Oliver Harris, "Beating the Academy," 221.
78. Mourning Dove, *Coyote Stories* ed. Heister Dean Guie (Lincoln: University of Nebraska Press, 1990), 7.
79. For each Native narrative discussed, I present the related tribe, translator, and authors whenever possible in order to help situate each new telling and to recognize the multiple stakeholders and voices involved.
80. Chief Eaglewing, *Peek-Wa Stories: Indian Legends of California* (San Francisco: Mercury, 1938), 18.
81. Ibid.
82. Ibid.
83. Ibid.
84. Ibid., 19.
85. Evan T. Pritchard (retold and annotated by), *Native American Stories of the Sacred: Annotated and Explained* (Woodstock: Skylight Paths, 2009), 195.
86. Ibid.
87. Ibid.
88. Allen Ginsberg and Gary Snyder, *The Selected Letters of Allen Ginsberg and Gary Snyder*, 195.
89. Ibid.
90. Roland B. Dixon, "Some Coyote Stories from the Maidu Indians of California," *The Journal of American Folklore* 13, no. 51 (1900): 267–268.

Notes. Chapter 2

91. This development ultimately aided in the dismantling of much of the Maidu lifestyle and land — a fact that has been recently recognized by the Tibetan monks of the Gaden Shartse Monastery who, in the summer of 2009, met with members of the Tsi-Akim Maidu to share "an evening of culture" given the many similarities they see and feel existing between their communities (Baumgart, "Tibetan Monks"). Joseph Guida, who represented the Sierra Friends of Tibet, explained, "The California Gold Rush era"— 50 years prior to the C.P. Expedition —"and other events devastated the ... way of life of the [Tsi-Akim Maidu] tribe" (Baumgart, "Tibetan Monks"). The anthropologists who came to the Maidu of the higher Sierra (the Tsi-Akim are of the Foothills, not higher Sierra) during the 1899 expedition were meeting the Maidu fresh from the choking grips of the gold rush. Therefore, this history as well as the various prejudices and stereotypes against Native Americans at the time and the Maidu's unique relationship to Coyote ought to be born in mind when considering these versions of the narratives.

92. "Driving the Last Spike," *The Virtual Museum of the City of San Francisco*, accessed March 10, 2012, http://www.sfmuseum.org/hist1/rail.html.

93. I believe the translation provided here is in fact a preview or early release from this later 1912 publication (as this story is documented by the American Folklore Society's *Journal of American Folklore* as being originally published in 1900) as it was derived from the same expedition (namely, the Huntington Expedition) and was released upon permission of the Trustees of the American Museum of Natural History in New York (who were also responsible for sending the group of scholars and scientists on the C.P. Huntington Expedition in the first place). Thus, there is some confusion and discrepancies between publication dates offered as the documents provided by the *Journal of American Folklore* gives the date 1900 (with the expedition taking place during the summer of 1899), while William Shipley dates the expedition as taking place during 1902 and 1903 (Shipley 2).

94. William Shipley, "Introduction," in *The Maidu Indian Myths and Stories of Hanc'ibyjim*, ed. and trans. by William Shipley (Berkeley: Heyday Books, 1991), 3.

95. Jewell worked with several members of the Concow Maidu tribe, including Bryan Beavers and Frank Day, in order to write his work. And while he spells the tribe's name as "Concow," the tribal name is also spelled "Konkow."

96. Donald P. Jewell, *Indians of the Feather River*, 166.

97. Of course, this is also a part of the culture of the Maidu of the Foothills rather than of strictly the higher Sierra region and is a part that has been at least two times removed interpretively from the Concow Maidu themselves as it has been first interpreted from the words of various Maidu tribal members by Jewell and whose work, in turn, has thus been reinterpreted by myself.

98. Donald P. Jewell, *Indians of the Feather River*, 166.

99. The acronym NAGPRA refers to the Native American Graves Protection and Repatriation Act.

100. Eric Josephson, e-mail message to author, March 22, 2012.

101. Ibid.

102. Ibid.

103. Coyote Man received the Maidu narratives in the 1960s from Tom Epperson who "became an experienced singer and ceremonialist, a fixture at traditional bear dances in Indian Valley and Jaynesville" and whose "knowledge of Maidu oral literature was extensive" as he was also a "fluent speaker of the Maidu language" (Bibby and Aguilar 5).

104. Eric Josephson, e-mail message to author, March 25, 2012.

105. Ibid.

106. Roland B. Dixon, "Some Coyote Stories from the Maidu Indians of California," *The Journal of American Folklore* 13, no. 51 (1900):267.

107. The grant Ginsberg refers to here is most likely from the Committee on Poetry (COP), which was "a non-profit organization" Ginsberg founded and used to distribute grants to "writers and friends down on their luck" (Bill Morgan, 434, *An Accidental Autobiography*).

108. Allen Ginsberg and Gary Snyder, *The Selected Letters of Allen Ginsberg and Gary Snyder*, 194–195.

109. Bill Morgan, "Footnote no. 261," in *An Accidental Autobiography: The Selected Letters of Gregory Corso*, ed. Bill Morgan (New York: New Directions, 2003), 434.

110. Gregory Corso, *An Accidental Autobiography: The Selected Letters of Gregory Corso*, ed. Bill Morgan (New York: New Directions, 2003), 406, 407.

Notes. Chapter 2

111. Roland B. Dixon, "Some Coyote Stories from the Maidu Indians of California," *The Journal of American Folklore* 13, no. 51 (1900): 267–268.
112. Evan T. Pritchard (retold and annotated by), *Native American Stories of the Sacred: Annotated and Explained* (Woodstock: Skylight Paths, 2009), 164.
113. Ibid.
114. Roland B. Dixon, "Some Coyote Stories from the Maidu Indians of California," 268.
115. Ibid.
116. Lawrence Aripa, "Coeur d'Alene: Story: Coyote's Identity," *Lifelong Learning Online: The Lewis & Clark Rediscovery Project*, last modified 2002, http://l3.trailtribes.org/ShowOneObjectSiteID50ObjectID693.html.
117. Ibid.
118. Bingo, SiJohn, "Coeur d'Alene: Story: Coyote and the White Man," *Lifelong Learning Online: The Lewis & Clark Rediscovery Project*, last modified 2002, http://l3.trailtribes.org/ShowOneObjectSiteID50ObjectID438.html. Part I: http://l3.trailtribes.org/Sites/ShowOneContentFilenameBingoCoyoteandMan1txt.html.
119. Ibid.
120. Ibid.
121. Ibid. Part II: http://l3.trailtribes.org/Sites/ShowOneContentFilenameBingoCoyoteandMan2txt.html.
122. Ibid.
123. Ibid.
124. Gary Snyder, *The Back Country*, 3.
125. Ibid., 7.
126. William Bright, *A Coyote Reader* (Los Angeles: University of California Press, 1993), 18.
127. Peter Blue Cloud, "Talking with the Past," in *Survival This Way: Interviews with American Indian Poets*, ed. and interviewed by Joseph Bruchac (Tuscon: Sun Tracks and University of Arizona Press, 1987), 30–31.
128. Peter Blue Cloud, "Coyote's Anthro," in *Elderberry Flute Song: Contemporary Coyote Tales* (Buffalo: White Pine, 2002), 117.
129. Ibid., 119.
130. Ibid., 120.
131. Ibid.
132. Barry Holstun Lopez, *Giving Birth to Thunder, Sleeping with His Daughter: Coyote Builds North America* (New York: Avon, 1977).
133. Ibid.
134. Ibid., 92–93.
135. Ibid., 93.
136. Ibid., 88.
137. Ibid.
138. Ibid., 89.
139. Ibid.
140. It should be noted that Opler's work does not really account for the major cultural and community changes impacting the Jicarilla Apache during the 1930s and that the bulk of his work and interpretation is based almost solely upon individual testimonies (he utilized translators) rather than upon testimony and significant observation/ethnographic study. He worked during a time when it wasn't necessary or even expected for an anthropologist to give credit or reference to those he or she consulted, interviewed, and collaborated with. Nor did he work during a time when Native opinions concerning the final product of such research mattered to the anthropological discipline. These should all be kept in mind when considering his interpretation of the relationship between the Jicarilla Apache and Coyote. (See the Introduction to Opler's *Myths and Tales of the Jicarilla Apache Indians* for more details on these matters.) Morris Edward Opler, *Myths and Tales of the Jicarilla Apache* (Lincoln: University of Nebraska Press, 1994), 263. Originally published by the American Folk-Lore Society in 1938.
141. Ibid.
142. Tom Robbins, "In Defiance of Gravity," *Harper's Magazine*, September 2004, 58.
143. Ibid.
144. Ibid.
145. Ibid.
146. Richard Erdoes and Alfonso Ortiz, *American Indian Trickster Tales: Myths and Legends* (New York: Viking, 1998), 34.
147. Ibid.
148. Ibid.
149. Ibid.
150. Ibid.
151. Ibid., 35.
152. Ibid.
153. Ibid.
154. Ibid., 36.
155. Ibid., 35.
156. Lewis Hyde, *Trickster Makes This World: Mischief, Myth, and Art* (New York: North Point Press, 1998), 8.
157. However, there are many stories in which Coyote does have at least one son. He presumably had this son with his wife, Mole. There are other stories, such as "Coyote Mar-

ries a Man" and "Coyote Makes Human Beings" (provided by Barry Lopez in *Giving Birth to Thunder*) wherein Coyote produces offspring. Nevertheless, given the rarity of this as well as Coyote's apparent ability to control when he does or does not impregnate a sexual partner, it seems fair to agree with Hyde that, despite certain outliers, Coyote's extramarital affairs are, typically, sexual without being procreational.

158. The name "Crow" is actually a mistranslation by non–Natives from the actual tribal name, Apsáalooke, which means "children of the large-beaked bird" (Crow Nation, Our Mother Tongues).

159. Rodney Frey, *The World of the Crow Indians: As Driftwood Lodges* (Norman: University of Oklahoma Press, 1987), 8, 67.

160. Fred W. Voget, introduction to *Old Man Coyote (Crow): The Authorized Edition*, Frank B. Linderman (Lincoln: University of Nebraska Press, 1996), 2.

161. Ibid., 3–4.
162. Ibid., 3.
163. Ibid., 4.
164. Barry Holstun Lopez, *Giving Birth to Thunder, Sleeping with His Daughter: Coyote Builds North America* (New York: Avon, 1977), 69.
165. Ibid.
166. Ibid.
167. Ibid.
168. Ibid.
169. Ibid.
170. Ibid.
171. Ibid., 170.
172. Ibid., 170–171.
173. Ibid.
174. Ibid., 170–171
175. Ibid., 171.
176. Ibid.
177. Ibid.
178. Ibid.
179. Ibid.
180. Ibid.
181. Ibid.
182. Richard Erdoes and Alfonso Ortiz, *American Indian Trickster Tales*, 12.
183. Frank Lapena, *Legends of the Yosemite Miwok* (Yosemite, CA: Yosemite Association, 2007), 5.
184. Ibid., 7.
185. Ibid.
186. Ibid., 8.
187. Simon J. Ortiz, "Review: *Coyote Tales from the Indian Pueblos* by Evelyn Dahl Reed; *The Other Side of Nowhere: Contemporary Coyote Tales* by Peter Blue Cloud (Arpmoawentate)," *American Indian Quarterly* 16, no. 4 (1992), 599.

188. Ibid.

189. Kimberly M. Blaeser, "Gerald Vizenor," *The Cambridge Companion to Native American Literature*, ed. Joy Porter and Kenneth Roemer (Cambridge University Press, 2005), 262.

Chapter 3

1. Gordon Ball, "Reader's Guide — Biographical Note: The Decade Preceding These Journals," in Allen Ginsberg's *Journals: Early Fifties, Early Sixties*, ed. Ball (New York: Grove, 1977), xiv.

2. Ibid.

3. Allen Ginsberg and Jack Kerouac, *Jack Kerouac and Allen Ginsberg: The Letters* (New York: Viking, 2011), 39.

4. Allen Ginsberg and George Plimpton, "Allen Ginsberg," in *Writers at Work: The Paris Review Interviews*, ed. George Plimpton (New York: Viking, 1967), 291.

5. Allen Ginsberg and Jack Kerouac, *Jack Kerouac and Allen Ginsberg: The Letters* (New York: Viking, 2011), 39.

6. Terrie Waddell, *Wild/Lives: Trickster, Place, and Liminality on Screen* (New York: Routledge, 2010), xiii.

7. Allen Ginsberg, "Howl," *Collected Poems*, 134, 138, 139.

8. Anne Doueihi, "Inhabiting the Space Between Discourse and Story in Trickster Narratives," in *Mythical Trickster Figures: Contours, Contexts, and Criticisms*, ed. William J. Hynes and William G. Doty (London: University of Alabama Press, 1993), 201.

9. These are the definitions utilized by Doueihi in her examination of the trickster's liminal existence between discourse and story. However, I continue to utilize the term "narrative" rather than these terms in order to maintain as clear and simple an understanding as possible, considering the multiple levels, variances, and transformations Coyote and trickster narratives have undergone over the centuries, moving between cultures, communities, and eras, between orality and the written word to form discourses, stories, myths, sacred texts, cartoons, vignettes, and all manner of other forms and interpretations of narratives. In order to further manage my complexity, I have chosen not to attempt to retrace this

fluid history but to classify these as "narratives" in order to be both as precise and all-encompassing as possible.

10. Jonathan Culler, *The Pursuit of Signs: Semiotics, Literature, Deconstruction* (London: Routledge, 1981), 189.

11. Allen Ginsberg, "Howl," *Collected Poems*, 139.

12. Anne Doueihi, "Inhabiting the Space Between Discourse and Story in Trickster Narratives," 197, 198.

13. Ibid.
14. Ibid.
15. Ibid.
16. Ibid.

17. Stephen Prothero, "On the Holy Road: The Beat Movement as Spiritual Protest," 210–211.

18. Ibid.

19. Arnold Van Gennep, *The Rites of Passage*, trans. Monika B. Vizedom and Gabrielle L. Caffee (Chicago: University of Chicago Press, 1960), 11.

20. Dennis Tedlock, "Ethnopoetics," in *Folklore, Cultural Performances, and Popular Entertainments* ed. Richard Bauman (New York: Oxford University Press, 1992), 82.

21. Victor Turner, *The Ritual Process: Structure and Anti-Structure* (New Brunswick: Aldine Transaction, 1969), 95.

22. Barbara Babcock-Abrahams, "'A Tolerated Margin of Mess': The Trickster and His Tales Reconsidered," *Journal of the Folklore Institute* 11, no. 3 (1975): 150.

23. Ibid., 150–151.

24. Devin Proctor, "Not Elf, *Not* Not Elf: Ritual and Mimesis in the Liminal Video Game Space of *Oblivion*" (master's article, George Washington University, 2011), 5.

25. Ibid., 9. (The quote is a reference to R. Schechner's *Between Theatre and Anthropology*.)

26. Yi-Fu Tuan and Steven Hoelscher, *Space and Place: The Perspective of Experience* (Minneapolis: University of Minnesota Press, 1977), 6.

27. Tim Cresswell interestingly expands upon this notion of "naming" as place creation from space within his, *Place: A Short Introduction*.

28. Yi-Fu Tuan and Steven Hoelscher, *Space and Place: The Perspective of Experience*, 6.

29. Terrie Waddell, *Wild/Lives: Trickster, Place, and Liminality on Screen* (New York: Routledge, 2010), xiii.

30. Graham Allen, *Intertextuality: The New Critical Idiom* (New York: Routledge, 2000), 1.

31. Karl Kerenyi qtd. in Paul Radin, *The Trickster: A Study in American Indian Mythology*, 185.

32. Franca Bellarsi, "Proxemics and Poetic Discourse: Spatial Relationships in the Work of Allen Ginsberg," (Barcelona: Proceedings of the 20th International AEDEAN Conference, 1996), 371.

33. Ibid.

34. Allen Ginsberg, "Howl," *Collected Poems*, 139.

35. Allen Ginsberg, *Howl, 50th Anniversary Edition: Original Draft Facsimile* (New York: Harper Perennial, 2006), 57.

36. Allen Ginsberg qtd. in Allen Ginsberg and George Plimpton, "Allen Ginsberg," 320.

37. Thomas Clark qtd. in Allen Ginsberg and George Plimpton, "Allen Ginsberg," 281.

38. Anne Waldman, "Premises of Consciousness," in *The Poem That Changed America: "Howl" Fifty Years Later*, ed. Jason Shinder (New York: Farrar, Straus and Giroux, 2006), 268.

39. Ibid.
40. Ibid.

41. Christine Teresa Mazur, "Gothic Fiction, Liminality, and Popular Culture: Stephen King's Grotesque Social Commentary in '*Salem's Lot*" (master's thesis, University of Manitoba, 1997), 5.

42. Ibid.
43. Ibid.
44. Ibid.
45. Ibid.

46. Allen Ginsberg and Richard Eberhart, *To Eberhart from Ginsberg*, 18.

47. Allen Ginsberg, "Notes Written on Finally Recording 'Howl'" in *Deliberate Prose*, ed. Bill Morgan (New York: HarperCollins, 2000), 229.

48. Michael McClure, *Scratching the Beat Surface* (San Francisco: North Point, 1982), 13.

49. Ginsberg actually references Gary Snyder's *The Old Ways* within his annotations in the 50th Anniversary Edition of "Howl" in order to explain that within "Howl" he does actually and intentionally reference the concept of Native American vision quests, discussing them as a sign of reaching the post-liminal stage of life and that Snyder, through texts such as *The Old Ways*, attempted to take such traditions upon himself (Ginsberg, *50th Anniversary Edition*, 4, 128).

50. Allen Ginsberg, "Howl," *Collected Poems*, 136, 139.
51. Kenneth Lincoln, *Sing with the Heart of a Bear: Fusions of Native American Poetry: 1890–1999* (Berkeley: University of California Press, 2000), 124–125.
52. Ibid., 126.
53. Gary Snyder and Allen Ginsberg, *The Selected Letters of Allen Ginsberg and Gary Snyder*, 9.
54. Gerald Vizenor, *Interior Landscapes: Autobiographical Myths and Metaphors* (Minneapolis: University of Minnesota Press, 1990), 130.
55. Tim Cresswell, *Place: A Short Introduction* (Malden: Blackwell, 2004), 11.
56. This Latin phrase translates to "Father Omnipotent Eternal God."
57. Allen Ginsberg, "Howl," *Collected Poems*, 138–139.
58. Paul Portugés, "Allen Ginsberg's Paul Cézanne and the Pater Omnipotens Aeterna Deus," *Contemporary Literature* (1980): 441.
59. Ibid.
60. Ibid., 442.
61. Allen Ginsberg, "Howl," *Collected Poems*, 137.
62. Michael Castro, *Interpreting the Indian: Twentieth-Century Poets and the Native American* (Albuquerque: University of New Mexico Press, 1983), 55.
63. Ibid.
64. For further reference, see articles like Barbra A. Meek's "And the Injun goes 'How!': Representations of American Indian English in white public space," as was briefly discussed in the Introduction here.
65. Allen Ginsberg, *Howl and Other Poems*, 16–17.
66. Allen Ginsberg, *Howl, 50th Anniversary Edition: Original Draft Facsimile* (New York: Harper Perennial, 2006), 129.
67. Mahadev L. Apte, "Humor," in *Folklore, Cultural Performances, and Popular Entertainments*, ed. Richard Bauman (New York: Oxford University Press, 1992), 70.
68. Allen Ginsberg, *Howl, 50th Anniversary Edition: Original Draft Facsimile*, 129.
69. Gary Snyder, *The Old Ways* (San Francisco: City Lights Books, 1977), 71.
70. Webster Lardner Kitchell worked primarily as "minister emeritus of the Unitarian Universalist Congregation of Santa Fe" and utilized Coyote constantly within his sermons, personalizing Coyote as a "fictitious partner whom he met at doughnut shops to discuss current events, matters of theology, and the wonders of life" (The Rivera Family of Santa Fe Funeral Options).
71. Webster Kitchell, *God's Dog: Conversations with Coyote* (Boston: Skinner House, 1991), 84.
72. Allen Ginsberg, "Howl," *Collected Poems*, 135.
73. Allen Ginsberg, *Howl, 50th Anniversary Edition: Original Draft Facsimile*, 135.
74. Hart Crane, "The Bridge," in *Howl, 50th Anniversary Edition: Original Draft Facsimile*, ed. Barry Miles (New York: Harper Perennial, 2006), 135.
75. Stephen M. Llano, "Beating Rhetoric: Rhetorical Theory in the Beat Generation" (doctoral dissertation, University of Pittsburgh, 2009), 311.
76. Allen Ginsberg, "Howl," *Collected Poems*, 134.
77. Stephen M. Llano, "Beating Rhetoric: Rhetorical Theory in the Beat Generation," 317.
78. Lewis Hyde, *Trickster Makes This World: Mischief, Myth, and Art* (New York: North Point Press, 1998), 153.
79. Ibid., 157.

Chapter 4

1. Andrei Codrescu, "'Howl' in Transylvania," in *The Poem That Changed America: "Howl" Fifty Years Later*, ed. Jason Shinder (New York: Farrar, Straus and Giroux Paperbacks, 2006), 54–55.
2. Ibid.
3. The word choice in "hysterical" was actually originally "mystical," and was changed because, though Ginsberg had at first considered the poem to have an "idealistic impulse," he came to recognize that "Howl" more truly followed the hysteric than the "mystic" connoted (Ginsberg 124, *50th Anniversary Edition*). As he explains, the choice of "hysterical" was meant to encapsulate that negative capability between being "judicious" while remaining "overtly sympathetic" (Ginsberg 124, *50th Anniversary Edition*). In this way, Ginsberg was able to keep "Howl" focused and considerate as well as full of "comic realism" and "humorous hyperbole" (Ginsberg, 124, *50th Anniversary Edition*).
4. Allen Ginsberg, "Howl," *Collected Poems*, 134.
5. Ibid.
6. "Places" means "stanzas" here as well

as hearkens back to *Space, Place, and Traversing Boundaries*.

7. Allen Ginsberg, "Howl," *Collected Poems*, 134.

8. Ibid.

9. Allen Ginsberg, *Howl, 50th Anniversary Edition: Original Draft Facsimile*, 125.

10. Ibid.

11. Here this phrase, "cock and endless balls," is another rhetorical choice with various meanings, one being to "have a ball" (Ginsberg, 125, Original Draft Facsimile).

12. Allen Ginsberg, "Howl," *Collected Poems*, 134.

13. Ibid.

14. Ibid.

15. *Satori* is a Zen Buddhist term for a sort of spiritual enlightenment or sudden revelation. According to Kimberley Blaeser's *Gerald Vizenor: Writing in Oral Tradition*, satori may be "artistically expressed" in art or poetry that manage to "create not a work of art but a work of life," something that does not mimic but "attempts to ... point to 'the presence in us of a mystery that is beyond intellectual analysis'" (118).

16. "Jazz" functions as a symbol, an appetite for free expression and improvisation.

17. The phrase, "no crime but their / own wild cooking pederasty and intoxication," relates also to the earlier mentions of criminality and sexual desire.

18. It is a spelling Ginsberg invented; "gyzym" simply means jism, climax, ejaculate, cum, or orgasm.

19. Allen Ginsberg, "Howl," *Collected Poems*, 135, 136.

20. This particular narrative will be expanded upon within *Smearing Borderlines*.

21. Allen Ginsberg, "Thoughts on NAMBLA" in *Deliberate Prose*, ed. Bill Morgan (New York: HarperCollins, 2000), 170.

22. Allen Ginsberg, "Thoughts on NAMBLA" in *Deliberate Prose*, 171.

23. Cannastra was certainly a site of horror for Ginsberg (despite Ginsberg's appreciation for him as he served almost as an early, even wilder Neal Cassady) as he ended up beheading himself one night (not in the company of Ginsberg but of Jack Kerouac and a couple of other Beats) while moving from party to party and playing one too many games on the subway. He was also known to play games such as "see who can hold their head in the oven with the gas on the longest"—a truly wild and reckless "best mind" if ever there was one (Ginsberg, Original Draft Facsimile).

24. Allen Ginsberg, *Howl, 50th Anniversary Edition: Original Draft Facsimile* (New York: Harper Perennial, 2006).

25. Allen Ginsberg, "Howl," *Collected Poems*, 137, 139.

26. Richard Erdoes and Alfonso Ortiz, *American Indian Trickster Tales*, 12.

27. Allen Ginsberg, "Howl," *Collected Poems*, 139.

28. Ibid.

29. Ibid., 139–140.

30. Ibid., 139.

31. Rockland County is the location of an institution for mental patients and ex-convicts called Hope Hall that went up around 1906; it is not the institution where Ginsberg and Solomon met but stands as a clear symbol nonetheless.

Chapter 5

1. Lewis Hyde, *Trickster Makes This World: Mischief, Myth, and Art* (New York: North Point Press, 1998), 2.

2. Allen Ginsberg, "Howl," *Collected Poems*, 135.

3. Ibid.

4. Ibid., 137.

5. A.L Kroeber and E.W. Gifford, *Karok Myths*, ed. Grace Buzaljko, informant Mary Ike (Berkeley: University of California Press, 1980). In fact, A.L. Kroeber and E.W. Gifford's *Karok Myths* actually provides the version wherein Coyote attempts to prop his eyes open with sticks in order to get the best bow. Thus, my retelling of this particular story should be understood as more mine than theirs, representing a piecemeal that, to the best of my ability, remains true to the basic construction, point, and plot devices of the story, though with some details changed according to what I also found in a variety of other translations.

6. Allen Ginsberg, "Howl," *Collected Poems*, 137.

7. Roland B. Dixon, *Maidu Myths* (Whitefish: Kessinger Publishing, 2006), 44. Extracted from the Bulletin of the American Museum of Natural History.

8. Ibid.

9. Allen Ginsberg, "Howl," *Collected Poems*, 139.

10. Mark Doty, "Human Seraphim:

'Howl,' Sex, and Holiness," in *The Poem That Changed America: "Howl" Fifty Years Later*, ed. Jason Shinder (New York: Farrar, Straus and Giroux, 2006), 15.

11. Allen Ginsberg, "Howl," *Collected Poems*, 140–141.

12. Ibid., 141.

Chapter 6

1. Jonah Raskin, *American Scream*, xx.

2. Allen Ginsberg, "Howl," *Collected Poems*, 134.

3. Ibid.

4. David Turnbull, *Masons, Tricksters, and Cartographers: Makers of Knowledge and Space* (Amsterdam: Overseas Publishers Association, 2000), 91.

5. Regina Marler, ed., *Queer Beats: How the Beats Turned American on to Sex* (San Francisco: Cleis, 2004), xv.

6. Jack Utter, *American Indians: Answers to Today's Questions, 2nd Ed.* (Norman: University of Oklahoma Press, 2001), 147.

7. Ibid.

8. Ibid.

9. Ellen Rosenberg, "Native American Coyote Trickster Tales and Cycles," 157.

10. For more information on these sorts of issues, see Amanda E. Lewis' *Race in the Schoolyard: Negotiating the Color Line in Classrooms and Communities.*

11. Allen Ginsberg, "Howl," *Collected Poems*, 134.

12. Ibid. 134, 139

13. Ibid., 134.

14. Henri Lefebvre qtd. in Edward W. Soja, *Thirdspace: Journeys to Los Angeles and Other Real-and-Imagined Places* (Cambridge: Blackwell, 1996), 146.

15. Stephen King, *Just After Sunset* (New York: Pocket Books, 2009), 287.

16. Kenneth Lincoln, *Sing with the Heart of a Bear: Fusions of Native American Poetry: 1890–1999* (Berkeley: University of California Press, 2000), 129.

17. Jarold Ramsey qtd. in Ellen Rosenberg, "Native American Coyote Trickster Tales and Cycles," 162.

18. Kenneth Lincoln, *Sing with the Heart of a Bear*, 129.

19. Allen Ginsberg, "Howl," *Collected Poems*, 135.

20. This mischief may be observed through examples not only found in "Howl" but in other contemporaries of Ginsberg such as the prolific poet Bob Dylan with songs like his "Freight Train Blues." Here we find another example of how the engines meant for progress, meant for plowing through borderlines, often end up creating more and more boundaries; they become trapped by their own tracks. It's especially trickster-poignant with the mention of his "rambling shoes," which implies that, like Coyote in his tale with Skunk, he already had precisely what he wanted — means of travel in this case (meat in Coyote's) — but was done in by his lust for the prospect of more and ended up with nothing, ended up precisely where he started.

21. Allen Ginsberg, "Howl," *Collected Poems*, 139.

22. Ibid., 139–140.

23. Ibid., 140

24. Ibid.

25. Ibid.

26. Ibid., 141.

Chapter 7

1. Russ McDonald, "The Language of Tragedy," *The Cambridge Companion to Shakespearean Tragedy,* ed. Claire McEachern (Cambridge: Cambridge University Press, 2002), 24.

2. Gerald Vizenor, *Earthdivers: Tribal Narratives on Mixed Descent* (Minneapolis: University of Minnesota Press, 1981), ix.

3. Allen Ginsberg, "Howl," *Collected Poems*, 134.

4. Although, I must add, the beautiful thing about these fearful transformations, something Ginsberg gets to more in his "Footnote" than in the body of his "Howl," is that their power to transform in the opposite direction to holier, wiser, and more loving remains and can only be highlighted by the — pray for it — *temporary* slippage into the muck and the grim, the devilish curl of the trickster grin.

5. Allen Ginsberg, "Howl," *Collected Poems*, 138.

6. Ibid., 138–139.

7. Paul Portugés, "Allen Ginsberg's Paul Cézanne and the Pater Omnipotens Aeterna Deus," 441.

8. Richard Erdoes and Alfonso Ortiz, *American Indian Trickster Tales*, 36.

9. Allen Ginsberg, "Howl," *Collected Poems*, 139.

10. Ibid., 140–141.
11. Ibid., 141.
12. Roland B. Dixon, *Maidu Myths* (Whitefish: Kessinger, 2006). Extracted from the Bulletin of the American Museum of Natural History.
13. Allen Ginsberg, "Howl," *Collected Poems*, 141.

Epilogue

1. Franca Bellarsi, "Proxemics and Poetic Discourse: Spatial Relationships in the Work of Allen Ginsberg," (Barcelona: Proceedings of the 20th International AEDEAN Conference, 1996), 375.
2. Stephen Prothero, "On the Holy Road: The Beat Movement as Spiritual Protest," 208.
3. Nancy M. Grace, "Seeking the Spirit of Beat: The Call for Interdisciplinary Scholarship," *Contemporary Literature* 43, no. 4 (2002): 818.
4. Carl Waldman, *The Dictionary of Native American Terminology* (New York: Castle, 2009), 136.

Bibliography

Albanese, Catherine L. "Exploring Regional Religion: A Case Study of the Eastern Cherokee." *History of Religions* 23, no. 4 (1984): 344–371. http://www.jstor.org.proxygw.wrlc.org/stable/1062645.
Allen, Graham. *Intertextuality: The New Critical Idiom*. New York: Routledge, 2000.
Ammons, Elizabeth. Introduction to *Tricksterism in Turn-of-the-Century American Literature: A Multicultural Perspective*. Edited by Elizabeth Ammons and Annette White-Parks. Hanover: University Press of New England, 1994.
Apte, Mahadev L. "Humor." In *Folklore, Cultural Performances, and Popular Entertainments*, edited by Richard Bauman, 67–75. New York: Oxford University Press, 1992.
Aripa, Lawrence. "Coeur d'Alene: Story: Coyote's Identity." *Lifelong Learning Online: The Lewis & Clark Rediscovery Project*, in collaboration with the *Coeur D'Alene Tribe*. Last modified 2002. http://www.webpages.uidaho.edu/L3/ShowOneObjectSiteID50ObjectID693.html.
Babcock-Abrahams, Barbara. "'A Tolerated Margin of Mess': The Trickster and His Tales Reconsidered."*Journal of the Folklore Institute* 11, no. 3 (1975): 147–186. http://www.jstor.org.proxygw.wrlc.org/stable/3813932.
Ballinger, Franchot, and Gerald Vizenor. "Sacred Reversals: Trickster in Gerald Vizenor's 'Earthdivers: Tribal Narratives on Mixed Descent.'" *American Indian Quarterly* 9, no. 1 (1985): 55–59. http://www.jstor.org.proxygw.wrlc.org/stable/1184653.
Baumgart, Don. "Tibetan monks, Maidu Native Americans celebrate similar cultural experiences." *Indian Country Today*, July 8, 2009. Accessed through *The Buddhist Channel*. Accessed February 27, 2013. http://www.buddhistchannel.tv/index.php?id=65,8351,0,0,1,0.
Bednar, Robert. Discussion with author. Fall 2010.
Bellarsi, Franca. "Proxemics and Poetic Discourse: Spatial Relationships in the Work of Allen Ginsberg." Proceedings of the 20th International AEDEAN Conference, Barcelona, 1996. 371–375.
Bibby, Brian, and photography by Dugan Aguilar. *Deeper Than Gold: A Guide to Indian Life in the Sierra Foothills*. Berkeley: Heyday Books, 2005.
Blaeser, Kimberly M. "Gerald Vizenor: postindian liberation." In *The Cambridge Companion to Native American Literature*, edited by Joy Porter and Kenneth Roemer, 257–271. Cambridge: Cambridge University Press, 2005.
Blake, William. "London." *The Poetry Foundation*. Last modified 2013. Accessed on 15 Oct. 2012. http://www.poetryfoundation.org/poem/172929 .
Blue Cloud, Peter. "Coyote's Anthro." In *Elderberry Flute Song: Contemporary Coyote Tales*, 117–120. Buffalo: White Pine Press, 2002.
———. "Talking with the Past." In *Survival This Way: Interviews with American Indian Poets*, edited and interviewed by Joseph Bruchac, 23–42. Tucson: Sun Tracks and University of Arizona Press, 1987.

Bibliography

Bowers, John W., Donovan J. Ochs, Richard J. Jensen, and David P. Schulz. *The Rhetoric of Agitation and Control, 3rd Edition*. Long Grove: Waveland Press, 2010.

Breslin, James. "Allen Ginsberg: The Origins of 'Howl' and 'Kaddish.'" *Iowa Review* 8, no. 2 (1977): 82–108. http://www.jstor.org.proxygw.wrlc.org/stable/20158746.

Bright, William. *A Coyote Reader*. Berkeley: University of California Press, 1993.

Brooks, Nathan. "Indian Self-Determination and Education Assistance Act Contracts and *Cherokee Nation of Oklahoma v. Leavitt*: Agency Discretion to Fund Contract Support Costs." UNT Digital Library. March 31, 2005. Accessed on February 25, 2011. http://digital.library.unt.edu/ark:/67531/metacrs7890.

Brown, Alanna Kathleen. "The Evolution of Mourning Dove's Coyote Stories." *Studies in American Indian Literatures* 2nd ser., 4, no. 2/3 (1992): 161–180. http://www.jstor.org.proxygw.wrlc.org/stable/20736610.

Bruchac, Joseph, editor and interviewer. *Survival This Way: Interviews with American Indian Poets*. Tucson: Sun Tracks and University of Arizona Press, 1987.

Bucke, Richard Maurice. *Cosmic Consciousness: A Study in the Evolution of the Human Mind*. New York: Arkana Books, 1991. (First printed in 1901, Innes & Sons.)

Castro, Michael. *Interpreting the Indian: Twentieth-Century Poets and the Native American*. Albuquerque: University of New Mexico Press, 1983.

Chandarlapaty, Raj. *The Beat Generation and Counterculture: Paul Bowles, William S. Burroughs, Jack Kerouac*. New York: Peter Lang, 2009.

Charters, Ann, editor. *The Portable Beat Reader*. New York: Viking Penguin, 1992.

Chief Eaglewing. *Peek-Wa Stories: Indian Legends of California*. Whitefish: Kessinger Publishing, 2010.

Cloud, Dana L. "Foiling the Intellectuals: Gender, Identity Framing, and the Rhetoric of the Kill in Conservative Hate Mail." *Communication, Culture & Critique* 2, no. 4 (2009): 457–479. http://onlinelibrary.wiley.com.proxygw.wrlc.org/doi/10.1111/j.1753-9137.2009.01048.x/pdf.

Codrescu, Andrei. "'Howl' in Transylvania." In *The Poem That Changed America: "Howl" Fifty Years Later*, edited by Jason Shinder, 46–56. New York: Farrar, Straus and Giroux Paperbacks, 2006.

Corso, Gregory. *An Accidental Autobiography: The Selected Letters of Gregory Corso*. Edited by Bill Morgan. New York: New Directions Books, 2003.

Coymoon Creations. "Biography." *The Official Peter Coyote Web Site*. Last modified January 1998. Accessed on January 28, 2010. http://www.petercoyote.com/biography.html.

"Coyote." *Florida Fish and Wildlife Conservation Commission*. Last modified 2013. Accessed on December 13, 2009. http://myfwc.com/wildlifehabitats/profiles/mammals/land/coyote/.

Crane, Hart. "The Bridge." In *Howl, 50th Anniversary Edition: Original Draft Facsimile*, edited by Barry Miles, 135. New York: Harper Perennial, 2006.

Cresswell, Tim. *Place: A Short Introduction*. Malden: Blackwell Publishing, 2004.

Culler, Jonathan. *The Pursuit of Signs: Semiotics, Literature, Deconstruction*. London: Routledge, 1981.

Daly, Heather Ponchetti. "Fractured Relations at Home: The 1953 Termination Act's Effect on Tribal Relations throughout Southern California Indian Country." *The American Indian Quarterly* 33, no. 4 (2009): 427–439. doi: 10.1353/aiq.0.0065.

D'Ambrosio, Antonino. *A Heartbeat and a Guitar: Johnny Cash and the Making of Bitter Tears*. New York: Nation Books, 2009.

"Definitions of Folklore." *Journal of Folklore Research* 33, no. 3 (1996): 255–264. http://proxygw.wrlc.org/login?url=http://search.proquest.com.proxygw.wrlc.org/docview/85３064718?accountid=11243.

Deloria, Vine, Jr. *For This Land: Writings on Religion in America*. New York: Routledge, 1999.

———. "Intellectual Self-Determination and Sovereignty: Looking at the Windmills in Our Minds." *Wicazo Sa Review* 13, no. 1 (1998): 25–31. http://www.jstor.org.proxygw.wrlc.org/stable/1409027.

Bibliography

Dill, Bonnie Thornton. "Work at the Intersections of Race, Gender, Ethnicity, and Other Dimensions of Difference in Higher Education." *Connections: Newsletter of the Consortium on Race, Gender, and Ethnicity* (Fall 2002): 5–7. http://www.crge.umd.edu/pdf/RC2002_fall.pdf.

"Discover Navajo: The Official Navajo Nation Visitor Guide." *Navajo Nation Tourism Department*. Last modified 2008. Accessed on August 9, 2011. www.discovernavajo.com.

Dixon, Roland B. *Maidu Myths*. Whitefish: Kessinger, 2006. Extracted from the *Bulletin of the American Museum of Natural History*.

———. "Some Coyote Stories from the Maidu Indians of California." *Journal of American Folklore* 13, no. 51 (1900): 267–270. http://www.jstor.org.proxygw.wrlc.org/stable/532912.

Dotinga, Randy. "Peyote Won't Rot Your Brain." *Wired*. Last modified November 4, 2005. Accessed on December 15, 2009. http://www.wired.com/medtech/health/news/2005/11/69477.

Doty, Mark. "Human Seraphim: 'Howl,' Sex, and Holiness." In *The Poem That Changed America: "Howl" Fifty Years Later*, edited by Jason Shinder, 11–18. New York: Farrar, Straus and Giroux Paperbacks, 2006.

Doueihi, Anne. "Inhabiting the Space between Discourse and Story in Trickster Narratives." In *Mythical Trickster Figures: Contours, Contexts, and Criticisms*, edited by William J. Hynes and William G. Doty, 193–201. Tuscaloosa: University of Alabama Press, 1993.

Dove, Mourning. *Coyote Stories*. Edited by Heister Dean Guie. Notes by L.V. McWhorter. Introduction and notes by Jay Miller. Lincoln: University of Nebraska Press, Bison Book Edition, 1990.

"Driving the Last Spike." *The Virtual Museum of the City of San Francisco*. Accessed on March 10, 2012. http://www.sfmuseum.or/hist1/rail.html.

Dundes, Alan. "The Study of Folklore in Literature and Culture: Identification and Interpretation." *Journal of American Folklore* 78, no. 308 (1965): 136–142. http://www.jstor.org.proxygw.wrlc.org/stable/538280.

Dylan, Bob. "Freight Train Blues by Bob Dylan (1978)." *Bobdylan.com*. Last modified 2013. Accessed on January 5, 2010. http://www.bobdylan.com/us/songs/freight-train-blues.

Eckholm, Erik. "Gang Violence Grows on an Indian Reservation." *The New York Times* (Pine Ridge, SD), 13 Dec. 2009. http://www.nytimes.com/2009/12/14/us/14gangs.html?pagewanted=all&_r=0.

Engle, Gary. "'Knave, Fool, Genius: The Confidence Man as He Appears in Nineteenth-Century American Fiction' by Susan Kuhlmann, Book Review." *Modern Philology* 73, no. 2 (1975): 207–210. http://www.jstor.org.proxygw.wrlc.org/stable/436343.

Erdoes, Richard, and Alfonso Ortiz, editors. *American Indian Trickster Tales: Myths and Legends*. New York: Viking, 1998.

Folsom, Ed. "Commentary: Selected Criticism: Native Americans [Indians]." *The Walt Whitman Archive*. Accessed on 2011. http://whitmanarchive.org/criticism/current/encyclopedia/entry_34.html.

"Food Distribution Program on Indian Reservations." *United States Department of Agriculture: Food and Nutrition Service*. Accessed on January 29, 2010. http://www.fns.usda.gov/fdd/programs/fdpir/default.htm.

"French Parliament to Consider Burka Ban." *CNN.com/Europe* (Paris, France), 24 June 2009. Accessed on 23 Jan. 2010. http://www.cnn.com/2009/WORLD/europe/06/23/france.burkas/index.html.

Frey, Rodney. *The World of the Crow Indians: As Driftwood Lodges*. Norman: University of Oklahoma Press, 1987.

Geertz, Clifford. *The Interpretation of Cultures: Selected Essays*. New York: Basic Books, 1973.

Gennep, Arnold Van. *The Rites of Passage*. Translated by Monika B. Vizedom and Gabrielle L. Caffee. Chicago: University of Chicago Press, 1960.

Genter, Robert. "'I'm Not His Father': Lionel Trilling, Allen Ginsberg, and the Contours of Literary Modernism." *College Literature* 31, no. 2 (2004): 22–52. doi: 10.1353/lit.2004.0019.

Ginsberg, Allen. *Collected Poems, 1947–1997*. New York: HarperCollins, 2006.

_____. "A Definition of the Beat Generation." In *Deliberate Prose*, edited by Bill Morgan, 236–239. New York: HarperCollins, 2000.
_____. Foreword to *The Beat Book: Writings from the Beat Generation*. Edited by Anne Waldman. Boston: Shambhala, 2007.
_____. *Howl and Other Poems*. San Francisco: City Lights Books, 1956.
_____. *Howl, 50th Anniversary Edition: Original Draft Facsimile*. New York: Harper Perennial, 2006.
_____. *Indian Journals*. San Francisco: Dave Haselwood Books and City Lights Books, 1970.
_____. *Journals: Early Fifties and Sixties*. Edited by Gordon Ball. New York: Grove Press, 1977.
_____. "Letter to John Allen Ryan." In *Beat Down to Your Soul: What Was the Beat Generation?*, edited by Ann Charters, 206–208. New York: Penguin, 2001.
_____. *On the Poetry of Allen Ginsberg*. Edited by Lewis Hyde. Ann Arbor: University of Michigan Press,1984.
_____. "The Puritan and the Profligate." *Chronicles: A Magazine of American Culture*, reprinted in *Harper's Magazine: Readings*, "Interview: When Worlds Collide." Interviewed by John Lofton, 13–20. New York. January 1990.
_____. *Spontaneous Mind: Selected Interviews, 1958–1996*. Edited by David Carter. New York: HarperCollins, 2001.
_____. "Thoughts on NAMBLA." In *Deliberate Prose: Selected Essays, 1952–1995*, edited by Bill Morgan, 170–172. New York: HarperCollins, 2000.
_____, and Richard Eberhart. *To Eberhart from Ginsberg*. Lincoln: Penmaen Press, 1976.
_____, and Jack Kerouac. *Jack Kerouac and Allen Ginsberg: The Letters*. Edited by Bill Morgan and David Stanford. New York: Viking, 2010.
_____, and John Lofton. "John Lofton, *Chronicles*." In *Spontaneous Mind: Selected Interviews 1958–1996*, edited by Edmund White, 469–498. New York: HarperCollins, 2001.
_____, and Gary Snyder. *The Selected Letters of Allen Ginsberg and Gary Snyder*. Edited by Bill Morgan. Berkeley: Counterpoint,2009.
_____, Anne Waldman, William S. Burroughs, and Diane Di Prima. *First Thought Best Thought: The Art of Spontaneous & Inspired Writing Taught by Four Legendary Mentors of the Craft*. Edited by Chogyam Trungpa and David I. Rome. Boston: Shambhala Publications, 1983, Sounds True Inc., 2004. Audio CD.
Goldberg, Jonathan, and Madhavi Menon. "Queering History." *Modern Language Association* 120, no. 5 (2005): 1608–1617. http://www.jstor.org.proxygw.wrlc.org/stable/25486271.
Goldman, Ari L. *Being Jewish*. New York: Simon & Schuster, 2000.
Grace, Nancy M. "Seeking the Spirit of Beat: The Call for Interdisciplinary Scholarship." *Contemporary Literature* 43, no. 4 (2002): 811–821. http://www.jstor.org.proxygw.wrlc.org/stable/1209045.
Gross, Larry, and James D. Woods, editors. *The Columbia Reader on Lesbians & Gay Men in Media, Society, & Politics*. New York: Columbia University Press, 1999.
Gross, Lawrence W. "The Comic Vision of Anishinaabe Culture and Religion." *American Indian Quarterly* 26, no. 3 (2002): 436–459. doi: 10.1353/aiq.2003.0038.
_____. "Cultural Sovereignty and Native American Hermeneutics in the Interpretation of the Sacred Stories of the Anishinaabe." *Wicazo Sa Review* 18, no. 2 (2003): 127–134. http://www.jstor.org/stable/1409540.
Hale, Janet Campbell. "Claire." In *Reckonings: Contemporary Short Fiction by Native American Women*, edited by Hertha D. Sweet Wong, Lauren Stuart Muller, and Jana Sequoya Magdaleno, 87–110. New York: Oxford University Press, 2008.
Harjo, Joy. "The Story of All Our Survival." In *Survival This Way: Interviews with American Indian Poets*, edited and interviewed by Joseph Bruchac, 87–103. Tucson: Sun Tracks and University of Arizona Press, 1987.
Harris, Oliver. "Beating the Academy." *College Literature* 27, no. 1 (2000): 213–231. http://www.jstor.org.proxygw.wrlc.org/stable/25112504.
Heine, Steven. *Bargainin' for Salvation: Bob Dylan, a Zen Master?* New York: Continuum, 2009.
Hobson, Geary. "The Rise of the White Shaman: Twenty-Five Years Later." *Studies in Amer-

ican Indian Literatures 2nd ser., 14, no. 2/3 (2002): 1–11. http://www.jstor.org.proxygw.wrlc.org/stable/20737138.

Hoffman, Tyler. *American Poetry in Performance: From Walt Whitman to Hip Hop.* Ann Arbor: University of Michigan Press, 2011.

"Hope Hall's New Site in Rockland County; Ex-Convicts in Volunteers of America Home to Leave Flushing. Old Site Sold at Big Profit Exact Situation of the New Home a Secret for the Present—Scope of the Work." *The New York Times,* July 13, 1906. Accessed on Dec. 25, 2009. http://query.nytimes.com/mem/archive-free/pdf?res=FB0D10F6345913738 DDDAA0994DF405B868CF1D3.

"House Concurrent Resolution 108." In *Encyclopedia of Minorities in American Politics: Hispanics and Native Americans.* Vol. 2, edited by Jeffrey D. Schultz, Kerry Haynie, Anne M. McCulloch and Andrew Aoki, 629. Phoenix: Oryx Press, 2000.

Hyde, Lewis. *The Gift: Imagination and the Erotic Life of Property.* New York: Vintage, 1979.

———. *Trickster Makes This World: Mischief, Myth, and Art.* New York: North Point Press, 1998.

———, editor. *On the Poetry of Allen Ginsberg.* Ann Arbor: University of Michigan Press, 1984.

Hynes, William J. "Mapping the Characteristics of Mythic Tricksters: A Heuristic Guide." In *Mythical Trickster Figures: Contours, Contexts, and Criticisms,* edited by William J. Hynes and William G. Doty, 33–45. Tuscaloosa: University of Alabama Press, 1993.

"In Memoriam: Webster Kitchell." *The Rivera Family of Santa Fe Funeral Options.* February 9, 2009. Accessed on 2012. http://www.santafefuneraloption.com/sitemaker/sites/santaf 0/obit.cgi?user=webster-kitchell.

Isaacs, Jeremy. *Interview with Allen Ginsberg. Face to Face with Allen Ginsberg.* By Jeremy Isaacs. BBC Two, Face to Face, January 9, 1995. Television.

Jewell, Donald P. *Indians of the Feather River: Tales and Legends of the Concow Maidu of California.* Menlo Park: Ballena Press, 1987.

Johnson, Daniel Morley. "(Re) Nationalizing Naanabozho: Anishinaabe Sacred Stories, Nationalist Literary Criticism, and Scholarly Responsibility." In *Troubling Tricksters: Revisioning Critical Conversations,* edited by Deanna Reder and Linda M. Morra, 199–220. Waterloo: Wilfrid Laurier University Press, 2010.

Johnson, David K. *The Lavender Scare: The Cold War Persecution of Gays and Lesbians in the Federal Government.* Chicago: University of Chicago Press, 2004.

Johnson, Troy, Duane Champagne, and Joane Nagel. "American Indian Activism and Transformation: Lessons from Alcatraz." In *Contemporary Native American Political Issues,* edited by Troy R. Johnson. Walnut Creek: AltaMira Press, 1999.

Johnston, Allan. "Consumption, Addiction, Vision, Energy: Political Economies and Utopian Visions in the Writings of the Beat Generation." *College Literature* 32, no. 2 (2005): 103–126. http://www.jstor.org.proxygw.wrlc.org/stable/25115269.

Jones, David M., and Brian L. Molyneaux. *The Illustrated Encyclopedia of American Indian Mythology: Legends, Gods, and Spirits of North, Central, and South America.* London: Lorenz Books, Anness Publishing, 2009.

Josephson, Eric. Interview by Katherine Mead, via e-mail. March 22, 2012.

Kerouac, Jack. *Lonesome Traveler.* New York: Grove Press, 1988.

King, Stephen. *Just After Sunset.* New York: Scribner, 2009.

Kitchell, Webster. *God's Dog: Conversations with Coyote.* Boston: Skinner House Books, 1991.

Knoll, John. "Reconnecting to the spiritual muse." *Santa Fe New Mexican* (Santa Fe, NM), Aug. 12, 1988. http://newspaperarchive.com/santa-fe-new-mexican/1988-08-12/page-51?tag=john+knoll+littleburd&rtserp=tags/littlebird?pf=john&pl=knoll&page=2&ndt=by&py=1980&pey=1989.

Kroeber, A.L., and E.W. Gifford. *Karok Myths.* Edited by Grace Buzaljko. Informant Mary Ike. Berkeley: University of California Press, 1980.

Kuhlmann, Susan. *Knave, Fool, and Genius: The Confidence Man as He Appears in Nineteenth-Century American Fiction.* Chapel Hill: University of North Carolina Press, 1973.

"Lake Miwok." *Survey of California and Other Indian Languages.* Last modified 2009–2010. Accessed on July 3, 2011. http://linguistics.berkeley.edu/~survey/languages/lake-miwok.php.

LaPena, Frank, Steven P. Medley, and Craig D. Bates, compilers. *Legends of the Yosemite Miwok.* Berkeley: Heyday Books and the Yosemite Association, 2007.

Lardas, John. *The Bop Apocalypse: The Religious Visions of Kerouac, Ginsberg, and Burroughs.* Champaign: University of Illinois Press, 2001.

Leeming, David, and Jake Page. *The Mythology of Native North America.* Norman: University of Oklahoma Press, 1998.

Lefebvre, Henri. *The Production of Space.* Translation by Donald Nicholson-Smith. Oxford: Blackwell Publishers, 1991.

Leggatt, Judith. "Quincentennial Trickster Poetics: Lenore Keeshig-Tobias's 'Trickster Beyond 1992: Our Relationship' (1992) and Annhart Baker's 'Coyote Columbus Café' (1994)." In *Troubling Tricksters: Revisioning Critical Conversations,* edited by Deanna Reder and Linda M. Morra, 221–238. Waterloo: Wilfrid Laurier University Press, 2010.

Lincoln, Kenneth. *Sing with the Heart of a Bear: Fusions of Native American Poetry: 1890–1999.* Berkeley: University of California Press, 2000.

Lopez, Barry. "Barry Lopez, Home: Texas Tech." *Barry Lopez.* Last modified February 7, 2012. http://www.barrylopez.com/index.htm.

Lopez, Barry Holstun. *Giving Birth to Thunder, Sleeping with His Daughter: Coyote Builds North America.* New York: Avon Books, 1977.

López, Tiffany Ana. "María Cristina Mena: Turn-of-the-Century La Malinche, and Other Tales of Cultural (Re)Construction." In *Tricksterism in Turn-of-the-Century American Literature: A Multicultural Perspective,* edited by Elizabeth Ammons and Annette White-Parks, 21–45. Hanover: University Press of New England, 1994.

Luna, James. Interview by Katherine Mead, via telephone. August 14, 2011.

"L.V. McWhorter Native American Artifact Collection." WSU *Libraries: Digital Collections.* Manuscripts, Archives, and Special Collections, Washington State U, 2010. Accessed on 15 March 2010. http://content.wsulibs.wsu.edu/cdm/landingpage/collection/lv_mcwhorte.

MacNaughton, Anne. "'Taos Pueblo' reading features poetry." *Santa Fe New Mexican* (Taos Pueblo, NM), Oct. 12, 1990. http://newspaperarchive.com/santa-fe-new-mexican/1990-10-12/page-37?tag=anne+macnaughton+littlebird+poetry&rtserp=tags/littlebird-poetry?pf-anne&pl=macnaughton.

"Maidu People." City of Roseville, California; Maidu People. Accessed on March 21, 2012. http://www.roseville.ca.us/parks/parks_n_facilities/facilities/maidu_indian_museum/maidu_people.asp.Malotki, Ekkehart. *Gullible Coyote/Una'ihu: A Bilingual Collection of Hopi Coyote Stories.* Michael Lomatuway'ma, Hopi Consultant. Tucson: University of Arizona Press, 1985.

Marler, Regina, editor. *Queer Beats: How the Beats Turned America on to Sex.* San Francisco: Cleis Press, 2004.

Martin, Leisa A., and John J. Chiodo. "American Indian Students Speak Out: What's Good Citizenship?" *International Journal of Social Education* 23, no. 1 (2008): 1–31. http://www.eric.ed.gov/PDFS/EJ944022.pdf.

Mazur, Christine Teresa. "Gothic Fiction, Liminality, and Popular Culture: Stephen King's Grotesque Social Commentary in *'Salem's Lot.*" Master's thesis, University of Manitoba, 1997.

McCall, Leslie. "The Complexity of Intersectionality." *Signs* 30, no. 3 (2005): 1771–1800. doi: 10.1086/426800.

McCarthy, Timothy Patrick, editor. *Protest Nation: Words That Inspired a Century of American Radicalism.* Edited by John McMillian. New York: The New Press, 2010.

McDonald, Russ. "The Language of Tragedy." In *The Cambridge Companion to Shakespearean Tragedy,* edited by Claire McEachern, 23–49. Cambridge: Cambridge University Press, 2002.

Bibliography

McNally, Michael D. *Ojibwe Singers: Hymns, Grief, and a Native Culture in Motion*. New York: Oxford University Press, 2000.

McNeley, James Kale. *Holy Wind in Navajo Philosophy*. Tucson: University of Arizona Press, 1981.

"Maidu People." *City of Roseville, California; Maidu People*. Accessed on March 21, 2012. http://www.roseville.ca.us/parks/parks_n_facilities/facilities/maidu_indian_museum/ maidu_people.asp.

Meek, Barbra A. "And the Injun Goes 'How!': Representations of American Indian English in white public space." *Language in Society* 35, no. 1 (2006): 93–128. doi: 10.1017/S0047404506060040.

Miller, Jay. Introduction to *Coyote Stories*. Edited by Heister Dean Guie with notes by L.V. McWhorter. Lincoln: University of Nebraska Press, 1990.

Miller, John J. "The General Grubbiness of Allen Ginsberg." *National Review Online*. September 14, 2006. Accessed on July 4, 2011. http://www.nationalreview.com/articles/218704/general-grubbiness-allen-ginsberg/john-j-miller.

Morgan, Bill. *I Celebrate Myself: The Somewhat Private Life of Allen Ginsberg*. New York: Viking, 2006.

———, and Nancy J. Peters, editors. *Howl on Trial: The Battle for Free Expression*. San Francisco: City Lights Books, 2006.

Münch, Richard, and Neil J. Smelser, editors. *Theory of Culture*. Berkeley: University of California Press, 1993.

Niatum, Duane, editor. *Harper's Anthology of Twentieth Century Native American Poetry*. New York: HarperCollins, 1988.

Opler, Morris Edward. *Myths and Tales of the Jicarilla Apache*. Mineola: Dover Publications, 1994. Originally published by the *American Folk-lore Society* in 1938.

Ortiz, Simon J. "*Coyote Tales from the Indian Pueblos* by Evelyn Dahl Reed; *The Other Side of Nowhere: Contemporary Coyote Tales* by Peter Blue Cloud (Arpmoawentate)." *American Indian Quarterly* 16, no. 4 (1992): 598–600. http://www.jstor.org/stable/1185336.

———. "Towards a National Indian Literature: Cultural Authenticity in Nationalism." *MELUS* 8, no. 2 (1981): 7–12. http://www.jstor.org.proxygw.wrlc.org/stable/467143.

Ostriker, Alicia. "'Howl' Revisited: The poet as Jew." *American Poetry Review* 26, no. 4 (1997): 28–31. http://search.proquest.com/docview/220633768?accountid=11243.

Peiffer, Katrina Schimmoeller. *Coyote at Large: Humor in American Nature Writing*. Salt Lake City: University of Utah Press, 2000.

Peters, Nancy J. "Milestones of Literary Censorship." In *Howl on Trial: The Battle for Free Expression*, edited by Bill Morgan and Nancy J. Peters, 5–15. San Francisco: City Lights Books, 2006.

Plimpton, George, editor. *Writers at Work: The Paris Review Interviews, Vol. 3*. New York: Viking, 1967.

Portugés, Paul. "Allen Ginsberg's Paul Cézanne and the Pater Omnipotens Aeterna Deus." *Contemporary Literature* 21, no. 3 (1980): 435–449. http://www.jstor.org.proxygw.wrlc.org/stable/1208251.

Pritchard, Evan T. (retold and annotated by). *Native American Stories of the Sacred: Annotated and Explained*. Woodstock: Skylight Paths, 2005.

Prothero, Stephen. "On the Holy Road: The Beat Movement as Spiritual Protest." *Harvard Theological Review* 84, no. 2 (1991): 205–222. http://www.jstor.org.proxygw.wrlc.org/stable/1509800.

Public Speaking. Fran Lebowitz. Directed by Martin Scorsese. 2010. New York, NY: HBO Documentary Films, 2010. Documentary Film. DVD.

Raskin, Jonah. *American Scream: Allen Ginsberg's Howl and the Making of the Beat Generation*. Berkeley: University of California Press, 2004.

Reder, Deanna, and Linda M. Morra, editors. *Troubling Tricksters: Revisioning Critical Conversations (Indigenous Studies)*. Waterloo, Ontario: Wilfrid Laurier University Press, 2010.

Reesman, Jeanne Campbell, editor. *Trickster Lives: Culture and Myth in American Fiction*. Athens: University of Georgia Press, 2001.

Bibliography

Rich, Adrienne. "The Hermit's Scream." *Modern Language Association* 108, no. 5 (1993): 1157–1164. http://www.jstor.org/stable/462992.

Robbins, Richard H. *Cultural Anthropology: A Problem-Based Approach, 5th Edition.* Belmont: Wadsworth, Cengage Learning, 2006, 2009.

Robbins, Tom. "In Defiance of Gravity: Writing, Wisdom, and the Fabulous Club Gemini." *Harper's Magazine: Miscellany*, September 2004. http://archive.harpers.org/2004/09/pdf/HarpersMagazine-2004-09-0080199.pdf?AWSAccessKeyId=AKIAJXATU3VRJAAA66RA&Expires=1366969233&Signature=9ToMLhMHyMCKTzl%2FkJC9twhkIIk%3D.

Rosenberg, Ellen. "Native American Coyote Trickster Tales and Cycles." In *Fools and Jesters in Literature, Art, and History: A Bio-Bibliographical Sourcebook*, edited by Vicki Janik, 155–168. Westport: Greenwood Press, 1998.

Ruiz, Cathy. "Coyote, the Trickster, Comes to the Zen Buddhist Monastery and I Realize His Buddha Nature." *Raven Chronicles* 13, no. 1 (2007): 40–41.

Schutz-Gruber, Barbara G., and Barbara Frates Buckley. *Trickster Tales from Around the World: An Interdisciplinary Guide for Teachers.* Michigan: Schutz-Gruber, 1991.

Sherman, Sharon R. "Who Owns Culture and Who Decides? Ethics, Film Methodology, and Intangible Cultural Heritage Protection." *Western Folklore* 67, no. 2/3 (2008): 223–236. http://search.proquest.com/docview/212106730?accountid=11243.

Shipley, William, editor and translator. *The Maidu Indian Myths and Stories of Hanc'ibyjim.* Berkeley: Heyday Books, 1991.

SiJohn, Bingo. "Coeur d' Alene: Story: Coyote and the White Man." *Lifelong Learning Online: The Lewis & Clark Rediscovery Project*, in collaboration with the *Coeur D' Alene Tribe.* Last modified 2002. http://www.webpages.uidaho.edu/L3/ShowOneObjectSiteID50ObjectID438.html.

Slotkin, Richard. *Gunfighter Nation: Myth of the Frontier in Twentieth-Century America.* Norman: University of Oklahoma Press, 1998.

Smoak, Gregory E. "Review: *The Mythology of Native North America* by David Leeming; Jake Page." *American Indian Quarterly* 22, no. 4 (1998): 512–515. http://search.proquest.com/docview/216856122?accountid=11243.

Snyder, Gary. *The Back Country.* New York: New Directions Books, 1968.

———. *Back on the Fire: Essays.* Emeryville: Shoemaker & Hoard, 2007.

———. *Earth House Hold.* New York: New Directions Books, 1969.

———. Foreword to *The Maidu Indian Myths and Stories of Hanc'ibyjim.* Edited and translated by William Shipley. Berkeley: Heyday Books, 1991.

———. *Myths and Texts.* New York: New Directions Books, 1978.

———. *The Old Ways.* San Francisco: City Lights Books, 1977.

———. "Re: Coyote Trickster Thesis Question," e-mail message to author, January 30, 2010.

Soja, Edward W. *Thirdspace: Journeys to Los Angeles and Other Real-and-Imagined Places.* Malden: Blackwell Publishers, 1996.

Spanbauer, Tom. *The Man Who Fell in Love with the Moon.* New York: Grove Press, 1991.

Storey, John. *Cultural Theory and Popular Culture: An Introduction, 4th Edition.* Essex: Pearson Education Limited, 2006.

Tedlock, Dennis. "Ethnopoetics." In *Folklore, Cultural Performances, and Popular Entertainments*, edited by Richard Bauman, 81–85. New York: Oxford University Press, 1992.

Toelken, Barre. "The Yellowman Tapes, 1966–1997." *Journal of American Folklore* 111, no. 442 (1998): 381–391. http://www.jstor.org.proxygw.wrlc.org/stable/541046.

Tuan, Yi-Fu, and Steven Hoelscher. *Space and Place: The Perspective of Experience.* Minneapolis: University of Minnesota Press, 1977.

Turnbull, David. *Masons, Tricksters, and Cartographers: Makers of Knowledge and Space.* London: Routledge, 2003, OPA, 2000.

Turner, Victor. *The Ritual Process: Structure and Anti-Structure.* New Jersey: Aldine Transaction, 1969.

Twain, Mark. *Roughing It.* 1886. New York: New American Library, 1962.

Tytell, John. *Naked Angels: Kerouac, Ginsberg, Burroughs: The Lives and Literature of the Beat Generation.* Chicago: Ivan R. Dee, 1976.

Bibliography

Utter, Jack. *American Indians: Answers to Today's Questions, 2nd Edition*. Norman: National Woodlands, 2001.

Vickers, Scott B. *Native American Identities: From Stereotype to Archetype in Art and Literature*. Albuquerque: University of New Mexico Press, 1998.

Viorst, Milton. *Fire in the Streets: America in the 1960s*. New York: Simon & Schuster, 1979.

Vizenor, Gerald. *Earthdivers: Tribal Narratives on Mixed Descent*. Minneapolis: University of Minnesota Press, 1981.

———. *Interior Landscapes: Autobiographical Myths and Metaphors*. Minneapolis: University of Minnesota Press, 1990.

Voget, Fred W. Introduction to *Old Man Coyote: The Authorized Edition*, by Frank B. Linderman. Lincoln: University of Nebraska Press, 1996. (Linderman's original publish date: 1931.)

Waddell, Terrie. *Wild/Lives: Trickster, Place, and Liminality on Screen*. New York: Routledge, 2010.

Waldman, Anne. "Premises of Consciousness." In *The Poem That Changed America: "Howl" Fifty Years Later*, edited by Jason Shinder, 260–272. New York: Farrar, Straus and Giroux Paperbacks, 2006.

Waldman, Carl. *The Dictionary of Native American Terminology*. New York: Castle Books, 2009.

Wheelan, Charles. *Naked Economics: Undressing the Dismal Science*. New York: Norton, 2010.

White, Edmund. *The Farewell Symphony*. New York: Vintage, 1997.

Whitfield, Stephen J. *The Culture of the Cold War (The American Moment)*. Baltimore: Johns Hopkins University Press, 1991.

Womack, Craig. *Art as Performance, Story as Criticism: Reflections on Native Literary Aesthetics*. Norman: University of Oklahoma Press, 2009.

Wong, Hertha D. Sweet, Lauren Stuart Muller, and Jana Sequoya Magdaleno, editors. *Reckonings: Contemporary Short Fiction by Native American Women*. New York: Oxford University Press, 2008.

Index

activism 19–20, 31
Alexie, Sherman 172
Allen, Paula Gunn 172
American Civil Liberties Union (ACLU) 54
Angulo, Jaime de 43
Anishinaabe 51–52, 61, 65, 144
Apache 95, 72, 85–86, 145, 166
Apsáalooke 88–89; *see also* Crow
Arapaho 72
Atsugewi 76

Babcock-Abrahams, Barbara 105
Ball, Gordon 152
Ballinger, Franchot 57
Bascom, William 58
Beat Generation 19, 30, 33, 43, 121, 159
Bednar, Robert 41
Bellarsi, Franca 107, 172
Beltrametti, Franco 43
Benzedrine 127, 152, 154
Bernini, Gian Lorenzo 132
Blake, William 34–35, 73, 99–101, 107, 149–150, 164
Blue Cloud, Peter 83, 139, 150–151, 154, 174
Bowers, John 51
Breslin, James 46, 73
Bright, William 71, 82
Bruchac, Joseph 82
Bucke, Richard 17, 34
Buckley, Barbara 72, 74
Buddhism *see* Zen Buddhism
Burroughs, William 21, 29–30, 173

Cannastra, William 131–132, 141, 154
Carr, Lucien 29
Cassady, Neal 12, 29–30, 119
censorship 19–22, 32, 46, 50–51, 53–56, 61, 73–74
Cézanne, Paul 114, 166, 173
Charters, Ann 3

Chemehuevi 57
Cherokee 72
Cheyenne 72
Clark, Thomas 100, 108
clowns 42, 65, 69–70, 134
Codrescu, Andrei 20, 125
Coeur d'Alene 38, 81, 137
Cold War 53–54, 56, 63, 128, 148
Columbia Presbyterian Psychiatric Institute 137
Columbia University 30, 76, 155
Communism 20, 63, 49, 52
Confidence Man 10
Corso, Gregory 43, 75–76, 78–80
cosmic consciousness 17, 34, 108
C.P. Huntington Expedition 76
Crane, Hart 39, 115–116, 120–121
creative destruction 47, 135
Cresswell, Tim 113
Crocker, Charles 76
Crow 72, 88–89; *see also* Apsáalooke
cultural hero 32, 53, 66, 71, 82, 93, 134, 138, 141, 156, 163, 170
cultural studies 15–16, 33

Deloria, Vine, Jr. 67
Dixon, Roland B. 76–77, 143, 152, 169
Doty, Mark 20, 144
Doueihi, Anne 102
Dove, Christine Mourning 55–57, 66
Dylan, Bob 3, 13–14, 45

Eaglewing, Chief 74
Eberhart, Richard 33, 46, 110
Eisenhower Administration 63
Emerson, Ralph Waldo 29, 34
Engle, Gary 10
Erdoes, Richard 70, 87, 93, 133, 166–167

FBI 53, 63, 119–120, 138–140
Ferlinghetti, Lawrence 54

Index

"Fie My Fum" 30–31
free speech 54, 131
Frey, Rodney 81, 89

Gaines, David vi, 2,
Gennep, Arnold Van 104
Ginsberg, Louis 29, 104, 150
Ginsberg, Naomi 33, 39, 113, 122, 150, 162
Goldberg, Jonathan 16
Goldman, Ari 39, 132
Grace, Nancy 21, 174
Gross, Lawrence 50–52, 57, 144

Hale, Janet Campbell 38
Harjo, Joy 5
Harris, Oliver 73
Heine, Steve 13–14
Hemingway, Ernest 5, 38
Hendrick, Wally 37
Hobson, Geary 5
Hollywood Injun English 24, 116
Holmes, John Clellon 30
Holterhoff, Kate 99
Hoover Administration 62
Hopi 65
Horn, Clayton W. 54
House Concurrent Resolution One Hundred and Eight 63–64
Hudson River 35
Hunke, Herbert 127
Hyde, Lewis 45, 66, 115, 122–123, 147
Hynes, William J. 12

Indian Bureau of the Department of the Interior 35
Indian Journals 36
Interior Salish 122
intersectionality 13, 16–17
intracategorical complexity 16–17
Isaacs, Jeremy 44

Jackson, Shirley 138
jazz 3, 37, 129
Jewell, Donald 76
Johnson, Daniel Morley 13
Johnston, Allan 43
Josephson, Eric 77
Judaism 1, 9, 39, 49, 52, 119, 132

Kaddish 46, 162
Karok 141
Keats, John 35
Keck, Bill 44
Kerenyi, Karl 107
Kerouac, Jack 3–5, 9, 12, 19, 21–22, 29, 30, 37–41, 52, 54, 99, 127, 147, 173
King, Stephen 109, 156

Kinsey Reports 63
Kitchell, Webster 117–118
Klamath 74, 79, 81
Koch, Kenneth 70
Kuhlmann, Susan 10–11
Kupferberg, Naphtali Tuli 116
Kurath, Gertrude P. 58

La Farge, Peter 63
Lamantia, Philip 38
Lapena, Frank 93
Lardas, John 173–174
Lebowitz, Fran 7
Leeming, David 10, 12, 15, 22, 66
Lefebvre, Henri 155
Leggatt, Judith 61
Lincoln, Kenneth 112, 130, 156, 174
Littlebird, Harold 42
Littlebird, Larry 42
Llano, Stephen M. 121
Lofton, John 22, 32–35
Lopez, Barry 57, 64, 68, 84–85, 89–90, 145, 166
Luiseño 4
Luna, James 4–5, 38–39, 59, 172

Maidu 43, 70, 72, 76–77, 143, 152, 169
Makarius, Laura 12
Malotki, Ekkehart 65
marijuana (tea) 121, 127, 152–153
Mattachine Society 63
Mazur, Christine Teresa 109
McCall, Leslie 16
McClure, Michael 37–38, 42, 110
McDonald, Russ 163–164, 166
McWhorter, L.V. 56
Mello, Kenneth vi, 2, 3
Menon, Madhav 16
Miller, Jay 56–57, 66
Miller, John 72
Miwok 93–94, 133, 140, 166
Morgan, Bill 37
mother-in-law 90, 129
Myth of the Frontier 10, 60

Naropa University 54, 78–79
Nash, Henry 6
Navajo 59–60, 65, 72, 84
negative capability 35, 46, 109, 126, 134
New Mexico 42
New York 24, 47, 99, 116–117, 121, 127, 132, 152
Nez Perce 72, 90
Niatum, Duane 71
North American Man/Boy Love Association (NAMBLA) 131
Northern Paiute 130, 156

Index

obscenity 41, 50, 53–55, 63, 73, 81, 100, 106, 122, 128, 156, 164–165, 174
On the Road 29–30, 40, 52
Opler, Morris Edward 86
Ortiz, Alfonso 70, 87, 93, 133, 166–167
Ortiz, Simon J. 5, 94
Outrider 108–109, 155

Page, Jake 10, 12, 15, 22, 66
Pater Omnipotens Aeterna Deus 24, 113–114, 165, 173
Paterson 29, 149, 151
Peiffer, Katrina Schimmoeller 60
Peters, Nancy 54
Peyote 44, 121, 152–153
Podhoretz, Norman 52
Portugés, Paul 114, 173
Post Apocalypse Stress Syndrome (PASS) 52
Potter, Charles Francis 58
Pritchard, Evan T. 75, 79, 81
Proctor, Devin 105
Prothero, Stephen 103, 172–173
Pueblo 9, 42, 72, 87, 167
"Pull My Daisy" 30, 40

queer theory 15–16, 24, 126

Radin, Paul 66
Ramsey, Jarold 156
Raskin, Jonah 33, 35, 148, 174
Rathbun, Robert (Coyote Man) 77
reader-response theory 15–16, 33
Reesman, Jeanne 52
regional religion 49, 51
Rexroth, Kenneth 38, 119
Rich, Adrienne 19
Robbins, Tom 22, 31–32, 86
Rosenberg, Ellen 2, 36, 67, 151
The Roth Standard 54
Ryan, John Allen 37, 41

St. Teresa 132
San Francisco 1, 9, 29, 47, 119
Santo Domingo/Laguna Pueblo 42
Schumpeter, Joseph 135
Schutz-Gruber, Barbara 72, 74
Shakespeare, William 35, 163
Sherman, Sharon 59
Shinder, Jason 171
Shoshone 72

SiJohn, Bingo 81–82, 137, 169
Silko, Leslie Marmon 5
Six Gallery 1, 9, 37, 41, 110
Slotkin, Richard 15
Smoak, Gregory E. 15
smorgasbording 39
Snyder, Gary 3–4, 9, 12, 18, 38–39, 41–43, 49, 58, 60, 70, 72, 75–76, 78, 82, 113, 117
Solomon, Carl 11, 55, 123, 137, 168, 170
Spanbauer, Tom 1, 112
Spengler, Oswald 174
Stanford, Leland 76
Stewart, Joffre 119, 139
stream of consciousness 49, 72, 126

Taoism 31, 86
Thomas, Dylan 53, 148
Tibetan 31
Toelken, Barre 59–60
Trail of Tears 35
Trilling, Lionel 104
Truman Administration 62
Tuan, Yi-Fu 100, 106
Turnbull, David 149
Turner, Victor 104–105
Twain, Mark 72

Utter, Jack 150

Vision quest 110, 150
Vizenor, Gerald 4, 57, 61, 95, 113, 163
Voget, Fred 89

Waddell, Terrie 11–12, 101, 106–107
Waldman, Anne 18, 30, 53, 108–109
Waldman, Carl 175
Warrior, Robert Allen 7
White, Edmund 6
Whitestream 60, 149
Whitman, Walt 31, 34–36, 39–40, 113
Wile E. Coyote 72, 86
Williams, William Carlos 44, 151, 172
Womack, Craig 7
Wounded Knee Massacre 35

Yellowman, Hugh 59
Young, Tom 76

Zen Buddhism 1, 9, 13–14, 31, 36–37, 39, 42, 86, 103

www.ingramcontent.com/pod-product-compliance
Ingram Content Group UK Ltd.
Pitfield, Milton Keynes, MK11 3LW, UK
UKHW042003140426
5217IPUK00015B/956